THE CURIOUS ADVANTAGE

PAUL ASHCROFT SIMON BROWN GARRICK JONES

LAÏKI

The Curious Advantage

Published by Laïki Publishing

ISBN
978-1-64871-369-9 (Hardcover)
978-1-64871-351-4 (Paperback)
978-1-64871-334-7 (Ebook)

British Library Cataloguing in Publication Data

For our families and loved ones for their love and support and for above all, inspiring our curiosity

Paul - for Zsanett, Ben and Leanne
Simon - for Rachel, Oliver and Lucinda
Garrick - for Georgia, Leila, Emma, Matilda, Oscar, Pietro, Pauline, Alex & Jeremy

TABLE OF CONTENTS

A NOTE FROM THE AUTHORS

The Curious Advantage is an exploration of the idea of curiosity and its increasing importance for thriving in the digital age.

Taking the widest possible exploration of things curious—historical, contemporary, neuroscientific, anthropological, behavioural, semantic and business-focused. *The Curious Advantage* contextualises curiosity within the cultural, social, organisation and individual perspectives. We provide pragmatic tools for enabling a culture of curiosity for leaders and make the case for how curiosity is a value driver in the new digital reality.

Curiosity is at the heart of the skills required to successfully navigate our digital reality. When all futures are uncertain, curiosity shines a light.

As a cultural mindset, curiosity has profound implications for organisations, leaders and individuals inhabiting the digital reality. This book aims to bring those implications to life by being fact-based, entertaining and memorable as we seek to answer our own question—*why is curiosity the greatest driver of value in the digital age?*

The authors
June 2020

FOREWORD

Curiosity, once forgotten but now an essential part of business life

By Josh Bersin

What is the most wonderful thing we love about children? It's their wide-eyed curiosity about everything in life. In fact, many say children are blessed by this trait: they are too young to judge so everything in the world seems new, interesting, and filled with promise.

Why is curiosity such an important trait in business? Because today, perhaps like never before, work has become surprising, disruptive, and changing faster than ever. Rather than worry, predict, or try to engineer our way through it, maybe we should just 'be curious' about what's going on.

In my career as a businessperson, analyst, and consultant, I constantly hear about 'innovation' and 'disruption.' These are 'action words' that sound like something you 'do' with force and vigor. You can buy 'innovation workshops' that drive innovation, start 'innovation sprints' to force new ideas to come out, and forcibly decide to 'disrupt the market' or 'disrupt our competition' through sheer effort.

Well, as valuable as all that seems, the real secret to business success is not forcing new ideas to come forward, it's listening and sensing why things are as they are. And from there new solutions become clear and unique in form. Curiosity is what makes this happen.

Some of the most successful scientists (Albert Einstein, for example), including my own father, are just very curious souls. They have wonder about the world and they look at things with an open mind, fresh eyes, and a limitless potential to change. These behaviours, which fall into the category of curiosity, are what business needs more than ever.

There's another element to curiosity I find important. Not only is it open-minded, learning-centric, and inquisitive, but it's non-judgmental and expansive in form. When you experience a failure or a problem, you can just 'be curious' about why it happened. Rather than think about your effort as a 'mistake' or a 'failure,' you can simply think to yourself, 'I wonder why I behaved that way,' or, 'I wonder what happened that we could do differently?'

Finally, curiosity is a behaviour that creates energy—energy driven from wonder and the potential to do more. Rather than think, 'Well that's a good idea but it's too hard to do,' curiosity lets you imagine the future in a new way, which suddenly seems more possible than you thought.

I want to thank Paul, Simon and Garrick for an important and wonderful book. We can all learn to be more curious, and as a result become more joyful, happy, and successful.

Josh Bersin
Global Industry Analyst
Oakland, California

INTRODUCTION

'Curiosity is the one thing invincible in nature.'

Freya Stark

I was sitting in a small taverna, up a mountain, the sea below us some seven minutes away by jeep. It was evening and most of us had finished our evening meal when a young man, damp from diving, walked in. The immediate reaction of the patron instantly got my attention. He rushed over, as did most of the staff in the kitchen, clustered around the young man and they whispered conspiratorially. After a minute, the patron exclaimed, and came directly to my table with half a plastic water bottle. It was full of sea water, and the oddest, strangest, ugliest objects. What are these? I thought to myself. It looked like a plastic bottle of flotsam and jetsam. Could it be the steel wool used to scour pots and pans—now rusted?

'*Fouska*,' he said, looking at me. You have to try this. We'd known each other for some time. He's a friend. He knows I'll give most things a go—at least once! He also knows I love seafood. I sat up, intrigued. Something genuinely new.

The patron reached into the bottle and brought out one of the strangest objects—*fouska* means 'bubble,' said my friend. With a gusto I see rarely, the patron set to cutting it in half with his penknife. It seemed to be something between an oyster, a mussel and a rock. However, its casing was a strange, soft disguise. They have to be dived for—they are not found deep—but they are difficult to detect.

As he cut it in half, he revealed the pink, yellow, red-flecked flesh of something organic, something protein. It squirted sea water in a little stream as it was pierced. Then it was revealed. Visceral. I was overwhelmed by the iodine sharpness of the sea, here on the table. The patron ate one himself, then attacked the next. Spooning out half of the creature he handed it to me. I smelt, I ate, I swallowed. The sea, the waves, the kelp, the spray. It hit me. As he handed me another, I felt a warm glow, I felt a smile creep onto my face, I felt the blood rush to my face. I looked around at the room. 'Oh,' said the patron, 'meet the world's most powerful aphrodisiac.' He was not joking. After three spoonfuls it was clear I had a glint in my eye! Everybody was smiling and joking around! *What on earth is this?* I thought. These are the mechanisms by which we propagate, evolve and ensure the survival of the species. I laughed to myself.

I thought of Patrick Süskind's book *Perfume*—all manner of things may have happened that night, if this were a magic realist novel. Curiosity leads us down strange pathways.

It is vital to our survival.

Albert Einstein said, 'We cannot use the same thinking or order of thinking that got us into a situation to get us out of that situation.' Some of the skills we learn in the kitchen are not necessarily useful in the kindergarten, but they might be. Context is everything. Alexander the Great conquered the mightiest empire of his time using an entirely new order of battle and warfare. The Persians who outnumbered him were blind to his manoeuvres. They could not read what he was doing tactically until it was too late—and Darius had fled the field. So, too, the skills and forms of organisation that dominated the agrarian age were no longer of use in the industrial age. Many of the skills taught in schools today, many of the techniques taught in MBAs today, are fit for an age that is quickly passing. The digital age requires entirely new mindsets, codes, education and organisational abilities. Curiosity, and its practical, active, constructive application are slap bang at the heart of thriving in the digital realm. Curiosity is like the molecules of potassium, magnesium and iodine that flood our blood and our brain and attach to our neuro-receptors from the *fouska*.

Curiosity is the aphrodisiac of the digital age.

Not just any curiosity, mind you. Not just a random stumble through the Internet, fixating on YouTube videos, newspaper articles and advertisements. Rather the kind of curiosity that drives passionate enquiry, throwing ourselves into new communities, creating for the first time, learning new languages, experiencing different ways of understanding the world, prototyping, testing the water, becoming proficient, making and building things—the kind of curiosity that is sparked by the question, 'I wonder if…' and causes us and our networks of geographically diverse, global friends to thrive in this digital age.

Becoming more curious

This book is about that kind of curiosity and the advantage curiosity brings to us as individuals and to our organisations, especially now as we adapt to the digital age. We explore why nurturing curiosity as a specific value is a vital ingredient to individual, organisational and societal success. We aim to show why we believe that curiosity is the greatest driver of value in the digital age.

The book is structured in three sections. In the first, we look at what is curiosity, and what does it mean for individuals, organisations and society? We pepper each chapter with stories from history, as there is not much new under the sun. We include references to other books that have done a great job in illustrating each of the points we wish to make. We include cases and stories from amazing individuals and the worlds we work in. Each of us, as authors, has years of working with the world's greatest brands at the highest levels, and we include these stories to illustrate how powerful curiosity is in practice.

We will reference interesting organisations where we have witnessed a culture of curiosity being applied with great impact and who have been starting to understand the value of curiosity. In particular we tell many stories from Novartis, a global medicines company, as we have been fortunate to have many years' experience seeing how this organisation has worked to put curiosity at the centre of its culture.

It's important to note that this book is a personal project of the three of us as friends and has not been commercially sponsored. We decided to write this book as a means to document the incredible conversations we had as we began to reflect on our experiences of curiosity.

In Part 1, we explore how curiosity is at the heart of being human and central to the most successful societies we humans have created, including this new digital society.

In Part 2, we explore how to put curiosity to work for us and for our organisations. We ask what encourages curiosity? What is required to put wonder into action?

We have identified seven elements that individuals, leaders and organisations can employ to create competitive advantage by building a culture of curiosity. These we call 'sailing the 7 C's.' Mostly because it's a great pun. It also really helps us remember the idea, as each of these elements is described by a word beginning with C.

SAILING THE 7C's OF CURIOSITY

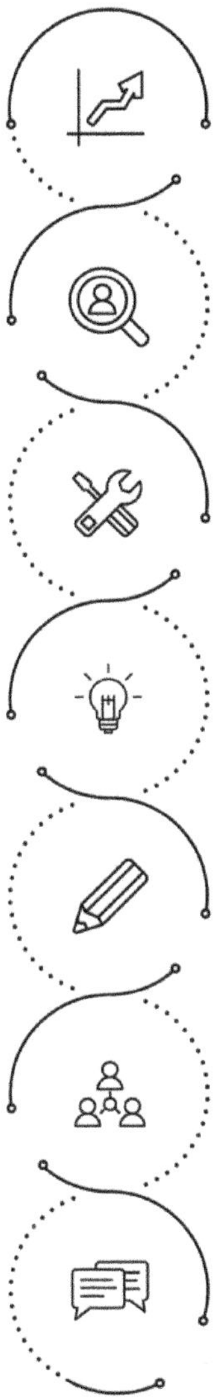

7. CONFIDENCE

Confidence grows with curiosity. The two grow with each other. If we approach something new with a curious mindset, being open to trying, failing and improving – we build our confidence.

6. CRITICALITY

Asking questions is deeply connected to being curious. It is the questions that prompt us to discover and find solutions. The type of questions we apply are important if we want to know if there is a different or better way. We also need to be aware of our own biases.

5. CONSTRUCTION

Curiosity is not just wondering. It is putting your wonder into action. This means making or constructing something to learn about it. Whether it's making new connections, building something physical, writing a document, a piece of music, building a business or just figuring out how something works.

4. CREATIVITY

Our exploration into new worlds may require us to think differently, connect something in a new way and make a leap of faith. Sometimes, it's the spark that starts a new cycle of curiosity.

3. CURATION

We need to make choices and intentionally curate our curiosity to synthesize and focus our thinking, our ideas and the information we are gathering.

2. COMMUNITY

Curiosity is powered by our community. Societies or organisations with curiosity as a specific part of culture are more productive and people are more engaged in learning and in their work.

1. CONTEXT

The broader the context you expose yourself to, the more likely you will find new ideas that stimulate you to explore further.

In Part 3, we show how these seven elements work together for learners and leaders in the digital era and how to sail the 7 C's so as to nurture a culture of curiosity in digital organisations.

In short, the book is about you as a curious individual; about your organisations and about how to nurture curiosity as a leader.

Throughout the book you will find curious examples from our own experience and more broadly from the disciplines we find most fascinating. For consistency and to make it easier for the reader, we write referring to 'we' and 'us,' although the stories, experiences and viewpoints may come from any one or all of us.

Here are 12 curious ideas we explore in this book—

1. Curiosity is key to thriving in the new digital reality.
2. Curiosity is a state of mind that enable us to further anything.
3. Curiosity is deeply tied up with learning—how we learn, how we apply what we learn and the future of learning.
4. Curious learning learns from failure. It is the root of confidence.
5. Curious learning is essential for the evolution and survival of the contemporary business.
6. Investing in a culture of curious learning will directly impact the value in a business.
7. There are new rules for leadership in the digital economy.
8. Encouraging curiosity in a workforce will achieve greater and faster innovation.
9. Moving to a culture of curiosity and continuous learning is complex but achievable.
10. New technical platforms for learning will promote, enable and support curiosity.
11. The future of organisational learning is underpinned by networks of curious individuals.
12. Curiosity can be ignited in individuals.

Part 1
Understanding Curiosity

1.
CURIOSITY AND ME

'The important thing is not to stop questioning. Curiosity has its own reason for existence. One cannot help but be in awe when we contemplate the mysteries of eternity, of life, of the marvellous structure of reality. It is enough if one tries merely to comprehend a little of this mystery each day.'

Albert Einstein

Why Am I Curious?

Curiosity is a fundamental part of being human. Think about it... It drives us to learn and to grow, to form friendships and new relationships, to discover new things and new places, and to question the world around us.

We are born curious. Have you ever watched a baby explore the world? They are wide-eyed as they take in the sights, sounds and smells around them, touching and tasting everything. Curiosity is an innate ability we all have. From the day we are born, we are on a voyage of exploration and discovery.

In this chapter we will explore why we are curious as humans and why curiosity is important to us. We'll also describe what we mean by curiosity and start to see how we can use curiosity to power up our own learning and performance. We'll explore it from many different perspectives and disciplines, all with the purpose of understanding why this very human part of our nature is vital to our survival, now and into the future.

Our curious brains

Why are we curious? We have powerful brains that exist because of stimulus. Curiosity physically changes the physiology of our brain. When we are curious, our body releases powerful hormones that enable us to create new connections within our brains. Research shows that the act of wanting and desiring new information directly involves the mesolimbic pathways (often called the reward pathways) of the brain, which are responsible for the release of dopamine. This dopamine release stimulates, amongst other things, our sense of reward. It happens when we anticipate receiving pleasure or a benefit such as receiving a prize, eating food or exercising. Dopamine makes us happier, more focused, motivated and productive. Anticipation of reward is at the heart of curiosity.

Being curious gives us pleasure and is addictive. This positive feedback encourages us to explore further, to learn and discover more. Learning moment to moment with, as the saying goes, 'child-like wonder.'

Our brains need constant stimulation. If we stop learning and challenging ourselves, particularly later in life, our brain begins to atrophy. Antonio Damasio, the eminent neuroscientist, has written about how the act of learning to sing makes us more curious, as it rapidly establishes the patterns of neurons linked to activity in the body. Curiosity lays down neural pathways. Being exposed to different languages makes us comfortable with ambiguity, and more comfortable with the stress hormones we generate when out of our comfort zone, hence we are less afraid of new contextual situations. Antonio Damasio is a Professor of Psychology and Philosophy, as well as Neuroscience, and is answering his own curious questions about the brain from each of those disciplines.

We have evolved through curiosity

We have evolved to be continually curious. As our species becomes more developed, we humans spend less energy on basic survival and have more time to explore and be creative.

Curiosity has driven all human development. From where we live, how we live, the tools and technology we use. If we were not curious, we would be still living in caves to shelter from the weather and struggling to feed ourselves, whilst avoiding being eaten, trampled on or otherwise eradicated.

Psychologist-educators G. Stanley Hall and Theodate L. Smith (1903) provided one of the earliest modern studies on the development of curiosity. They compiled surveys and biographies of children from mothers relating to the development of their child's curiosity. In their findings, they describe that children go through four stages of early development. The first is stage is 'passive staring,' which begins as early as the second week of life and then moves on through each stage ultimately to what they call 'curiosity proper' as early as their fifth month. This 'curiosity proper' then stays with us for the rest of our lives.

Curiosity is required for survival

The need for survival is inherently connected to curiosity. At the most basic level, successful reproduction requires being curious outside our own immediate family. We need to be curious enough to find others to reproduce with. Consider the Khoisan people, more commonly known as Bushmen, who survive the almost barren land of the Kalahari Desert. Their curiosity over the ages has led them to survive and thrive even in that context. They are able to feed themselves from the berries and grubs that they can find in what urban individuals consider hostile territory. They are able to find water hidden underground and when water is not available from the ground, they can take it from the large tubers of plants that present minute indications on the surface. They have lived in that terrain for over

100,000 years. They also know that in order to survive they have to mate with members from other families and tribes. For that to happen they had to continually move to ensure they met with others on the edges of their territory.

We learn about context through our curiosity—defining what's safe, what's dangerous, what feeds us and what poisons us. Our best knowledge is gained mostly from making mistakes, hopefully not fatal ones.

The urge for safety may be behind why so many people are curious of, or even obsessed with, gossip. We cannot help but be intrigued by information about others that in some way should be unknown or secret.

Think about when we are told a long list of how great someone is—their achievements, qualifications and experience. How memorable was that list? Compare this to hearing a single piece of gossip we might hear about them. 'Did you know that so and so ….?' We far more readily pay attention to and remember the gossip rather than a list of achievements. Gossip is providing contextual information that is stored in the social area of the brain. Neuroscientists think we prioritise the retention of this information because it creates a sense of safety. We have learned information about somebody that may be useful to us in the future. We know this because gossip fires the attention and survival receptors in our brain.

What stimulates our curiosity?

Curiosity is often driven by surprise or uncertainty or, as renowned astrophysicist Mario Livio describes it, 'confounded evidence.'

We are surprised when we expect one thing to happen and then something else happens instead. We naturally become curious to close the gap between our expectations and reality. Surprise is part and parcel of being curious. We enjoy surprises. Our brain fires more of the pleasure-providing endorphins when it happens. It's why we often end up with a smile on our faces when we've been surprised.

Livio describes 'confounded evidence' as a situation where there are many possible answers to a problem or many potential futures that may occur. This ambiguity stimulates our curiosity through our desire for certainty. As psychologist Dr. Susan Engel says, curiosity 'can be understood as the human need to resolve uncertainty.' Another survival mechanism.

Surprise is helpful for learning. One of the main areas of the brain connected with processing and storing new sensory information is the hippocampus. Surprising stimuli activate the hippocampus more than familiar stimuli. When stimulated with novelty, the hippocampus compares the new information with existing stored knowledge. If there is a difference the hippocampus sends a pulse of dopamine to the midbrain, which activates the synapses in the nerve cells, creating stronger connections, leading to better long-term memory storage. Surprise or novelty seems to promote better memory and therefore more effective learning. It is the 'difference that makes a difference.'

Neuroscience shows us that the laying down of new pathways is related to learning and memory. What is very interesting is that there is a difference between whether we are making new knowledge ourselves or whether we are receiving something related to a body of knowledge from someone else. We know this because neuroscientists can monitor where glucose is consumed in the brain through live scanning. The hippocampus stores new information, then searches for related information already stored and associates the new information with these memories. Memory is a function of multiple connections. Which is why learning new things is easiest when linked to existing things we know. For example, the words for the numbers one and two in Japanese are '*ichi*' and '*ni*' and can be easily memorised as together they sound like 'itchy knee.'

The laying down of information that is in itself new, happens in a completely different part of the brain. If we see someone else experiencing pain, we react in a mirror-like way. In the presence of cortisol (a stress hormone) and the HPA (hypothalamic–pituitary-adrenal) axis we experience empathy and our knowledge that is learned socially is activated.

Curiosity and jokes

Many jokes work because they are based on the principles of surprise or confounded evidence. The arc of a good joke tantalises our curiosity because it takes us on a little journey. The set-up of a joke creates a particular expectation with something out of the ordinary and then a punchline which is unexpected. For example—

> **Patient:** Doctor, doctor, I've swallowed a twenty-dollar note.
> **Doctor:** Hmm. Take this and we'll see if there's any change in the morning

Sometimes jokes combine 'confounded evidence'—with ambiguity. For example—

> Why did the mushroom always get invited to parties?
> Because he was a fun-guy (fungi).

We thrive on ambiguity and the unexpected. It evokes a visceral response in us. It seems that some of the most effective ways to improve learning is to stimulate our curiosity by combining it with elements of surprise, uncertainty and humour.

Programming curiosity out

At some point in our lives, we often stop becoming curious. Why?

As children, we explore and explore, until at some point we hit a first point of failure. We try and we fail. We taste and we don't like. We reach and we fall. All of a sudden, the world has become a little more dangerous, a little less forgiving, and we start to lose confidence that our experiments will work out for the best.

As we progress further through childhood, our innate curiosity is often tempered further by well-meaning parenting—'don't touch that,' 'don't do that,' 'don't eat that,' 'come back here,' 'stop with all the questions.' Often for good reasons, parents rein back the constant questioning and exploration in the interest of safety or fear of allowing their child to fail. Research has shown that typically our curiosity peaks at around age four or five, and then gradually declines as we become more self-conscious and fearful about getting things wrong.

Is it any wonder that the first response we receive when describing this book on curiosity to others is 'well, you know that curiosity killed the cat!' Such sayings literally tell us to avoid being curious because it might be dangerous!

Ancient philosophers saw curiosity as a virtue—for example Socrates interpreted the practice to 'know thyself' to be a moral virtue. This mindset no doubt led to the growth and expansion of these societies. By contrast, in the Middle Ages curiosity was specifically described as a vice. In his influential *Confessions*, St. Augustine railed against curiosity. He considered the three kinds of temptation to be lust, curiosity, and power. His belief was based on an idea that all knowledge should exist within the religion and the canon of Christian scripture. It wasn't until Galileo's discoveries in the 17th century demonstrated the benefit of increased knowledge through scientific experimentation. We rediscovered and recognised that curiosity about the natural world in itself has value for the individual, for society and for how we organise ourselves.

In the modern-day workplace, many jobs stifle curiosity. From our very first day we are told that 'this is how things are done around here,' 'just follow the manual, 'don't worry about why, just do it.' At least for many physical or transactional jobs, consistency and standardisation are valued most. Deviation from the process is penalised in the name of efficiency. This was the essence of Taylorism, and although it may be good for factories and machines, it has proven to be detrimental for humans. Most notably through the Second World War.

Our mechanistic post-war world seems sometimes to have been designed to engineer curiosity out of our system. We became a species of implementers rather than innovators. In fact, those who would call themselves 'inventors' or 'innovators' are seen as outliers, possibly even strange individuals who do not quite fit in. Consider this perspective, people who we may think of as insane (from *in sana*—unhealthy mind) actually may just be living in a different context—literally outside of our conventional frames of reference.

The digital age is changing all of that. The greatest single advance in human technology has been the invention of the personal computer and the hyperconnected worldwide web. We are only just getting to grips with the implications for us and our societies. We are only now learning about how politics has been changed by social media companies like Facebook and Twitter. How our children are used to a world where they are engaged with constant Snapchat or WhatsApp conversations and messages from 'influencers.' Where there is a vast amount of information available to us and no clear pathways through it all.

We believe that curiosity is the power skill that helps us navigate in this hyper-ambiguous world of the future.

What does curiosity mean?

The origin of the word 'curious' in English comes from the old French word *curiosité*, which means 'the tendency to ask and learn about things by asking questions, investigating, or exploring.' The Greeks have two words that have slightly different meanings that evoke curiosity. The main word they use is *periergia* (Περιέργεια) which means curiosity, intrigue, nosiness. The noun *periergos* means curious, having an inquisitive mind, eager to learn, but it also means to be difficult to be understood, weird, meddling, or to be a busybody. The German word for being curious is '*neugierig*' also meaning to be nosy or prying.

However, the Greeks have another word for curiosity, *oestros* (οίστρος). This word has many meanings, it is linked to the passion for life, creativity and inspiration awakening. *Oestros* is related to the female cycle (think oestrogen) and so it is linked to ideas of cycles of creation, birth, growth as well as spiritual and mental inspiration. *Oestros* also relates to the idea of the gadfly that irritates or annoys animals and drives them to react. Constant irritation or returning to something is part of the idea. The concept also relates philosophically to existential concepts—when we become aware of our own death we become more focused on living life, not wasting time. Being full of passion and energy and not living as if we were eternal. Curiosity in language is related to ideas of being in the world and to life itself—it is a condition.

It is about questioning to discover and create new understanding, through the process of exploring, being in the world, being alive to opportunity, not being afraid and taking action.

Specific and general curiosity

The 19th century philosopher and psychologist William James described curiosity as 'the impulse towards better cognition.' James interpreted curiosity as wanting to understand more about something you do not know.

In the 20th century, psychologist Daniel Berlyne was one of the foremost figures with regards to the study of curiosity. He described two main types of curiosity, specific curiosity and general curiosity. Specific curiosity is connected with seeking out a particular piece of information, filling the gaps in our knowledge. For example, looking up the definition of a new word. Berlyne described 'general' curiosity as being either perceptual or epistemic. Perceptual curiosity is our motivation to find new stimuli, the exploration of things we have not encountered before. Epistemic curiosity relates to not only finding stimulating information, but also acquiring useful knowledge. Cicero, the Roman statesman and philosopher, wrote that curiosity is 'the innate love of learning and of knowledge…without the lure of any profit.'

So, we have (at least) two main types of curiosity to keep in mind. General curiosity which relates to learning about things that are new or unfamiliar. Specific curiosity is the deep dive into the details, establishing how or why something is or works.

What stimulates our curiosity?

The Greek philosopher Aristotle wondered what motivates us to do the things we do. He wrote that 'If we ask why we chop wood, the answer may be to build a fire; and if we ask why we build a fire, it may be to keep warm; but, if we ask why we keep warm, the answer is likely to be simply that it is pleasant to be warm and unpleasant to be cold.' In Aristotle's view, the ultimate answer to every question relating to why we do something is what he called *eudaimonia.* This Greek word is usually translated as 'happiness,' but it can be better understood in a broader sense, of living a satisfying life.

If we are stimulated towards happiness or at least avoiding pain, what pricks our curiosity to explore in the first place? As we have seen, we are curious about something surprising, or where we feel we have a lack, or where we can imagine knowing and doing something new to make us more satisfied. The feeling of lack could be of knowledge, experience or simply about another individual or community.

Subconscious curiosity

This is a synthesis of ideas and feelings that form an intuition that creates a desire to explore. In fact, recent research on the brain has shown that we process all information subconsciously at first, before it moves into our conscious mind. In mathematics there is a concept called strange attraction. Even with a wide variety of initial settings, a strange attractor tends to gravitate towards or cluster around a specific set of numbers. Humans also can act like strange attractors. We are subconsciously drawn to things depending on the questions we ask and how we feel about the answers we receive. Examples of subconscious curiosity are feelings that we may need to call a relative or friend, to move to another country or to have a child.

Conscious curiosity

In every moment, we continually curate the thoughts and feelings we bring into our conscious mind. As these thoughts pass through our mind, we will choose to focus on certain ideas. Something about it intrigues us and we want to know more. We then make a decision to explore and be curious about it. An example of conscious curiosity is the decision to find out why something is the way it is, or to learn a new subject area, skill or language. It is a conscious decision motivated by interest and curiosity.

External curiosity

When we are exposed to something different or unusual, we often wonder 'what if?' We are hard-wired to notice the unusual and for these things to get our attention. Once something does get our attention it might attract or repel. A new food, a different sport, a news bulletin or piece of technology. We constantly curate these external stimuli and make judgements about whether to investigate further. An example of externally driven curiosity would be a common reaction to seeing emergency lights on a police car or many people running in the street. We become curious about what is happening and try to establish the cause, even if we don't consciously choose to or even want to.

Intentional external curiosity

These are the things that are suggested to you to be curious about. Your attention is specifically drawn to a new topic area or activity. For example, your manager may suggest learning a new skill at work. A friend might recommend a new recipe to try, a new class to try or knowledge area to learn about. At work you might become curious to learn a hot new skill, knowing that it could open up interesting future opportunities. These stimuli prompt a new world to discover that we might not have otherwise considered.

We can power up our curiosity by giving ourselves opportunity for all four stimuli to be present in our lives. By paying attention to our inner voice. Being open to the people and the things around us and by seeking out diverse experiences.

In each of these situations, our interest is sparked. We start to wonder. What happens next? What if I do this? It is the grandest storytelling of all.

The difference between wonder and curiosity

What's the difference between curiosity and wonder? Researchers have also classified curiosity as being *state* or *trait* curiosity. State curiosity is being curious for the sake of it—for example, wondering why the sky is blue or where a stranger is heading. Trait curiosity relates to actively wanting to learn—trying a new activity or language.

In the context of this book, we focus on curiosity relating to being engaged in making, testing and exploring in the world. We believe curiosity requires action. To wonder is to just keep it in your head. To be curious is fundamentally to engage in the world.

Curiosity is often born out of frustration of not knowing. The word 'knowledge' in Greek is *gnosi* (γνώση) which means knowing through observation or experience. Many languages distinguish between knowing 'in your head' and knowing 'in your body.' For example, in French we distinguish between co*nnaître* and *savoir*, or in German *kennen* rather than *wissen*. It is the difference between knowledge gained through experimentation or realisation versus theoretical knowledge.

Kissing and curiosity

Take, for example, an activity perhaps every human on the planet has at least considered, if not regularly participated in—kissing. At some point, in almost everyone's life they become curious about kissing. We might see our parents kiss. We see actors kiss on our screens. We can even see animals kissing each other. As children, we wonder about this strange invention—often with feelings mixed equally with excitement and fear. The difficult thing about learning to kiss is it usually requires a willing partner. It can be practised solo but cannot be experienced properly without another. We have to take the plunge, risk getting it wrong and hopefully learn from the experience to improve. Wondering what it is like does not deliver the answers, it takes curiosity to act, to find a willing accomplice and then experience.

Curiosity goes beyond being inquisitive. As we have seen, the roots of the word come from busy-bodying or getting involved in cycles of things. It implies activity and uncovering. It implies action. In short, curiosity is putting wonder into action.

Wonder in the palm of your hand

If 'to wonder' is to keep something in your head and curiosity is putting it into action, that doesn't mean that wonder doesn't play an important role. Wonder can be a powerful trigger for curiosity. Think of the power of the question 'I wonder if...?' I wonder if we could create a machine that lets us fly like a bird? I wonder if we could put a man on the moon?

Vas Narasimhan, CEO of Novartis, encourages Novartis associates to ask the question 'I wonder if...' in their pursuit to reimagine medicine. To push the boundaries of current thinking and experiment with new approaches to science, technology and ways of working. It can be applied to almost any situation and when coupled with the power of curiosity, curiosity converts that wonder to action.

Narasimhan also talks of the physical embodiment of wonder, when he describes the power of medicines to improve and extend people's lives—that a small pill is 'wonder in the palm of your hand.'

Vas Narasimhan is actively promoting a culture of curiosity by asking simple questions that spark wonder and give permission to be curious.

Your curious power skill

The activity or action that is generated from curiosity can be harnessed to bring benefit across a range of skills. It supercharges the skills that we already have or that we are working to develop. Curiosity is a 'power skill' that super charges our ability to learn, make decisions and innovate.

Research undertaken by the University of California found that if curiosity is invoked alongside learning then the impact is to strengthen the learning experience. Approaching learning with curiosity actually helps you to learn better. As we have described, when you pair curiosity and learning it sparks the reward part of your brain, perking up the hippocampus and strengthening the new memories being created.

If you are looking to learn something, particularly if it is something that does not immediately excite you, make yourself curious about it. It will improve your likelihood of retaining it.

Curiosity improves your decision making

A study published in the *Harvard Business Review* also highlighted benefits that curiosity brings in improving the decisions that you make, through reducing decision-making error. It was found to reduce conflict, because being curious leads you to better understand others' points of view and to be more open to understanding the ideas that they propose. In addition, being curious works to enhance your communication skills, therefore leading to better performance with others in a team, as information is shared more openly. A curious person will listen to others more attentively.

A study at INSEAD found that greater curiosity leads to greater innovation. If you are more curious then that leads to being more creative and therefore more innovative.

The skills being boosted are what would traditionally be called soft skills. The term 'soft skills' does not do them justice, though, as these are skills that are increasingly in demand by employers—we prefer the term 'power skills.'

Curiosity makes you more attractive in the workplace

These skills are also becoming more valuable. An IBM report in 2019 showed that between 2016 and 2018, the most in-demand skills switched from hard skills, like software programming or technical skills, to power skills taking four out of the top five places.

Source: IBM: The enterprise guide to closing the skills gap, 2019

We look specifically at curiosity as a power skill or even a 'super-power skill' in the chapter 'Becoming a Curious Learner.'

With curiosity boosting these increasingly in-demand power skills, being curious will help not just in your current role, but also in any future career progression.

This is reinforced in the 2018 book *The Expertise Economy: How the Smartest Companies use Learning to Engage, Compete and Succeed* by Kelly Palmer and David Blake. Kelly is the former Chief Learning Officer from LinkedIn, and now, with David, is an executive at learning company Degreed.

They describe how 'Today, the vital skill set for success includes learning agility (the ability to learn new things quickly), collaboration and teamwork, perseverance, curiosity and the ability to question the world around you. If you aren't ready and willing to learn every day and keep up with the rapidly changing world, you can't and won't stay competitive.'

This applies at both an individual level, but also at an organisation or company level, and even at a society level.

Summary

We are all innately curious. You were curious enough to put time aside to discover what *The Curious Advantage* is all about. We can promise that it gets even more curious as you read on.

We are a curious species. As humans, curiosity has been key to not only our survival, but also our ability to flourish. We find curious the things that surprise us or stimulate us to explore, whether that motivation comes from within or from outside. We can bring our curious mind into our work and our everyday life to improve the way we learn, make decisions, even form better relationships. Curiosity gives us pleasure.

As our world becomes more digital and more automated it seems that curiosity is once again a key for humans to make sense of this new world. It might even be the power skill required to ensure we continue to thrive alongside artificial intelligence and whatever new technological developments await us in years to come.

Our curiosity can help us by acting as a supercharger for our other power skills. Curiosity helps us to learn better, it can enable us to make better decisions, and to communicate better with the people around us. It will even make us more innovative. How many other traits can have this level of impact on us as individuals?

In the next chapter, we will explore how our societies throughout history have used curiosity to power up their world.

References

Dunbar, R. (2004), 'Gossip in evolutionary perspective,' *Review of General Psychology*, Vol 2, 100-110

Fiebelkorn, I.C., Pinsk, M.A., and Kastner, S., 'A Dynamic Interplay within the Frontoparietal Network Underlies Rhythmic Spatial Attention,' *Neuron*, 2018, 99:4, 842-852

Gino, F., 'Why Curiosity Matters,' *HBR*, 2018, Sept-Oct, https://hbr.org/2018/09/curiosity

Gruber, M.J., Gleman, B.D., Ranganath, C., 'States of Curiosity Modulate Hippocampus-Dependent Learning via the Dopaminergic Circuit,' *Neuron*, 2014, 84:2, 486-496

Habibi, A. and Damasio, A. (2014), 'Music, Feelings, and the Human Brain, Psychomusicology: Music, Mind, and Brain,' 24:1, 92–102 https://dornsife.usc.edu/assets/sites/1247/docs/Music_Felings__the_Human_Brain.pdf

Hord, S.M., Roussin, J., Sommers, W.A., (2010), *Guiding Professional Learning Communities: Inspiration, Challenge, Surprise*, Wiley

IBM Report (2019), 'The enterprise guide to closing the skills gap'

Immordino-Yang, M.H., Damasio, A., (2017) *We Feel, Therefore We Learn: The Relevance of Affective and Social Neuroscience to Education*, Wiley

Kidd, C., and Hayden, B. Y., 'The psychology and neuroscience of curiosity,' *Neuron* 2015, Vol 88. No. 3, 449-460

Livio, M., (2017), *Why? What makes us curious.* Simon & Schuster, https://onlinelibrary.wiley.com/doi/full/10.1111/j.1751-228X.2007.00004.x

Palmer, K., and Blake, D., 2018, *The Expertise Economy: How the Smartest Companies use Learning to Engage, Compete and Succeed*, Amazon Barnes & Noble IndieBound

Peng X, Li Y, Wang P, Mo L, & Chen Q (2015), 'The ugly truth: negative gossip about celebrities and positive gossip about self entertain people in different ways,' Social neuroscience, 10 (3), 320-36

Stanley Hall, G. and Smith, T.L. (1903), 'Curiosity and Interest, The Pedagogical Seminary,' 10:3, 315-358, DOI: 10.1080/08919402.1903.10532722, https://www.tandfonline.com/doi/abs/10.1080/08919402.1903.10532722

2.

CURIOUS SOCIETY

'The paradox of education is exactly this—that as one begins to become conscious one begins to examine the society in which one is being educated.'

James Baldwin

When we organise ourselves as human beings into societies, communities, cities or countries, we are attempting to find ways to achieve more from our resources than if we are distributed and living alone. Some societies in history have been incredibly successful and we think one of the reasons for that has been the way they organised themselves to be curious. Curious societies find, store and transmit applied knowledge in ways that make them more efficient and powerful with the resources they have access to. This chapter is about how they have done so. How have successful societies organised themselves to be curious and applied it to survive and thrive?

Through our research process, we've come to understand how curious societies increase the diversity and sophistication of knowledge within their population, and in doing so, open up their ability to trade, create new products that others want, and attract others to them. In short there exists a direct relationship between curious societies and wealth.

In chapter one, we looked at the benefits of curiosity for individuals; in this chapter we go broader and look at the impact of curiosity on society as a whole. How has curiosity led to some of the most successful societies in history? How has curiosity aided us in times of crisis and what can we learn from how curious societies organise themselves?

Curious capacity

Before the advent of computers, we used organisations and institutions to orchestrate our societies. We invented political systems such as monarchies or democracies, with their various ministries and societies, to do so. From one perspective we can understand societies and civilisations as pre-computers.

We can define the ability of a system such as a society to achieve things collaboratively by organising and motivating their resources, including people, as its *capacity*. In this context, the amount of capacity a system has for achieving things is a combination of the number of links that exist between the agents in that system, how similar connections are chunked together, the speed with which knowledge transfer and learning take place, and most importantly, how it costs in resources to achieve this. The greater the number of connections between the people in a society, the greater the capacity for that society to problem-solve and create.

Let's take a look at some of the most famous societies in history, and their capacity to be curious.

Alexandrian hierarchies

When Alexander the Great conquered Persia he established the hierarchical cascading system of 'command and control' that has dominated the Western organisational thinking until the present day. It was the only way that he was able to communicate with such a vast empire and control the local kings and governors who brought their territory to him. The communications channels, the institutions for tax collection, the establishment of centres of knowledge, the appropriation of local gods, the inclusion of himself in the pantheon of local gods, the organisation of the military—these were the mechanisms that Alexander had to control the vast empire in his day.

He died young, aged only 32. When he died, his four favourite generals distributed the wealth accumulated and established the four post-Alexandrian kingdoms of Cassander, Lysimachus, Seleucid and Ptolemy. Through them they distributed the legacy of Alexander—not without battles and wars. Ptolemy established Alexandria in his honour. They kept his body there for a thousand years. They also established the greatest and most renowned centre of learning—the Great Library. It was built on the ideals of Alexander's tutors, Lysimachus, who taught him reading, writing and music; Aristotle who taught him statecraft, philosophy and the practical arts such as architecture and construction; and Leonidas who taught him about fitness and horsemanship. These skills and tutors had provided Alexander with the confidence to take on the mightiest powers of his age and conquer them, propelling him to become one of the most famous leaders of all time.

The Great Library at Alexandria was an academy that not only collected the best manuscripts and libraries of the age, but also created new knowledge by encouraging the greatest minds of that time to study and teach in and around it. Doing so formalised the knowledge archives, the learning and the curiosity of the Ptolemites (the people of Ptolemy), providing them with the institutional mechanisms to thrive all the way through to Cleopatra some 300 years later. The Ptolemites may well have been the wealthiest family in all history, relatively speaking. Their line continued to survive and rule by intermarrying into the Roman Imperial Elite. The last Ptolemite Queen was Cleopatra. Her curiosity, supplemented by her access to the knowledge and learning available to her, it could be argued, enabled her to understand the contextual and strategic changes that were coming to the region and establish the relationships and prestige necessary to enable her family's line to make the transition and survive.

Societies (and by inference organisations) that formalise the institutions of curiosity—whether by design, or through evolution—achieve more learning, more powerful links between people and ideas, in the fastest possible time at the cheapest possible cost. These societies possess a culture of curiosity and possess an edge. They possess strategic advantage.

Alexander's army was a culture on the move. Alexander was curious to such an extent that he explored the world with all the resources he could muster. Wise men, advisors, generals, soldiers and the court. They were a tented city on the move, who would often talk together late into the night and reflect on all they had encountered. Alexander wanted to take over the world and conquer the peoples he met. That was how he was trained from birth. He was wise in his curiosity, though; he learned to assimilate new cultures. To merge his gods with theirs, and to take on their practices where it was strategically advantageous. His was a culture of recombination and assimilation.

As he conquered new territory he left behind generals as governors and had them marry with the local people in order to squire a new generation of Alexandrians. He set up new cities—all called Alexandria—many of which still exist. In one, close to the borders of India, they still to this day speak a form of Hellenic Greek. He was able to leave behind all the elements of a culture that would last for thousands of years. The institutions he carried with him in his travelling army were reproduced and put in place when groups were left behind to establish colonies.

Alexander had established an effective machine for learning. They needed to learn about all that was required to run and administer an army on the move; to create and establish societies that were sustainable; to understand the shifting contexts they encountered as they moved through Asia. What are these institutions and ways of organising and how can they assist us in enabling curious societies today, two thousand years later?

The Ming dynasty

The Chinese Ming dynasty is considered one of the most successful empires of all time—if success is measured by its bureaucratic organisation and the promotion of peace. The formalisation of bureaucracy, the introduction of administrative exams, the institutionalisation of knowledge-gathering, creation of archives and organisations of knowledge and the standardisation of systems enabled the dynasty to rule over the territory that had been conquered by the Mongols. The Yongle Emperor created the Forbidden City which contained the headquarters of all these institutions, constructed to further and transmit knowledge and power. The Forbidden City effectively activated as a ritualistic and administrative engine for the management of the Empire. The wealth of the ruling class was substantially increased by their connections and trade with countries abroad. This outward focus caused much innovation. For example, chilies from South America were introduced into Szechuan cuisine. A vast amount of silver from abroad was accumulated through trade, that resurrected the economy after their paper money had been devalued. The printing press was invented to support the promotion of Chinese culture throughout the region.

The Ming dynasty was able to bureaucratise curiosity and create an administrative machine that went beyond tax collection. They specifically advanced knowledge through exams, and advanced knowledge within the technical crafts. They were able to provide a lens of criticality to their efforts. They were creative in their problem-solving and curated information in formal manners that promoted peace amongst the largest group of people for the longest period in their history.

There is some speculation that the Ming dynasty may even have equipped fleets of ships to circumnavigate the world. It is clear that the Ming dynasty was outward-looking, curious about the greater world, and felt confident enough to explore it.

The Ming dynasty collapsed as a result of a giant standing wave of calamity during the minor ice age in the 17th century. It led to famine, in turn rebellion and economic collapse. Combined with a devastating earthquake, the dynasty did not have the resources to turn things around, and it succumbed to internal warfare and a new dynasty that promised resurrection.

Although the Ming dynasty established powerful institutions, bureaucratic success and extensive, outward-looking curiosity—they were not the most technically advanced Chinese dynasty. That title belongs to the Song dynasty. Four hundred years previously they had mechanical clocks, cannons, mechanical fountains and many technological advances, much of it created through the cultural dialogue with the Mongols. This history was effectively destroyed by the later dynasties, as they sought to discredit them. There is often a political purpose behind curiosity in societies. Let's not forget that many innovative technologies are funded by military research. The point being that curious societies are curious for reasons very different from individuals. Politics, economics, warfare and prestige are more likely to be the drivers of curiosity at a social level. However, it is clear that the most successful societies in history have been very curious.

High-capacity societies

Beyond Alexander or the Mings, there have been many epochs defined by the most successful societies of their times—the Egyptians, the Persians, the Europeans, Great Zimbabwe, the Aztecs, the Americans—each in turn has managed enormous amounts of resources, organised their inhabitants, innovated, solved their problems, promoted their culture, and explored. One thing they all have in common is that they evolved mechanisms for processing enormous amounts of information. They each had the ability to combine curiosity with constructivism—that is to be curious and turn the data acquired into useful, pragmatic knowledge. As we step forward in time, we can see similar levers at work with successful high-capacity societies that are still with us today.

Knowledge fueled the Industrial Revolution

The Industrial Revolution in Britain emerged as a direct result of the invention of the steam engine. The ability of Britain to improve the efficiencies of these engines, and the fuel required for them, had an impact on Britain's ability to produce the goods required by the rest of the world. The scale and speed was unprecedented and led directly to the wealth and reach of the British Empire.

Underpinning the rapid advancement of technologies and innovation were multiple civil societies that emerged to share knowledge and solve problems. The Lunar Society (1775) was a broad group of people centred around Birmingham, but also from around all of Britain, made up of industrialists and philosophers. This group was constantly mutating and was characterised more by the fact that its members were in daily communication, rather than having specific meetings. The members included Erasmus Darwin (father of Charles), James Watt and Josiah Wedgwood. The most successful members were known for their practical and pragmatic research, and a constant commitment to innovation. The archive of Josiah Wedgwood's experiments in pottery, colour, durability and form is astonishing in its documentation and thorough application of science. He was truly curious—about everything connected to his craft and he developed laboratories, archives and detailed records to document his experiments and discoveries.

The Society of Art that became *the Royal Society of Arts for the Encouragement of Arts, Manufactures and Commerce* (RSA) in London is still going strong in its beautiful building just off London's Strand. It was formally established by William Shipley in 1754. It was based on an idea that had been established in Dublin called the *Society for Improving Husbandry, Manufacturers and Other Useful Arts.* They offered prizes, called premiums, to those who came up with patentable ideas for solving problems. Shipley had the idea of awarding prizes when he saw how effective horse racing was at motivating people to invest heavily in training and stables, for the simple prize of a small cup or medal, together with a great deal of prestige. The problems to be solved included better processes for manufacturing porcelain and inventing an alternative source material for the colour blue that would not require expensive importing of raw materials. At the heart of much of the competition was the need to beat France as a rival.

The same principle of organisation of prizes for results has been recreated by organisations such as InnoCentive today. InnoCentive awards prizes for the solving of the greatest challenges faced by the medical and pharmaceutical industries. It successfully enables laboratories to be funded for solving the micro problems that all add up to momentous breakthroughs.

Leveraging this same underlying motivation is re-emerging as 'gamification' (the application of game elements like scoring to other areas of activity) and leverages our in-built motivation for recognition or reward. We find this in so many walks of life now, particularly in app design (Strava or Duolingo as examples for exercise and language-learning), where the reward may only be a digital badge or virtual points, yet it drives our behaviours.

Digital society

The biggest shift in human communication arrived with the advent of telecommunications. The digital age has upped the bandwidth and breadth of our communication to the extent that we are able to collaborate as human beings across space, distance and time.

This vast increase in bandwidth means the command and control type communications, organised by hierarchies in the past, have been entirely supplanted by this mass of hyperconnected, self-organising agency that has become known as the cloud.

This is new. It has not been done before on this scale and its impact is proving seismic. One could argue that much of the unsettled politics we are experiencing around the world is the reaction of an older system of power and organisation, confronting the new.

Through social media, individuals now have direct communication channels to world leaders and vice versa. Similarly, in organisations the most junior can now access and communicate directly with the top leaders.

The problem for the older establishment is that the Internet is so hardwired into our economic supply chains that one cannot simply switch it off, although some societies are trying hard to at least censor it. To switch it off though would risk economic catastrophe. Our dependency on it has been demonstrated clearly during the COVID-19 pandemic and has meant that many businesses, communities and friendships have been able to stay connected. Without the Internet, the COVID-19 virus would have forced even more of the world to shut down completely. A pattern that has been seen in societies before—whether it was bubonic plague or typhoid—massive pandemics have often led to huge changes in social organisation around the world.

What does this digital reality for society mean for how we organise ourselves and why do we believe that curiosity is so important for the digital human, the digital organisation and the digital society?

Capacity for problem-solving

By digitally connecting everyone, we are effectively organising society as if it were itself a giant brain. The greater the number or opportunity of links between individuals, as with the cells in the brain, the greater the capacity to solve problems and to self-organise. What this means for how society eventually organises itself is yet to play out—however, we believe we can wager that governance of society, if we continue in this direction, will be significantly different from what exists today.

Organisation as a brain

If our society is now organising something like a brain, what does this mean for the productive processing capacity of our current society, and what does it mean for how we need to behave as individuals within it? The research around this question focuses on something called the *Network Effect.* The best definition of this is related to economies of scale, which means the more the network increases in size, the more the value to the user increases. The bigger the network, the greater the value. The more options, the more diversity. Therefore, the safer the exploration and ability to be curious to your advantage.

The quantification of the Network Effect is defined by Metcalfe's Law which states that the value of a network grows exponentially to the number of users on it. The assumption, though, is that every user can interact with every other user equally. This is not necessarily true for an organisation as there are constraints in place such as the extent to which a network is open or closed and where each member of the network is located relative to one another.

Openness leads to more of the network effect within an organisation. However, it should not be completely open, as this may destabilise the system. Our brain does it, our societies do it and our digital societies are doing it. Openness of the network is a function of discoverability, familiarity, language, and lack of idiosyncrasies. Things need to be obvious and easy to be open. This means that the degree of openness has an impact on the capacity of the organisation. If location is a constraint on being a member of a network, then the network cannot scale infinitely. The network effect has to be location-independent, otherwise the network cannot not survive.

To be effective as a curious system, our society needs to strike the right balance between being open enough and being connected enough to grow and sustain, without descending into complex chaos.

Strange attractors

One of the effects of curiosity is that it enables more and more connections to be made within a system. As existing context is explored, new connections of interactivity, content, interests and attraction are made. Complexity science, which uses multi-disciplinary theories to study systems, has looked at the groups of people and ideas that cluster together using the idea of strange attractors mentioned above.

Strange attractors are not unlike what happens when our brain makes neural connections between connected concepts. The greater the number of connections, the greater the capacity of the brain to function.

In pre-computer society we would suggest that the organisation of these strange attractors can be likened to the societies, professional bodies and institutions that exist to further particular bodies of knowledge. These can be scientific, or academic, or civil or general. Today these institutions are under pressure as the role they played in our current epoch is being undermined by the digital societies and clustering that's taking place online. There was huge questioning as to whether smartphones would be allowed into the debating chambers of the Westminster Parliament. Once permitted, MPs were able to text and tweet, and shift the conversation out of the Chamber. Hansard, the creators of the official documentation, shifted from being the single record. Reporting shifted from being mediated by the parliamentary press to being mediated within Twitter and other social media.

The pandemic has led to the Parliament at Westminster looking to digitise the parliamentary procedures, an idea that previously was considered unthinkable given the physical organisation of parliamentary process at Westminster. Discourse is central to Parliament, informal and formal. Voting is organised across lobbies, and people are required to be physically present. All of these functions are now being reproduced online.

The traditional knowledge bases are becoming increasingly undermined by social media—and the traditional mediation of politics, the law, the academy, science or news reporting is considered to be under threat. We think they are not so much under threat as transitioning to different digital forms within society.

This shift to knowledge being digital and being open to all should be good news for the curious, as there is so much more to explore!

Post-truth

The traditional sources of knowledge have been undermined to the extent that the record of 'truth' has shifted. We are sure that in time our society will figure out mechanisms to ensure that knowledge that is proven, validated and impactful is distinguishable from populist knowledge. The tyranny of the thumbs up and thumbs down feedback system, based on feelings or political persuasion, will be replaced. How will we test knowledge that enters the canon of learning to ensure that it satisfies a set of criteria for validity? How will we ensure knowledge is free from bias? Will blockchain provide the solution for tagging data and sources to ensure the traceability of information in time?

Why do societies fail

Jared Diamond's book *Collapse* used a comparative methodology to tell the story about societies that have collapsed in the past. For example, he tells the story of the Greenland Norse who held a taboo about fish and died out despite the abundance around them.

According to Diamond, the primary reason for collapse is where the impact on the environmental resources required is too much to sustain the society—basically not enough resources—these may be due to habitat destruction, soil fertility, water management, overhunting, overfishing, destruction of native species, overpopulation and the increased impact of people. These may lead to climate change, toxins in the environment, energy shortages, and full use of the earth's photosynthetic capacities, leading to desert. Illness, politics and war may escalate the decline.

However, he also suggests that when faced with signs of failure two things may save the society—

- Long-term planning or bold, anticipatory decision-making before crises are reached
- And willingness to consider core values

We would suggest that curiosity as a value within a society is core to its long-term survivability. Ideological thinking, that may be the norm in a society, but that cannot shift or change in the face of change, may contain the seeds of its own destruction. That means that continuous change is key to survivability, change requires options for consideration, and curiosity is key to identifying options and creating new contexts.

Today, the rise of populism, that ferments increasingly polarising views based on biases or prejudice, may indicate a lack of curiosity and feelings of threat from 'the other.' Travel may expand the mind and open up wider perspectives as it acquaints us with other ways of viewing the world, but not always. If individuals are curious and open to new ideas, if organisations embrace curiosity, then these may lead to a positive wider impact on society.

According to research studies, curiosity reduces conflict. Expanding on this, at its simplest using a phrase such as 'tell me more' rather than directly challenging someone else's opposing position, enables us, through curiosity, to understand different perspectives.

Stephen Covey's book *The 7 Habits of Highly Effective People* has a similar suggestion, 'Seek first to understand, then to be understood.' A more curious society could help to, at least in part, counter the polarisation of society.

What are the implications for organisations and society

The concept of the organisation as a brain has been around for some time and was identified by systems theorists such as Herbert Simon in the 1940s and 1950s. A great synthesiser of these ideas was Gareth Morgan in his book *Images of Organization* (1986).

In the 1950s organisations came to be viewed as information-processing systems—and functionalities were put in place that enabled them to be so. These included the capacity to sense, monitor and scan their environments; the ability to relate this information to operating norms to guide the behaviour of the system; the ability to detect significant deviations from these norms; and the ability to initiate correcting actions.

As Morgan writes, the problem with this is that it is an example of single-loop learning—a single loop that consists of an action and a reaction. If the reaction is not what is required then a new action is tried, but the thinking is constrained. A learning organisation is one that can learn, self-organise, mutate and evolve.

Morgan identified the things that get in the way of being a learning organisation as

- the division of responsibilities that cause fragmentation of knowledge and attention;
- bureaucracy and asymmetric access to knowledge, producing

deception in the system;
- collective delusions where espoused theories are different from what actually goes on.

How do we build an organisation or a society that is like a brain?

Morgan synthesises four things that should be done to encourage double- and triple-loop learning—

1. Encourage and value openness and reflectivity, accept error and uncertainty
2. Recognise the importance of e xploring different viewpoints
3. Avoid imposing structures of action and allow intelligence to emerge
4. Create organisational structures and principles that help implement these principles.

He adds four more criteria that enable the organisation to function as a brain—or something he calls the 'holographic' organisation.

- Redundancy of function - Each individual or team should have a broader range of knowledge and skills than is required for the immediate task at hand, thus building flexibility into the organisation
- Requisite variety - The internal diversity must match the challenges posed by the environment. All elements of an organisation should embody critical dimensions of the environment
- Minimal critical specification - Allow each system to find its own form
- Learning to learn - Use autonomous intelligence and emergent connectivity to find novel and progressive solutions to complex problems.

These principles are exactly why we encourage curiosity at every level within the organisation—as it specifically requires learning to learn and soundings from what is taking place in reality.

It takes a village

There are many ideas that cannot be achieved by an individual—it takes a community, well organised, with purpose and motivation to solve a problem and move our civilisation forward. There are many ideas or objectives that are beyond the powers of an individual to explore. For example, 'I wonder what's beyond the horizon?' can only be answered safely by changing the question to 'What if I sail beyond the horizon?'

Some things can't be discovered on their own. They require a community to explore curiously and extend beyond what's possible within a 'reasonable time frame.' Some ideas can only be answered by working from what others have done or as we say, standing on the shoulders of giants. For example, the creation of lenses and optics required first the understanding of glass and glass-blowing. Then came the knowledge of how to create lenses through sand-grinding and polishing. The interaction with other civilisations spurred these ideas on. In addition, explorations into the nature of light had to be coupled with the technology of glass-making. This required a community that was diverse enough, sophisticated enough and small enough to make these connections. Such as Galileo's University in Padua, which was financed by the Serene Republic—Venice!

Preserving and transmitting knowledge

Christopher Columbus may have discovered the so-called New World and the Americas; however, what is little known is that he could not have done so without the navigational expertise of Basque navigators. The Basques' culture and methods of organising themselves, and their knowledge, throughout their ancient culture, enabled them to explore, survive and return to their homes. Not only did they have a sophisticated ability to navigate but they also routinely fished for cod off the banks of Newfoundland, an ocean away. They also created salted cod, which enabled them to preserve their catch.

The Basques have systems for finding new knowledge, preserving existing knowledge and transmitting it amongst their community. How they arrived at this is not known. What is known is that the Basques have been in their land from before recorded history. There are families that live in caves attached to their houses that have belonged to their families before they can remember. We also know that their language is unlike any other language group on the planet. Every part of Basque society is organised into multitudinous interest groups that meet regularly and that compete between each other as individuals, as well as between each other as groups, to advance their knowledge and skills.

The importance of being open

Curiosity is important in open society. Where things are shut down or are too rules-based, we cannot progress. The digital society requires online institutions that are furthering knowledge—both personal and canonical knowledge. Curiosity drives how we approach all the access to knowledge that exists with openness and the willingness to discover things that may unsettle us.

We would suggest that it is not enough to just have access to knowledge; the curious society needs to be able to provide mechanisms for individuals to understand things and to further canonical or formal knowledge. The curious society needs to be constantly testing and inventing.

Museums as archives

One of the most interesting repositories of knowledge in London is the area called Albertopolis. Established in 1851, it consists of the Victoria and Albert Museum, Imperial College for Engineering and Science, the Royal College of Art and Design, the Royal College of Music, the Royal Geographical Society, the Royal Albert Hall and various other institutions devoted to the research and development of practical knowledge. It is a complete organic set of institutions that drive human activity and it thrives when discourse takes place between them all.

It was established by the Victorians with the profits generated by the Great Exhibition in the Crystal Palace. It is a mini-city of curiosity that enables ideas to be stimulated through culture and the arts, formulated and created through science and engineering and then launched in the market through design. It contains institutions for promoting music and the arts that promote the stimulation, joy and motivation that comes from being humanly creative. The Victorians coupled the machines of the Industrial Revolution with the organisation of knowledge and culture. They understood that rich context was vital to stimulate the dynamics of meaning, narrative and enthusiasm that drive discovery. These ideas were informed by Prince Albert and his advisors on the continent, most notably in Bohemia. Curiosity was at the heart of Victorian England.

Curiosity furthers technical advances

In Paris there is a wonderful museum called *Musée des arts et métiers*, or the French Museum of Arts and Crafts. It contains many curiosities that document the development of ideas. For example, it contains the primary Foucault Pendulum which gives evidence of the earth's rotation. It contains a collection of the tools of a cardinal who established a laboratory for the exploration of physical phenomenon.

The museum has within it a room that shows the progression of technology, from the pipe organ to the Cray computer. The story begins with the pneumatic and lever systems of a pipe organ. Next it shows the mechanical switching mechanisms that were created for organs when they were first electrified. These switches were used in the first telephone exchanges. Then it shows transistors and how they were created to miniaturise these switches. Next came PABX systems. These in turn led to the development of diodes and circuit boards and finally at the end is a Cray computer. It was the fastest in existence. There is a direct relationship between all these developments—curiosity—and specifically the ability to make connections between things from one domain that may solve the problems in another.

Scientific and technical advance is formalised through such academies of science and arts. Their advances are laid down in patent law, and knowledge is maintained and distributed through media, museums and archives.

Curiosity and experimentation

Being curious inevitably bring us to the question, 'How do we know this to be so?' The history of a scientific method always brings us to an understanding of *inductive reasoning* and *deductive reasoning.* 'Deductive' being that which we deduce from our system of logic and 'inductive' being that which we learn from interrogating the thing itself, or nature.

Buddhist Lamas, Indian mystics, Arabic philosophers and Western science have all developed systems of thought for answering fundamental questions, with a major advance being created by Francis Bacon's *Advancement of Learning* in 1605. Bacon suggested experiments should be carried out to eliminate ambiguities. Sir Isaac Newton shifted these ideas forward again with a focus on inductive reasoning as the sole basis for knowledge—and shifted laboratory work away from alchemy towards knowledge through experimentation.

Speculation and experimentation are at the heart of the scientific method—and developments since Newton have attempted to reconcile the two—by enabling a dialogue between that which is speculated and that which is tested.

Karl Popper developed the idea of *critical rationalism* in 1934 in *The Logic of Scientific Discovery* that essentially required scientific theory to speculate, based on the canon of accepted understanding, and for science to pursue experiments that could show these theories to be false, in which case they were discounted.

In 1962, Thomas Kuhn wrote *The Structure of Scientific Revolutions,* which held that the paradigms that science exists within are themselves constructs and relative. This has led to the predominance of peer review as the basis for evaluation of scientific work.

What this means is that however sophisticated the scientific philosophy held by a culture, all knowledge is only advanced through experimentation and communication. Where it can be applied, then it can be useful.

There is a broad requirement to establish criteria to differentiate between science and the proliferation of pseudoscience in order to answer the question, how do we know this to be true? A similar challenge to the current situation of determining what is real news and fake news.

The curiosity to cure

As we write this book the world is going through the global COVID-19 crisis. Countries, communities, families and individuals are being impacted like nothing we have seen for generations. Billions of people are confined to their homes and travel has all but ground to a halt. Lives are being lost or forever impacted and the global economy will take years to recover. In the midst of all this, though, curiosity is providing a glimmer of hope.

Around the world, scientists and medics are applying curiosity and scientific endeavour to find potential solutions or ways to help. The focus is dramatically accelerating developments across this field, whether it is looking for ways to create a vaccine, or revisiting existing medicines to see which may have an impact to alleviate the symptoms of those suffering.

The global community is coming together, leveraging technology to share ideas, data and findings. Engineering firms are asking, 'I wonder if… we could help,' and repurposing their factories to make everything from ventilators to personal protective equipment. There are stories of car companies like GM and Ford or vacuum cleaner companies like Dyson all stepping in to apply their innovation to save lives.

Creativity and curiosity are being applied in the most surprising of ways. For example, a local brewery in Switzerland, on finding that they had an excess supply of beer due to the cancellation of the local carnival, further distilled the alcohol and turned it into hand sanitiser to address the short supply. There are further stories of diving masks being adapted as hospital breathing apparatus or ventilators being adapted to support two patients instead of one to save lives. These stories highlight the ingenuity that people are showing as the global community rapidly iterates and innovates. We are sharing, questioning and improving together to address these challenges.

Summary

Bringing together what we can learn from past curious societies, we would summarise the ingredients of these as—

- A culture of curiosity and openness
- Curiosity being held as a value
- A broad philosophical understanding of bias in thinking
- Forums for questioning and connecting people
- Broad and continuous exposure to new contexts, new ideas and difference
- Broad understanding of the value of diversity
- Safety in the exploration of and meeting of 'otherness'
- Processes and language for the organisation of ideas through experimentation and testing
- The regulation of curiosity to avoid disaster—long-term thinking and scenario work
- Institutions that organise knowledge and document outcomes
- Funding

The capacity of societies to be successful is linked to how curiosity is systematised and knowledge advanced, enabling the greatest number of connections for as low a cost to society as possible. It is the connections that we make to each other and to different sources of knowledge that have an impact on how a Curious Society may thrive.

In the next chapter we take a look at what all this might mean for the Digital Society.

References

The Albertopolis Companion (2015), RCA
Arrian, Mensch, P., & Romm, J. S. (2010), *The Landmark Arrian: The Campaigns of Alexander.* Anabasis Alexandrous: a new translation (1st ed). New York: Pantheon Books
Brook, T., *The Troubled Empire: China in the Yuan and Ming Dynasties*, Harvard Cover
Covey, S. (1989), *The 7 Habits of Highly Effective People*, Free Press
Diamond, J. (2005), *Collapse: How Societies Choose to Fail or Succeed*, Viking Press
Fuentelsaz, L., Garrido, E., Maicas, J.P., 'A Strategic Approach to Network Value in Network Industries,' *Journal of Management*, May 2012
Howes, A. (2020), *Arts & Minds: A history of the Royal Society Arts for the Encouragement of Arts, Manufactures and Commerce* (RSA), Princeton University Press
Kauffman, S.A. (1993), *At Home in the Universe*, Oxford University Press
Kuhn, T. (1962), *The Structure of Scientific Revolutions*, University of Chicago Press
Lane Fox, R. (2005), *Alexander the Great*, Penguin London
Morgan, G. (1986), *Images of Organization*, Sage
Popper, K. (1959), *The Logic of Scientific Discovery*, ed. 2005, Routledge
Naiden, F.S., *Soldier, Priest, and God: A Life of Alexander the Great*, Oxford, Oxford University Press
Romm, James S. (2011), *Ghost on the Throne: The Death of Alexander the Great and the war for Crown and Empire*, New York: Alfred A. Knopf
Struve, L.A. (1993), *Voices from the Ming-Qing Cataclysm*, Yale University Press

3.
DIGITAL CURIOSITY

'Life is full of electronic desires
where one dream spliced with currents of wires
Leading our footsteps to the online shore,
we expect the waves to bring us some more
of those binary tides to wash us away
to the cyber beach for a lonesome day'

Munia Khan

'In the digital age, the simple and the complicated become more and more automated, and so you're left with the complex. The only way you can navigate complexity is to have a mindset of inquiry where you're constantly asking questions, navigating, understanding there's not going to be any absolute answers. You have to almost be an explorer, and to explore you have to be very curious.'

Vas Narasimhan

We are seeing a dramatic resurgence in curiosity as a specific response to the realities of the new digital epoch. One of the biggest trends during the COVID-19 lockdown has been the increase in people taking part in online classes and courses and furthering their knowledge.

In this chapter we look at some of the digital developments that will underpin our ability to be curious in the moment.

Digital capacity

The digital revolution has dramatically increased the connectivity between people and knowledge. The telephone connected many, and fax machines upped the bandwidth of knowledge we were able to move around; however, the digital revolution has gone infinitely further. By 2017, over half of the world's population was online, providing practically instant connectivity to each other anywhere on the planet. Currently two-thirds of the world population have a mobile phone and 57% (4.4 billion people) are online. Digital has also seen a proliferation of different types of devices for us to connect with knowledge and each other, to the point where many people on the planet have multiple computers, smartphones and IoT (Internet of Things) devices ready to be connected wherever they are.

The price point for this has been driven so low that the potential capacity of our digital society has increased phenomenally. However, it's not enough just to be connected. The knowledge that is exchanged by groups who form within this hyperconnected cloud has to be organised and used. The speed, efficiency and clarity of this organisation of knowledge are the things that set one group apart from another.

What this means is that *how* our digital societies or organisations, or interest groups, or communities organise themselves to process the knowledge is important to their success.

Triple-loop learning

Chris Argyris took the ideas of *single-loop learning* further. He suggested that single-loop learning satisfies the question *what to do?* For example, rules for behaviour that govern the stabiliser on a plane. *Double-loop learning* answers the question *what should we do* or *are we solving the right problem?* For example, reframing whether we really should be stabilising the plane, do we want to climb or dive, perhaps it's an engine problem? This requires the kind of learning that leads to insight. *Triple-loop learning* interrogates context and asks *how do we decide what is the right thing to do?* This is about perceptions, principles and learning how to learn effectively. Why did we come to those conclusions and what underpins our assumptions?

Curiosity requires us to question everything, to do so critically, to reflect on our biases, to test our assumptions, and to learn by doing whilst interrogating our context. Curiosity provides us with the opportunity to ask whether this is the right thing to be doing given what we are trying to achieve, question or understand. Curiosity is at the heart of enabling networked digital organisations to thrive.

What does this mean for how we construct the platforms that support the curious digital society?

An open society is driven by openness between people—relationships and the questions that people ask between each other, avoiding group think and totalitarianism. The open society has forums that enable people to present their ideas, to present their experiments, to test their experiments, and to receive real-world feedback.

Open access

The open exchange of this knowledge is influenced by how knowledge is organised. Google achieved ascendance because it simply enabled people to find information easily. It took out other great search engines, such as AltaVista (remember that?), simply because the interface was faster and more intuitive. The key thing is to have a platform that not only creates the connections between groups, but also guides people through the labyrinth of information.

The platform needs to enable a journey to be easily defined. It needs to serve information in a timely manner, provide contextually relevant information and enables people to explore both General and Specific Curiosity.

For example, many organisations are creating partnerships where their employees have free-to-use access to complete online university courses, provided by the best branded universities in the world. Novartis is providing full access to catalogues like Coursera (3,500 online programmes from 200 global universities) and Linkedin Learning (14,000 online video-based courses). These catalogues allow people to be curious around a *specific* topic. For example, employees could dive into a four-week programme on Essentials of Global Health from Yale University, or explore more *general* curiosity with short videos across a range of topic areas. People are actively encouraged to spend 100 hours a year, approximately 5% of their working time, engaging in learning activities.

After open access - learning in the flow?

The next development has work-related information being served to people where and when they need it, in a manner that has integrity with the work experience and doesn't disrupt it. This is where artificial intelligence (AI) will play its role in this revolution. Josh Bersin calls this 'learning in the flow of work.'

Some imagine learning in a Netflix-like scenario, where we will automatically be served the learning we are most likely to be interested in. However, there are complexities with learning in the flow of work that are different from simply serving media based on choice algorithms.

Learning in the flow of work requires external awareness by the algorithm, it needs to be anticipatory based on the context of work. Imagine someone in a lab conducting experiments—their process, lab results and questions will need to be sufficiently online to enable useful information and learning to be served in a useful manner. Perhaps the scientist will be wearing a heads-up display mask and be able to ask questions such as, 'I have found this data in this sample, what will happen if we add the following to it?' and, 'how do I test for *x*?' The companion tool will then serve answers or offer a short video that shows how to do things. It's not unlike Tony Stark in Iron Man building things with his holographic simulator. A key skill for us humans will be to know how to ask intelligent questions.

New technologies and digital societies

In the palms of our hands we can access almost the entirety of human thought. We are improving the way we organise all this information and data. We can make the world we live in as contextually wide, or as specifically detailed as we want.

We are continually served new information, new pathways to explore through adverts, streaming news, never-ending data feeds. How many times have we started reading an article or looking at a product online, only to discover something new, thinking, 'That's interesting,' and deviating from our current path to explore an adjacent or different topic. Our devices are encouraging us to explore and be curious again. A whole industry has sprung up designing 'click-bait' (enticing questions or statements) to try to lure us into following our curiosity by clicking on links and then gaining our attention.

The 2020 coronavirus pandemic showed us how rapidly new technologies and platforms can now be adopted, whether it was corporations that rolled out new collaboration tools such as Microsoft Teams in days, when this would normally take months, or consumer uptake of platforms like Khan Academy. Khan Academy, a non-profit online learning platform created by Sal Khan, provides free access to virtual schooling. Khan saw millions of new learners flock to the platform as schools closed around the world, driving a 250% increase in usage in a matter of weeks. People young and old embraced new forms of communication such as the Zoom video communications platform, as family and friends looked for ways to stay in touch virtually, resulting in the share price more than doubling in three months from the start of 2020.

Curiosity in an age of robots

For many years we have seen factories and assembly plants filled with robotic arms replacing or augmenting the human workers, but this is not where the greatest short-term scale for robots will come. Many of the robots that we are seeing today and will see more of in the short term are not like metallic humanoids in the sci-fi movies, but are in fact software, lines of computer code, bots that are written to perform tasks that replace the transactional or repetitive aspects that exist in so many of our human jobs today. They may be chatbots in a contact centre, bots dealing with reconciliations in an accounting department, watching for fraud on your credit card, or taking your order at your local hamburger restaurant.

This is widespread. Already, 62% of companies are using automation to eliminate transactional work and replace repetitive tasks, and 41% of companies are extensively using automation. This is coming fast. The market is growing at 20% per year.

While some roles may eventually be replaced by these electronic bots or perhaps in the long term by physical robots, far more roles will be augmented. Repetitive tasks will be done for us by bots and the human focus will be on the non-repetitive elements, the unusual, the creative, the personal, the discovery and the innovative.

Even in the most advanced areas of work there are robots today. Surgeons' work can be assisted by robots to support a wide range of procedures. Robotic-assisted surgery is particularly helpful with operations requiring a high level of precision and control. Advanced robots can perform some of the most exacting keyhole surgery, such as tying a surgical knot or laser cauterisation, deep in the stomach of a patient with minimum invasion, meaning less pain, faster recovery and less chance of infection for patients.

So here we see another force driving the need for greater curiosity. *Automation* is leading to an increased demand for soft skills like creativity, disruptive thinking and asking critical questions.

New skills required

Layer onto this world another force, the *acceleration of reskilling.*

As the world changes, so do the roles and skills required of the workforce. This requires us to accelerate the reskilling of our people, and ensure our associates are supported, and have the right tools and knowledge to develop the skills they need to develop in their new roles. With an increased speed of change, the ability to learn efficiently in a sea of information and evolving content is essential to acquiring the knowledge and skills needed in our roles.

In 2019, a third of people surveyed by Gartner, the global analyst firm, recognised that they had learned a 'new to world' skill in the last three years. A 'new to world' skill being something that did not exist before—examples would be, 'robotic process automation,' 'machine learning,' or 'blockchain.' At the same time, their research predicts that 19% of the skills that we have today will be irrelevant in three years' time. Things are moving fast and getting faster. Research by consulting company Deloitte goes further, stating that 54% of employees will require significant reskilling and upskilling in just three years. Skills are changing. The hard skills or technical skills that we have relied on are having shorter and shorter 'lives' and therefore we need to be on the lookout for the next skill to help us. We need to be curious about what we can learn. In a change from the past, it is the softer skills—communication, service, critical thinking and collaboration—that will be enduring and therefore will increase in demand.

Staying relevant or don't be a liability

Given the speed that skills are evolving, not investing in continuous learning means that we may be bringing out-of-date approaches, methodologies or thinking to a problem by not using the latest tools. Digital marketing is a great example of this. Many companies work to an annual marketing cycle—develop the message, create the campaign, execute, then assess the impact and effectiveness. For the next year, they simply refine or adapt the message then repeat. This model applies across many industries, with the only variable being the length of the cycle. With changes in digital and data over recent years, the method has been significantly disrupted. Cycle times are being dramatically reduced to weeks, days or even hours. We can access large datasets with real-time dashboards to understand which messages are landing best with which customer profiles. People and companies not using these techniques will find their messages lack the impact of their competitors. Bringing out-of-date skills to work means we risk becoming a liability.

What about expertise?

The Internet has changed the way we view knowledge. The world's information is now only a Google search away or a question posed to Alexa, Siri or other personal digital companions. Despite a few populist anomalies, expertise is still highly valued. In many industries, experts can still command high rewards for their knowledge and skills. Increasingly there are areas where our traditional or stereotypical view of expertise is being challenged. However, expertise is not going away. The application of knowledge through assiduous questioning can only be gained through experience. The speed with which we assimilate these skills may be increasing—consider the number of younger and younger prodigies who are emerging in many fields—but what is changing is the immediate availability of expertise. Just as 'learning in the flow of work' will bring immediate learning to the task at hand, so, too, will it provide immediate access to experts in a just-in-time manner.

Artificial intelligence (AI) and machine learning (ML)

AI and ML bring new and exciting opportunities into the world, such as research and development, customer engagement and production. In the world of learning, they are providing predictive analytics, powerful personalised learning journeys or smart learning assistance.

According to a World Economic Forum report in 2020, we will need to upskill billions of people to meet the requirements of the future as AI replaces existing roles.

AI and ML fall within the area of data science, which has become one of the hottest skills areas over the last few years. A drive around the high-tech city of Hyderabad, India, demonstrates how it is the skill of the moment, with adverts in the streets everywhere you look, for courses and training to build your data science skills and become a data scientist.

Whole humans

As a reaction to virtual working, having more time and being more digitally connected we are seeing a trend both inside and outside of the workplace—a desire in society to be 'whole humans.' We are a social species and the vast majority of people want to be in a community. We are becoming more aware of the importance of our mental and physical health, of gaining broad, holistic knowledge from multiple sources and fulfilling our sense of our whole self. We are no longer satisfied with a job defining our entire identity or *raison d'être*. We are increasingly becoming identified by our interests and the projects that create meaning for us beyond the workplace.

New organisational shapes with skills at the heart

As organisations adapt to a faster, more connected world, new organisational shapes are emerging—such as those that can be characterised by the brain or holographic organisation. We are moving towards less hierarchical organisational structures and more fluid value chains. In this context, we need to evaluate how learning is embedded in our systems, as applied skills and knowledge become the main currency of work.

IBM is a business that has put skills at the heart of their organisation powered by AI. Their HR processes motivate and reward their employees to invest time in learning the latest hot skills. They have opened up opportunities for new roles and increased compensation (with the counter being that not having up-to-date skills will limit these opportunities and pay). AI-based algorithms help in suggesting annual pay increases and recommend personalised learning paths based on their employees' own aspirations.

Gordon Fuller, IBM Chief Learning Officer, says, 'IBM remains a test bed for innovation and we have created a movement within IBM for continuous learning. We are not doing this because it is a cool idea but because our world is changing and we need to ensure we support our employees as they reinvent themselves and future-proof their career…we explore a deep understanding of the learners' behaviours, enabling them with the right assortment of skills for today and future-proofing via original and curated content that stimulates our employees' learning appetite.'

A new demographic mix

Demographic shifts are putting pressure on organisations to find new ways to attract, retain and develop talent across different locations and generations. Understanding the expectations, value and challenges of employees is key for delivering learning experiences that equip us for this rapidly emerging future.

Summary

Digital is creating a fundamental shift again in our society and forcing us to ask questions of ourselves as a species. How do we stay relevant? What is the future for 'the human?' How much technology should we allow?

Digital is also nudging societies to become more permissive of exploration and challenging the status quo. We see that we are coming into a phase where we have more time and therefore more inclination to explore. We are rediscovering being curious in all aspects of our lives.

In the next chapter we will see what this means in the content of organisations and how organisations can gain competitive advantage simply by being more curious.

References

Argyris, C. (1995), *Organizational Learning II: Theory, Method, and Practice: Theory, Method, and Practice*, FT Press

Gartner Group Research (2019), *Emerging Risks Survey*

World Economic Forum Research Report (2019), *Shaping the Future of Technology Governance, AI and Machine Learning*

4.
CURIOUS VALUE

'Our only limit to our realization of tomorrow will be our doubts of today.'

– Franklin D. Roosevelt

In this chapter we look at the changing landscape within which our organisations operate today and consider how they need to adapt to this new world. We take a look at why curiosity is vital for our organisations. Through being curious, organisations can adapt faster, identify change and risk, increase quality and take full advantage of the opportunity the incredible digital changes present. Organisations that have invested in curiosity as a value are shifting their culture, becoming more innovative and delivering better results. In short, there is identifiable value to be had in investing in curiosity.

As we write we will refer to 'organisations' but don't take this to only mean businesses, as what we describe can be as readily applied to clubs, charities, educational institutions, societies, teams or any other collection of people.

How has the landscape changed?

The global business landscape is undergoing a massive transformation from the industrial to the digital. At the same time, the digital evolution of business is causing a shift from a standardised engineering (Industrial Revolution) model of how things work to a VUCA world of *volatility*, *uncertainty*, *complexity* and *ambiguity*. Complexity, flux and transformation are the new norms. With complex retooling of production, rapid shifts in product, continuous change in response to customer requirements and the rapid changes in the market, organisations can no longer rely on a known and consistent set of conditions in which they operate.

The next new product or new competitor could come from a completely different market or domain. We have seen Amazon move from books to products and now to dominating cloud computing. Supermarkets are now providing financial services. In the travel world, the main competition for hotels is from a pure-play tech model—Airbnb, which owns no hotels. Car manufacturers are looking over their shoulders at Google and Apple, with whom they already collaborate, but at the same time are building competitive products. Online businesses are becoming physical, and physical manufacturers are moving into intangibles. Car manufacturers have become financial organisations and Google is providing physical phones and companions.

Organisations today are on their own continuous journey of discovery. They continually need to adapt and evolve. Manufacturing is being retooled with rapid, modular production lines that can reconfigure themselves in real time. The old models of rigid, top-down structures are being torn down by digital technologies that are enabling smaller, more agile businesses not only to compete, but to win. Describing how a large organisation works today would invoke metaphors closer to nature rather than machines. A swarm, an ecosystem, a network of agents. They are a symbiosis of machine and humans working together and learning from each other.

These forms of organisation can spiral quickly out of control. Either by growing too fast or simply by missing customer needs and leaving gaps in their wake. Consider the Facebook mantra of 'move fast and break things.' Even just a few years ago that seemed a bold, pioneering approach. Today we have seen the problems this causes as issues emerge with privacy, security and trust. Society's reaction is then to control and limit. As we write there is talk of breaking up these large technology companies and imposing greater regulation. We are still struggling with the battle to promote individual agency, rapid responses, real-time data use and entrepreneurialism whilst avoiding chaos.

Can curiosity pull us through a VUCA world?

Is this an accurate scenario? Is everything really getting faster, or does it just feel like it? Thomas Friedman looks at a set of accelerations in his book *Thank You for Being Late.* He proposes that the age of accelerations began in 2007, launching an era, that we are still in, of 'constant adaptation.' Three forces came together in 2007 to cause a great disruption, that may have gone somewhat unnoticed at the time. The first iPhone was launched, Twitter reached global scale, and Airbnb was conceived.

He identifies three very large-scale forces that mean the new normal is a constant state of destabilisation. These are—

1. Climate Change - and the resulting biodiversity loss
2. Technology - seen through Moore's Law, that computer processor power is doubling every two years
3. Markets - with the increasing impact of globalisation and rise of populism.

These forces are transforming the realms of the workplace, politics, geopolitics, ethics, media and community. According to Friedman, in the past there have been destabilising periods, and normal life was a stable, known world. This world is gone, never to return. Constant change is now the new normal.

Justin Trudeau, Canadian Prime Minister, observed at the World Economic Forum in Davos Switzerland in 2018, 'The pace of change has never been this fast, yet it will never be this slow again.'

Friedman suggests that there can still be a new form of stability—a dynamic stability using the helpful metaphor of *riding a bike.* You need to be constantly shifting to the environment and forces around you, but once you master this, you can smoothly travel wherever you choose.

Continuing this metaphor, when as a child you cycled to the top of a hill to enjoy the long descent, gravity was the force that pulled you along, helping you accelerate and minimising the effort you needed to exert.

These new VUCA conditions require us to have a different approach to data. Everybody across an organisation becomes an observer or a horizon watcher. Processing information from multiple sources needs to bubble through the organisation. The hyper-linked organisation enables people, acting as strange attractors, to gravitate towards information, or to swarm around it. Constant reorganisation around data and responding to it is the way things work now. Organisations will provide capacity for teams to swarm and deliver things into the market. We are all knowledge workers now.

One of the key behaviours that enables this new form of organisation is curiosity. Increasingly, a healthy exercise of curiosity will be the gravity that powers us through the VUCA world, helping us to gain momentum and speed us faster towards our collaborative goals.

Investing in Curiosity

We think that there is a serious case to be made for why organisations should invest in promoting curiosity.

In 2018, McKinsey published a report called 'Delivering Through Diversity' that made a direct link between curiosity as a mindset, with the resulting openness and diversity in the workplace and the value generated. The study found that curiosity in organisations leads to more openness, more exploration, more connections with things that are different, better problem-solving and more innovation—all of which lead to more value within the system.

There are several companies that already incorporate curiosity into their culture or DNA. Microsoft adopted the concept of a growth mindset—a culture that moved from know-it-alls to learn-it-alls. Satya Nadella was the architect of this shift. In his book *Hit Refresh*, he describes that the organisation he took charge of was struggling with internal fighting and a 'not invented here' mentality. In 2014, Microsoft was being written off in the media as a has-been.

Nadella focused on building new partnerships, making Microsoft open to innovation and shifting the culture. Nadella says he likes to think that the C in CEO stands for 'culture,' that the CEO is the curator of an organisation's culture. He centred the change at Microsoft to exercising a growth mindset (see the chapter on confidence for more on growth mindset).

A growth mindset at Microsoft required the following, every day—

1. Be customer-obsessed - 'At the core of our business must be the curiosity and desire to meet a customer's unarticulated and unmet needs with great technology.'
2. Seek diversity and inclusion - 'If we are going to serve the planet…we need to reflect the planet.'
3. Be One Microsoft - 'We are one company…innovation and competition doesn't respect our silos, so we have to learn to transcend those barriers.'

Microsoft is once again a destination for the best talent. Over 95% of Fortune 500 companies choose Azure, Microsoft's cloud computing service, and Microsoft is rated as one of the world's top five AI companies to work for. Since hitting a share price as low as $16 in 2009, since the start of 2020 it has been regularly trading above $160 per share.

Faster adaptation

'The only sustainable competitive advantage is an organisation's ability to learn faster than the competition.' This was said by Peter Senge is his 1990 book *The Fifth Discipline* and we believe still holds true 30 years later. Eric Ries reiterated this in 2011 in his bestselling book *The Lean Startup* saying, 'The only way to win is to learn faster than anyone else.'

We have described how pairing curiosity with learning helps an individual to learn better, but what about an organisation—why do Senge, Ries and others put such importance in the ability to learn fast, or more specifically faster than others?

Maybe a story best illustrates how curiosity and faster learning can generate an advantage for an organisation.

Two companies, QuickCo and Snail Inc., are both operating in a highly competitive industry. QuickCo, filled with curious people, learns from their customers and tests out a new feature idea, which their customers love. There curious culture enables QuickCo to gain an advantage over Snail Inc. Snail Inc. is a company that doesn't push people to be curious. After a quarter of trading, Snail Inc. realises there is a new feature that they need to offer, based on what QuickCo has been selling. Snail Inc. spends another quarter introducing it to their product, after two quarters, six months, they have caught up with QuickCo's offer. But over this time, QuickCo had a whole quarter of sales before Snail Inc. even realised the feature was needed, and then a further quarter while they learned how to adapt their product to respond.

QuickCo is constantly curious, though, so after introducing their first new feature idea and finding that successful, they also learned quickly from their customers that there was another complementary feature that would meet a further customer need. If their learning cycle is twice that of Snail Inc., then they can innovate and bring this to market in a single quarter, just as Snail Inc. is getting to understand the first problem that needs solving. Even if the launch of QuickCo's new feature tips them off to the problem, based on Snail Inc.'s longer learning cycle of a quarter to understand the problem and another to learn how to solve it, QuickCo has a major lead now.

From the launch of the second feature, QuickCo has a full quarter's lead, that Snail Inc. will need to take to address the first feature, then another quarter to realise there is a further customer problem that needs addressing, and then a third quarter to address it—giving QuickCo market leadership for nine months. If QuickCo continues to learn more customer issues and learn how to solve them with new features, always at a faster cycle time than that of the competitor, then they should dominate this market. Snail Inc. will never catch them with their slower learning cycle.

It's deliberately a simple story but it serves to illustrate that if all is else is equal, then any sustained reduction in the time to learn will propel a company forward and it is healthy curiosity that will fuel this learning advantage.

Simple rules for complex times

As everything becomes more complex the solution in fact may lie in greater simplicity. We see curiosity as one of the 'simple rules' or priorities that should sit at the heart of the culture and mindset of organisations seeking to create competitive advantage in this changing world.

We think that modern organisations evolve best through simple instructions sets. These are a set of principles that can guide the behaviours and actions of all parts of the organisation's ecosystem—technological and human. Designing these rules is not a simple task. We know from system theory, for example, in Stuart Kauffman's wonderful book *At Home in the Universe*, that a system with too many rules or the 'wrong' set of rules quickly becomes stuck, unable to evolve and grow. The most effective set of simple rules are best discovered through experimentation. Then the rules should be allowed to evolve over time as the environment in which they exist changes. Importantly, though these rules might adapt, to be optimal, they must adhere to the principle of 'sufficient but not more.'

Consider a hive of bees. A bee colony operates based on a set of simple rules that every bee follows. These include protect and nurture the queen, find food, maintain the hive, and if the hive reaches a certain size, bifurcate to form a new hive. The rules are few enough and simple enough to govern the bees' behaviour, but are also self-limiting so the hive does not get too big or out of control.

We live in a constantly changing world that is being impacted by the digital revolution. To operate in this world, we need to no longer accept the status quo but be constantly looking for new and novel thinking, new and better approaches, discovery of new products, new services, new procedures, new tools or new models. For this world, curiosity becomes a critical requirement, for it powers the desire to ask, 'What if…?'

What if…?

Actors and especially those training in improvisation have many exercises that hone their skills. You may have seen these in evidence on game shows such as *Whose Line Is It Anyway?* One of these is a group exercise that asks each individual to walk around the room, but to keep their eye on an individual of their choosing, and to walk with that person between them and the wall at all times. As everyone moves around a curious thing happens—all of the actors find themselves clustering in the centre of the room. Next, they are asked to choose another person, but this time to keep themselves between the wall and this person—the shift in this simple rule causes all the participants to cluster against the walls. It's a simple rule that ensures a very different outcome in the group—entirely self-organised.

If all leaders in a business are asked to keep a simple rule of only asking questions, not providing answers, different leadership styles and different ways of working across that business will emerge. If an organisation has a simple rule to not create any team with greater than five team members, a different culture will emerge than if teams are allowed to have ten or more people within them.

The contemporary artist Tino Sehgal creates work where different sets of rules are defined that govern the interaction between people. The net effect of each set of rules leads to entirely different outcomes for each piece. Sometimes visitors to his work are greeted by people and find themselves in strange conversations; at other times they witness curious behaviour between the participants in the piece. Tino's works are essentially algorithms or sets of simple rules that lead to complex behavioural outcomes. Not unlike the experience of many of us, as the simple rule that we needed to stay at home and isolate during the COVID-19 pandemic has led to a spectacular shift in our societies, economies and interactions.

The Curious Advantage

In our experience, embedding curiosity as a core operating principle in our organisations delivers significant competitive advantage. A curious organisation learns faster than a non-curious organisation. It will create and innovate faster, work better together, evolve and mutate faster in response to external shifts and build better relationships. All this leads to competitive advantage.

As Vas Narasimhan, CEO of Novartis says, 'Whenever we make a move to support our people, show that we care about our people's well-being, how our people grow and expand their horizons, it leads to growth in our company overall, across all other performance measures. So if you take that as a starting place, and knowing that a sense of curiosity, learning, and mastery is so important to human motivation, it's almost a no-brainer to invest wherever you can in providing better learning opportunities for your people.'

Here are five advantages to be had by investing in curiosity.

1. Curiosity leads to more innovation

'We run this company on questions, not answers.'

Eric Schmidt, co-founder of Google

The benefits of curiosity have been recognised across several companies, and across industries. In the pharmaceutical industry, Merck also have a focus on curiosity. In 2018, Merck conducted a study of 3,000 employees from across the business. They found that 84% of respondents felt that curious colleagues were most likely to bring an idea to life at work. Innovation relies on people asking questions and challenging existing assumptions. As Dr. Stefan Oschmann, CEO of Merck, said, 'We have been focused on innovation for many years. What we want to understand better is how we can foster this innovation in the first place. Curiosity is the critical ingredient to the future breakthroughs society needs.'

The study published in *Harvard Business Review*, demonstrated that encouraging people to be curious directly leads them to be more innovative at work. They asked more questions and were better at problem-solving than those who were not encouraged to be curious.

Harvard Business School Professor Francesca Gino wrote, 'Maintaining a sense of wonder is crucial to creativity and innovation. The most effective leaders look for ways to nurture their employees' curiosity to fuel learning and discovery.'

2. Curiosity helps to attract and retain talent

Research now shows that the quality of development and learning an organisation provides is a key decision factor by which people choose which organisation to join. Is this their innate curiosity? Is it desire to learn and grow? Or is it just a mechanism to accelerate promotion/career prospects? A recent World Economic Forum study rated learning as the top attraction item over salary for new joiners.

Novartis looked at data from half a million applications to work over the latter half of 2019. Opportunities for personal growth was the number one reason to apply, with over 55% of the applicants citing this.

In the past, the knowledge specifically required to do the work in hand would rarely change. Looking back over history, this makes sense. During the Industrial Revolution, people were hired to perform a repetitive task. It was the technical ability to perform that task that was paramount. Still today, traditional recruitment has been focused on the existing 'hard' skills of the candidate, such as technical expertise or process knowledge, or extensive experience in a technical discipline.

In a 2018 *HBR* article by Tomas Chamorro-Premuzic (Chief Talent Scientist at ManpowerGroup) and Josh Bersin (one of the leading analysts on learning in organisations), said 'Hire Curious People.' 'If you hire people who are naturally curious and maximise the fit between their interests and the role they are in, you will not have to worry so much about their willingness to learn or be on their case to unlock their curiosity.'

Employees getting better at learning also bring economic benefit for employers. Josh Bersin, in a 2019 blog, says that 'building a data scientist costs one sixth of buying one.' This goes beyond just data science—enabling your existing employees to learn the skills required within the organisation to meet the needs of the transforming organisation is less expensive than simply buying in new skills.

However, for our hard or technical skills to rapidly evolve, our ability and capacity to learn quickly and adapt becomes vital. In the past, skills such as communication, adaptability, creativity, and listening have been considered secondary. They have even been described as being 'fluffy' (we think this means 'not understood') and therefore not of interest to the 'business'—they are something that 'HR focuses on.'

We are now seeing that the skills that are becoming most important for recruiters are those traits relating to curiosity, such as asking good questions, listening, willingness to learn, building strong relationships. We will talk more about the importance of building your soft skills in the chapter 'A Curious Learner.'

Being a curious organisation is a key differentiator in the battle for attracting and retaining the best talent.

3. Curiosity helps people to build better relationships

Being curious encourages us to consider ideas from another person's perspective. Curious people are less aggressive, and therefore have less conflict. They also deal better with rejection, therefore recovering from a set-back faster.

In a study by Todd Kashdan of George Mason University and his colleagues, they paired their research participants with a trained researcher to engage in a discussion to build rapport. They asked questions that became more intimate as the conversion progressed. For example, 'When did you last cry in front of another person?'

After the conversations the participants completed surveys which measured their curiosity and how well they felt they interacted with one another. The researchers rated how close they felt to their participant and the participants rated how well they felt they came across. The results showed that the researchers felt closer to participants who they felt were more curious. Equally, the participants who were more curious felt that they came across better.

As Kashdan summarised, 'Being *interested* is more important in cultivating a relationship and maintaining a relationship than being *interesting*; that's what gets the dialogue going…It's the secret juice of relationships.'

In a further study, Kashdan found that curious people are also better at 'reading' others. In this study, the researchers formed people into pairs to have a conversation for ten minutes. Afterwards, they asked them to guess the personality traits of their partner. The study found that those who considered themselves more curious were able to more accurately guess the personality traits than those who weren't. This may be because they were better at recognising verbal and non-verbal signals.

Being curious helps us connect better with other people, even with strangers.

Several studies have shown that curious people are better in social interactions. In particular, one study demonstrated that curious people demonstrated more 'positive emotional expressiveness, initiation of humour and playfulness, unconventional thinking, and a non-defensive, noncritical attitude' than non-curious people. Curious people enjoy socialising more and are more positive about communicating with others.

Rather than 'killing the cat,' curiosity tends to lead to better relationships with others, less conflict, and increased teamwork and communication.

4. Curiosity helps people learn faster

The faster a system or network can learn and adapt, the better chance of its survival. In this way, curiosity and learning are entirely connected in the context of an organisation. Learning is the method by which organisations adapt to new situations. Josh Bersin's research has demonstrated that curious learners enjoy the process of learning more and are more effective learners. They also have increased memory of learning content.

When we stimulate and allow ourselves to be curious, we have those 'ah ha' moments. That sense of anticipation and excitement when something new is about to be discovered can motivate and engage us throughout our career. It can happen in our day-to-day work, when a critical piece of information is learned to perform a job, or when a project is discovered that will sharpen new skills.

Take the COVID-19 pandemic, a completely unprecedented situation in which companies needed to react and react fast. Exactly how to react was unclear; many companies initially collaborated internally and put in place an initial response. Curious companies, though, very quickly turned to their professional communities for further inspiration on what could come next. Networks of people in similar roles (for example, the Conference Board Chief Learning Officer Network, or similar bodies for CHROs) provided a forum where we could ask questions, share thinking, learn from one another and provide a better response for employees. Linkedin also provided a global platform where the ways companies were responding could be shared and discussed, both positive and negative, and those with the curiosity to look could find, learn, adapt and apply.

Learning in the Flow of Work

We see the future of learning being inseparable from the day-to-day work. Josh Bersin's concept of *learning in the flow of work* suggests that learning should not be something that is always a separated activity, but an integral part of the delivery of work, to the extent that the individual hardly realises that they have learned something new to complete a task.

Harold Jarche, an international keynote speaker and workplace learning consultant, describes this integration as, 'Work is learning and learning is the work.' This reframing of what learning is, of becoming one and the same as work, can be the aspiration of a learning organisation.

Outside of our working lives, we often find this a natural process. If we want to use a new piece of software, learn how to take a certain type of photograph, fix a household item, or cook a dish in a particular way—almost without thinking about it, we will search for techniques and advice online. For homes with voice assistants such as Alexa, we might even ask for help whilst we are completing a task.

Of course, if a particular topic stimulates our curiosity, we might want to learn more about it and attend a course or a class. However, the role of learning, particularly in the context of routine work is about providing the relevant information through the right channel to enable the individual to accomplish their work in that moment.

Imagine the research scientist we wrote about in the previous chapter, working in a sterile lab, with no access to a computer due to their lab equipment or the sterile environment in which they work. The appropriate channel might be a set of augmented reality safety glasses, as they would naturally be wearing goggles anyway in the course of the work. Now, with this digital enhancement to a regular tool, the right content, data, schematics can be provided to assist their work, as they continue to conduct their experiments.

New approaches that integrate learning into work and life are key for delivering next generation learning. Organisations will need to provide solutions that are flexible, provide quick access to learning from multiple sources, digestible, easy to access and complete, engaging and fundamentally relevant.

5. Curiosity relates to increased performance

In an experiment at Harvard Kennedy School by adding curiosity to teams (through adding a task that heightened their curiosity), groups performed better than a control group as they shared information more openly and listened more carefully.

Curiosity supports salespeople in building stronger relationships by seeking to understand and solve customer problems. Developers find more creative solutions. Across all roles an increased motivation to understand and learn brings huge benefit.

If we go back to our definition of curiosity—that curiosity involves action (versus wondering, about something in your head). It is *action* that leads to *learning*. It is activity and action that satisfy curiosity. There is considerable research that organisations that continuously *learn*, that promote a culture of learning, or are 'learning organisations' outperform others.

Bersin reported in 2018 that 'The single biggest driver of business impact is the strength of an organization's learning culture.'

Novartis commissioned research by the Center for Evidence-based Research in June 2019, to understand the linkage between culture and performance. This was to support the company's culture aspiration of associates who are inspired, curious and unbossed. The findings were initially surprising. Their research found that culture does *not* drive performance, innovation or reputation. On delving deeper into the findings, though, this made sense. Culture in itself is too vague. A company culture could be anything—positive or negative, welcoming or toxic.

What is important is the specific *traits* of a culture. The findings here were reassuring for Novartis. A culture of being curious, inspired and unbossed had a strong correlation to performance, indicating that having curious employees, those constantly looking to question, learn and share, along with empowerment, a safe environment and clear sense of purpose, correlates highly with high performance for knowledge workers.

Factors predicting performance among knowledge workers

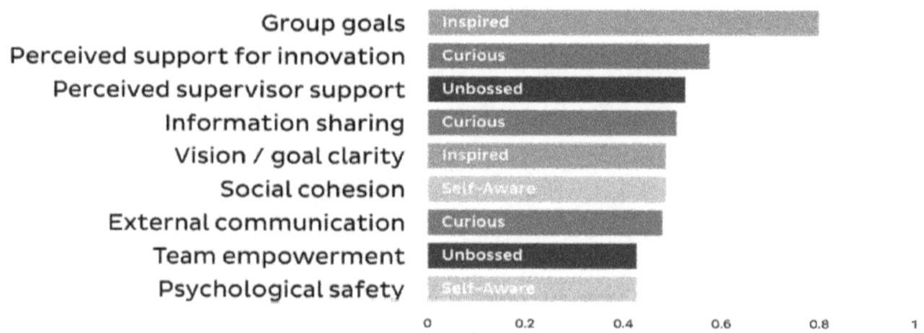

Source: 'What is known about scientific literature about factors associated with knowledge worker performance,' RapidEvidence Assessment meta-analysis, Center for Evidence-Based Management (CEBMa), June 2019, commissioned by Novartis

Therefore, the more curious a workforce is, the greater the likelihood of strong performance.

I don't have time to be curious

One of the frequent complaints we hear from people is that they 'don't have time to learn.' What is really being said, though, is that 'learning doesn't appear high enough up my priority list for me to get to it.' If learning was linked to an annual bonus as IBM have done, people would find time. People don't prioritise it for many reasons—it may be that the learning or training they have previously taken has not been relevant, impactful or effective. It may be a perception that they already know all they need to know to perform their role, or it may be anxiety about taking time away from the heavy workload constantly challenging them. Would we see the same response if we asked people if they have time to be curious?

Interestingly, and perhaps counterintuitively, spending time being curious has been shown to reduce stress, because it helps workers to build valuable instrumental and psychological resources. Two research projects by Zhang, Myers and Mayer, across multiple industries and organisations, found that near-term stressful problems and future stressors were addressed or even prevented by focusing time into learning.

'Psychologically, taking time to reflect on what we know and to learn new things helps us feel competent and capable of achieving goals and doing more.'

So, as well as curiosity working to boost various skills, it can also positively impact wellbeing by reducing stress and anxiety and leave you feeling capable of achieving more.

Summary

Investing in curiosity should be seen to drive both *direct* benefits such as increased performance, greater innovation and faster development of new skills to deliver strategy, as well as *indirect* benefits such as improved interpersonal interactions across the organisation and improved attraction and retention of the best people.

Becoming a curious organisation has demonstrable and direct benefits both for the organisation and the people who work within it. Individuals who are encouraged and given the time and resources to be curious are more open, evolve their skills and keep up to date.

Curiosity is a set of behaviours that are vital to the new organisational reality. In order to foster curiosity, organisations need to pay attention to the cultural values and the signals that are encouraged by leaders, the language that supports curiosity, and create an intelligent technology ecosystem that supports the curious individual.

Curiosity goes hand in hand with diversity and openness within a system, the ability to rapidly evolve in the face of continuous change, and these are being shown to have a direct impact on value and competitive advantage.

In this Part 1, we have looked at *what is curiosity* and asked why is curiosity important to us as humans, to the success of our societies over the ages and to our modern organisations?

In Part 2, we will look at *being curious*. How can we configure our societies, organisations and individual working lives, as leaders, to support successful curiosity—and how is it being realised in the world's most successful organisations?

References

Bennet, N., and James Lemoine, G. (2014) 'What VUCA means for you,' Jan-Feb, *Harvard Business Review*

Chamorro-Premuzic, T., Bersin, J. (2018), '4 ways to create a learning culture on your team,' *Harvard Business Review*, July 2018, https://hbr.org/2018/07/4-ways-to-create-a-learning-culture-on-your-team

Dweck, C. (2012), *Mindset*, Robinson

Friedman, T. (2016), *Thank you for being late*, Macmillan

Gino, F. (2018), 'Why Curiosity Matters,' *Harvard Business Review*, Sept-Oct 2018, https://hbr.org/2018/09/curiosity

Kashdan, T. (2010), *Curious*, Harper Perennial

Kauffman, S.A. (1993), *At Home in the Universe*, Oxford University Press

Ries, E. (2011), *The Lean Startup: How Constant Innovation Creates Radically Successful Businesses*, Portfolio Penguin

Senge, P. (2006), *The Fifth Discipline: The art and practice of the learning organization*, Random House

Sehgal, Tino: 'The fine art of human interaction,' June 2012, *The Economist*, https://www.economist.com/prospero/2012/07/12/the-fine-art-of-human-interaction

Zhang, C., Myers, C.G., & Mayer, D.M., 'To cope with stress, try learning something new,' September 2018, *Harvard Business Review*, https://hbr.org/2018/09/to-cope-with-stress-try-learning-something-new

Curious Conversations

The Future of Learning in Organisations with Josh Bersin

Josh Bersin is the president and founder of Bersin & Associates, and the author of *The Blended Learning Book*, *The High-Impact Learning Organization* and *High Impact Talent Management.*

On curiosity

For me the word curiosity expresses the idea that people have both an urge to explore and to understand why something is the way it is. It sort of wraps together some of the prior thoughts about innovation and creativity into the growth mindset. I think it's a wonderful trend. I think human beings are wired to learn and wired to be curious.

On disruption

Digital technology changes the way people behave. It changes the way people buy things. It creates a much tighter relationship between consumers and companies because you're sort of tethered to each other in a real-time basis. All of a sudden, your whole company has to operate in a different way. Well actually that creates a lot of need for curiosity about how to do that. Most of the business models and job models and career models in companies are not oriented towards that. They're oriented towards a functional hierarchy where my job is to produce this thing and make this widget or sell this stuff or whatever it may be. Curiosity is to me, the new way of rethinking this digital transformation. You know in some ways the coronavirus is the ultimate digital transformation because now everybody's working from home. We've got to be curious about that too.

On organisations being curious

The Big Reset, just to put some context around it, is that there is a de-layering or elimination of bureaucracy that's going on and it's speeding up. People are realising they can do things a lot faster than they did before. If you look at companies in general over a long period of time, the companies that go out of business or get bought or sort of fall apart have somehow been locked into their existing or old business model and been unable to either pay attention or were not curious. I'm not the first one to think about this, it goes all the way back to the innovator's dilemma. I think there has to be a healthy scepticism and questioning of how things work in every successful company, but not to the degree that you don't focus on executing what you have. It's kind of a tough balance.

On failure

I think failure is sort of a meaningless term in business. Everything you ever do has something about it that's not right. I've never worked for a company that did everything well. There's always a few things that are kind of botched up or they're not ready yet or they're not quite as good as they need to be or they need to be improved. If you don't accept and deal with all these little failures, you can't iterate to success.

On leaning technologies

A lot of the concepts that came out of the advertising industry are now being taken into learning. It's tough problem though, because serving up an ad is actually kind of simple, all we want people to do is click on it, we don't really care what happens next. Whereas a piece of learning has to actually help somebody do their job better. I think there's a big opportunity from the integration of technology ecosystems to really support people being curious.

On being personally curious

I think some of it is my wiring and some of it is my career. My father was a scientist and a musician. So, I think I have that nature in my brain. I'm very analytical, but I also did a lot of work in literature. I'm always interested in reading. I am lucky in that I can consume information pretty fast just because of the way I am. When I fell into HR and became an analyst, I became fascinated by the fact that it's very multi-disciplinary.

On confidence

If you looked at what I did when I started as an analyst, I was very timid. I think some of it was developing self-confidence and some of it was that so many people gave me feedback that they appreciated that I was curious and that I was trying to pattern match things that were hard to understand. I had this unique situation as an analyst where I could talk to a hundred companies, a hundred vendors and get involved in all their economic and other data. I found I could find ideas and patterns from all that data.

On staying relevant

We were always a more curious industry analyst firm than our competitors. I think that's why we became successful. The other thing that I've noticed in our domain, and I'm sure you feel the same way, it's changing so fast that the minute you write down something that seems to be true, you're like, 'Hmm, that's not maybe completely right.' So, I'm always questioning myself.

One piece of advice

I remember when my father was a physicist, he once said to me, 'If you can find one thing in the world and do that better than anybody else, you'll be happy your whole life. I found that for me, trying to be a generalist or a big shot business guy or whatever, didn't really appeal to me. I found something I was good at and I realised I could become better and better at it; it became a wonderful career. I give that advice to people all the time. Find something you really enjoy and dig in and be curious about that and your career will flourish.

Part 2
Being Curious

5.

SAILING THE 7 C'S OF CURIOSITY

In this chapter we explore how to put our curiosity to work and introduce the concept of the '7 C's of Curiosity'—the elements we think are vital to *being curious.*

Sailing the Seven Seas

The term 'Seven Seas' have been in our literature for thousands of years. The term today of course refers to the main regional bodies of water—the Arctic, North Atlantic, South Atlantic, North Pacific, South Pacific, Indian and Southern Oceans. However, this was not always the case.

Curiously, each civilisation referred to their 'own' set of Seven Seas, which referred to the bodies of water within their context and knowledge. In ancient Greek literature the Seven Seas were the Adriatic, Aegean, Black, Caspian, Mediterranean and Red Seas, along with the Persian Gulf. The Persians referred to the Seven Seas as being the streams forming the Oxus River in Central Asia.

Medieval European literature refers to the Seven Seas as being the Atlantic, Arabian, Baltic, Black, Mediterranean, North and Red Seas. In Arabian literature of similar times, the Seven Seas were those encountered as they voyaged east towards China. They were the Sea of Larwi (Arabian Sea), the Sea of Harkland (the Bay of Bengal), the Sea of Sanji (South China Sea), the Sea of Kalah (the Strait of Malacca), the Persian Gulf (the Sea of Fars), the Sea of Salahit (the Singapore Strait) and the Sea of Kardanj (the Gulf of Thailand).

Following the 'discovery' of the Americas, the Seven Seas changed once again. They then referred to the Atlantic, the Arctic, the Caribbean, the Gulf of Mexico, the Indian, the Mediterranean and the Pacific.

Which of the Seven Seas you sail, as with all things, depends on your *context*.

The 7 C's of Curiosity

We have identified seven elements that individuals, leaders and organisations can put into practice to live a culture of curiosity.

We call these the '7 C's of Curiosity.'

The Venetians used the expression 'to sail the Seven Seas' to describe someone having nautical skill, long before they ventured out into the oceans. Sailing the 7 C's of curiosity means to develop curiosity as a skill. Something we can improve and put to continual good use as we learn to apply it to our everyday practices.

What encourages curiosity? What's required to put wonder into action?

SAILING THE 7C's OF CURIOSITY

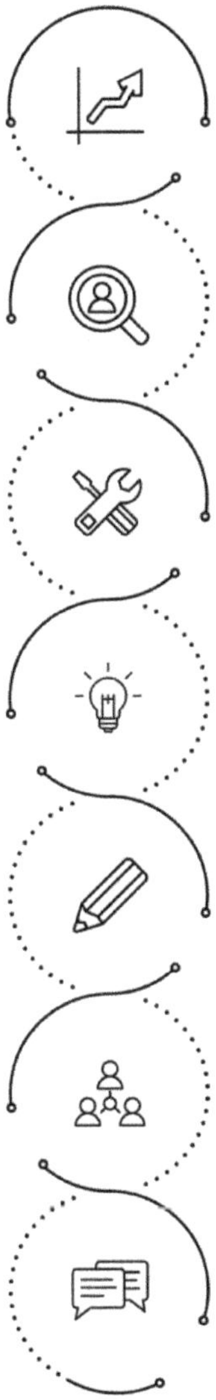

7. CONFIDENCE

Confidence grows with curiosity. The two grow with each other. If we approach something new with a curious mindset, being open to trying, failing and improving – we build our confidence.

6. CRITICALITY

Asking questions is deeply connected to being curious. It is the questions that prompt us to discover and find solutions. The type of questions we apply are important if we want to know if there is a different or better way. We also need to be aware of our own biases.

5. CONSTRUCTION

Curiosity is not just wondering. It is putting your wonder into action. This means making or constructing something to learn about it. Whether it's making new connections, building something physical, writing a document, a piece of music, building a business or just figuring out how something works.

4. CREATIVITY

Our exploration into new worlds may require us to think differently, connect something in a new way and make a leap of faith. Sometimes, it's the spark that starts a new cycle of curiosity.

3. CURATION

We need to make choices and intentionally curate our curiosity to synthesize and focus our thinking, our ideas and the information we are gathering.

2. COMMUNITY

Curiosity is powered by our community. Societies or organisations with curiosity as a specific part of culture are more productive and people are more engaged in learning and in their work.

1. CONTEXT

The broader the context you expose yourself to, the more likely you will find new ideas that stimulate you to explore further.

Like the oceans of our planet, the 7 C's of Curiosity are all connected. They are like a constellation of stars to navigate by, a set of principles rather than a process to follow.

All of the elements work together to enable our curiosity. If we're curious then we suggest the best thing to do is to first understand the *context*, next identify and establish a *community* to help us and to start *curating* the tools, content, *language* and people we need to support us. As our curiosity progresses through putting what we learn into action, we engage in cycles of *creativity*, *construction* and *criticality*, questioning our biases and gaining feedback as we come to a more complete understanding of our question. We may accelerate through these at any speed.

Fundamentally, being curious boosts *confidence*, and being confident increases our ability to be curious. The seven continue to work together and to adapt as we explore ever deeper new worlds of ideas.

1. Context

Context is about understanding the world that an idea, question or individual inhabits. It is being aware of what is in your peripheral vision. Context is the set of ideas and relationships between ideas that generates meaning. The broader the context we expose ourselves to, the more likely we will find new ideas that stimulate us to explore further. Encouraging curiosity in others, whether as a leader, parent or friend, means not only helping to provide access to greater context, but also providing the tools to read and map context, joining ideas together and helping others navigate into the unknown.

Tip: To be more curious we need to look constantly beyond our horizons and to broaden and expand our context.

2. Community

Curiosity is powered by our community. Societies or organisations with curiosity as a specific part of culture are more productive and people are more engaged in learning and in their work. Curious communities share what they learn and they value through learning. It is mostly done informally. A community has a language and lexicon that defines its understanding of its particular world. Individuals are encouraged to explore further and reinvest their learning back into the community: as a result the boundaries of knowledge are expanded. A community will help unlock the knowledge that we seek; it will have the language that holds the key to the architecture of meaning they inhabit.

Tip: Ideas and thinking are developed with regular engagement within a community.

3. Curation

Too much information and too many connections causes us to be overwhelmed and to stop. We are unable to move forward. For our curiosity to have focus, we need to make choices and decide where we are going. Our brain naturally and continuously curates the information it receives. If it didn't, we would be overwhelmed continuously with the sights, sounds, people and objects around us. In the same way, we need to intentionally curate and edit our curiosity to synthesise and focus. Go broad for context then curate back to what is most relevant to our quest.

Tip: As we develop our understanding of a topic by exploring context, content and building our community, ongoing *curation*, editing and focus are important to avoid information overload and also to keep focused on the objective.

4. Creativity

Being creative often comes from being curious. Generating new ideas, inventing new products or services, composing, authoring, problem-solving, all come from making new connections between things by being curious. Our exploration into new worlds may require us to think differently, connect something in a new way and make a leap of faith. Creativity emerges when many ideas clash together, forming new ideas. Sometimes it's the spark that starts a new cycle of curiosity.

Tip: Scanning broadly is the starting point for creative thinking. Apply active curiosity to your challenge, issue or need. Identify links, explore multiple pathways and then curate. It will all enhance your *creativity*.

5. Construction

Curiosity is not just wondering. It is putting your wonder into action. This means making or constructing something to learn about it. Whether it's making new connections, building something physical, writing a document, a piece of music, building a business or just figuring out how something works. Curiosity requires us to put our ideas to test in reality by building and making things. It requires a project—our own curious experiments. Without construction or putting into action, curiosity is just theoretical—like reading an article online and doing nothing with the information.

Tip: Being curious is not just theory—we put our curiosity into action by applying, *constructing* or experimenting.

6. Criticality

Asking questions is deeply connected to being curious. It is the questions that prompt us to discover and find solutions. The type of questions we apply are important if we want to know if there is a different or better way. We also need to be aware of our own biases. Are we developing something only for people 'just like us?' Is our view of a topic only based on our own experiences? Does our exploration simply further our own beliefs? Are we asking questions that may lead to uncomfortable answers? Bringing in diverse thinking helps keep a check on our inherent biases and makes our curious explorations more interesting, with richer outcomes.

Tip: Applying *critical thinking* and challenging our biases are likely to dramatically improve the answers to the questions we seek.

7. Confidence

Confidence grows with curiosity and, at the same time, being curious builds our confidence. The two grow with each other. If we approach something new with a curious mindset, being open to trying, failing and improving and thinking through the various outcomes, we build our confidence as we become secure in our knowledge or abilities to perform a task. The opposite is also true. When we stop being curious, we start being afraid—fearing the unknown. Our confidence grows when we form useful habits that builds our curiosity in our daily lives.

Tip: Our *confidence* is built through our failures rather than our successes. Being comfortable with ambiguity, difference and diversity enables us to be more secure, enhances our confidence and permits us to be yet more curious.

Summary

The 7 C's of Curiosity are also a map for discovering our own curiosity. In the following chapters we describe each of these in detail and how to successfully 'sail' these 7 C's to put our curiosity to work for us, our networks and for our organisations.

6.
CONTEXT

'There are things known and there are things unknown, and in between are the doors of perception.'

Aldous Huxley

'To see we must forget the name of the thing we are looking at.'

Claude Monet

Imagine something that nobody really knows what it is, something that is always shifting like sand dunes. Imagine something that's continually dynamic and always evolving. Something that can be known only by engaging with it, yet once we engage with it we become a part of it. This sounds like one of the great riddles of the Sphinx! What could it be? Context. This chapter is all about context. What is it? Why is it important for curiosity? How is context related to learning? Why do we believe that reading and understanding context is one of the key skills required for leadership in the Digital Age? Finally, how does an understanding of context enable us to go places we haven't been before?

Exploring context

There are a number of ideas about how to define context, and we'll take a look at each one in turn as they are all useful in their own way.

As ever, the intention of this book, you the reader are free to come to your own understanding of context and choose whichever you feel makes most sense for you.

Context is one of the most used words on all Wikipedia and yet it remains one of the most difficult to define. Let's start with the most basic example of context—context in action!

In the English language, the same word may be entirely changed by its context. The word 'club,' for example—a 'club' in the context of golf club (e.g. a 9-iron) is vastly different from 'club' in the context of a group of members or societies, or the 'club' used by a Neanderthal. How about 'tear'? Is it an emotion or something that happened to your clothes? It gets tricky, but context is implicit in the way we speak and write. It is vital to meaning and understanding. Consider the idea of scrubbing—this is a very different idea if it's used in the context of a hospital or of a kitchen. 'To surf.' If you are using the Internet, that's one thing, if you are on the water, that's another thing entirely.

How do we know the difference between 'fair,' the condition and 'fair' the place? These words are called 'homonyms' because they have the same spelling and pronunciation but mean very different things. It is only context that can help us distinguish between 'wound'—the thing we did with string—and 'wound'—the thing that happened when we tripped and fell. Our associations bring the context that enables us to make sense of the meaning. To put it simply, without context, which is a set of associations, no idea can exist.

Without context there is no meaning

Existing context has to be researched, learned, explored and fundamentally internalised. To find oneself in one particular context using the information and assumptions of a different context is not only naïve, it can be dangerous. Imagine going to dive to the bottom of the oceans, using the contextual information that had been accumulated on dry land.

Anyone who plays chess can understand the relative nature of context and finding how quickly context can change. From being on the attack and feeling one's king is well-defended within a context of safety, within the space of a move or two, the realisation can come that the context has completely changed and that things are no longer safe. Before you know it, checkmate may have materialised.

Context is contained in associations of data and narrative. If we want to go to a new planet and no one has ever been there before, we need to understand if it can support life. Data may exist about all kinds of parameters with regard to the terrain and atmosphere; however, outside of lived experience and narrative, this is purely conjecture—a best guess based on the information we have available. The real context arises when we want to put a machine or person on that planet. Now this gives meaning to the data, whether the atmosphere is life-supporting or not, the terrain is rocky or fluid—and all of this information has an impact on how we prepare to exist within that context.

Context is vital for bringing an idea into focus. Without context there can be no idea or concept. Context is central to how we engage in meaning-making. We build meaning by associating more and more ideas and understanding with an idea or question.

We make meaning through language

There is an old myth about the invisible ship phenomenon based on the story told by Joseph Banks in 1770, who was a botanist on Captain James Cook's *Endeavour.* In his notes, he describes that whilst sailing along the Australian coastline the local inhabitants paid no attention to the thirty-metre ship passing in front of them. He recorded that the fishermen on the shore '...seemd to be totaly engag'd in what they were about: the ship passd within a quarter of a mile of them and yet they scarce lifted their eyes from their employment...Soon after this an old woman followd by three children came out of the wood;...She often lookd at the ship but expressd neither surprize nor concern. Soon after this she lighted a fire and the four

Canoes came in from fishing; the people landed, hauld up their boats and began to dress their dinner to all appearance totaly unmovd at us, tho we were within a little more than ½ a mile of them.'

According to the story, these massive ships were so alien, so outside of the visual language of the current reality of the local people, that they could not even perceive them. Possibly. Or perhaps they just ignored them because they did not perceive them as a threat. Either way, the local people did not have the contextual awareness to recognise these strange visions and did not perceive them as relevant to their lives.

Research demonstrates that if something is out of our contextual awareness, we can be literally blind to it. Things do not exist to us if we don't possess the language of meaning to perceive them. Even if to others they may be present. This is not a limitation of our eyes but of our brains. We can only process a small proportion of the world around us at any one time. Think of a safari guide reading animal tracks or a crime scene investigator spotting evidence at a crime scene—their contextual awareness is finely trained for a specific purpose and they see meaning where others don't.

Philosopher Ludwig Wittgenstein, student of Bertrand Russell, and famed for his work on language, suggested that that which we have no language for cannot be spoken of, even though the concepts may exist within us. 'Of that whereof we cannot speak, thereof we must remain silent,' he wrote in his *Tractatus*. Throughout the course of his philosophical life he led the shift from the ideas of the *logical positivists* to the *pragmatic* and *behavioural* ideas that defined the late twentieth century. What Wittgenstein was suggesting was that all language, and indeed all experience and knowledge, is bound up in lived experience and community. Meanings shift continuously and that no meaning or language can be considered as fixed in time.

The exploration of context is an exploration of language. Language in all its forms, concepts, models, meaning, history, code—language enables us to explore context.

However, language is just the gateway. The context is an understanding of how all of these ideas may hang together within a certain set of circumstances.

For example, in a modern context, home automation illustrates this idea of the connection between language and context. Imagine a home that has been fitted with smart devices and lighting. It requires a shift in behaviour that is fairly profound. You may walk into such a place at night and be completely in the dark. Not even able to turn on a light—as light switches are redundant—and may not even be visible. Finding the control surface, the iPhone app, the sensor to wave in front of, or even knowing the right trigger word—'Alexa,' 'Hey Google,' 'Hey Siri'—and then the command to 'turn on the lights in the living room,' is a very different way of getting light into a room. As a learner in this situation, we could approach it as curiously as possible, but unless we understand the language of home automation, and that we might be able to find the switches in software apps available on iPhones or tablets—we would not understand how to turn on the lights—in the end we would still be stumbling around in the dark!

The boundaries of context

Ethics are determined by context. A practice in one context may be illegal in another. Killing another human being is somehow justifiable in a war situation, but not in everyday civil society.

This is why the law is founded on text. The law is essentially creating one of the contexts that governs our society. Disputes are disputes about context and meaning.

However, context is more than just text when it comes to being curious. It is everything that governs the meaning required to understand and answer a question. It is the internalised projections and shadows of lived experience.

An understanding of context can also be formalised as the canon of texts or books or visual imagery that are generally held to support a set of ideas. Our task is to imbibe these texts and, through this activity, inhabit the same architecture of the mind as those who share it.

Are we closer to understanding context? Perhaps if we tell enough of these stories from different perspectives, we will come to understand something that is in itself impenetrable.

What is context?

Context can be understood as an awareness of the meaning which is around you and the meaning which you inhabit. Being aware of what is in your peripheral vision is a form of sensitivity to context. Ideas may be formed by other concepts, language, visual things, experiences, histories, bodies of knowledge.

It is this bubble of bubbles that constitutes context. The broader the context you expose yourself to, the more likely you will find new ideas and the confidence that enables you to explore. In this definition, we can think of context as all the connections to a particular idea that exist and that are summed up by that idea. *So, context is the set of ideas that frame an idea.* For example, if we're curious about mountain climbing in the Alps, a good place to start is to read a book about the subject. We might watch films, do Internet research, and generally immerse ourselves in the contextually relevant research. However, we will only know what of that information is useful and relevant when we arrange to go to the Alps, find an experienced guide, rope ourselves up and head up the mountain. In this definition we work from the outside in. It is the context that defines the idea.

Another perspective

Another definition of context starts from establishing the concept or question and determining the context from there. This suggests that it is the networks of meanings, experiences and associations, that give rise to the idea itself. This is the reverse of the above—here it works from the inside out, it is the *idea that defines the context.*

The difference between the two is both philosophical and also physical. Linguists suggest considering both definitions and work, using one or the other depending on which is most helpful. Neuroscientists are starting to understand that the brain chunks similar information and may indeed create meaning through the association of vast arrays of networks that are laid down along electron pathways.

In summary, context can be viewed in many different ways. They all relate to defining and understanding the meaning of something. Whether it's the ideas and level of meaning that surround a central idea or whether it's a comprehensive network of connected ideas that give rise to meaning—we need to be aware of context and how to understand it in order to make meaning of the things we explore.

Whenever or wherever we go into a situation, context exists. Whenever we are being curious we are exploring a context. In fact, you might say that curiosity is fundamentally the exploration of a context outside of our existing context. Let's explore what context is from another perspective.

One city, multiple perspectives

A wonderful book was written by Italo Calvino, *Invisible Cities*, in 1972. It involved the story of the great explorer Marco Polo explaining the city of Venice to Kublai Khan. Calvino does so by narrating the story of 55 different cities which cover different perspectives of cities (for example, a city as a network of pipes or a city as a set of mercantile relationships, or a city as a group of buildings, or a set of families). He considers language, memory, desire, time and culture. By reading all of these different perspectives one gradually constructs a mental architecture of it all and derives a sense of this great city.

The genius of Calvino is that he understands that context is a complicated set of perspectives that inhabit entirely different systems of knowledge (like language or networks), and that context grows by exploring all of these different ways of understanding, simultaneously.

Context, curiosity and us

It's an interesting exercise to analyse our life in this way. Think of yourself as a set of relationships, or as a story of love affairs, or as the owner of different houses, or as a career pursued, or as a father or mother, as a set of transformations, recipes baked, cities visited, road trips taken, perhaps a medical history, languages spoken or hair colours. Each story reveals another facet to our incredible multi-dimensional lives. We are all of these things and we are each one in turn. The narrative we tell (or perform) is entirely dependent on context. Context shifts based on our perspective. There are many contexts for every situation. To be curious learners is to develop awareness of these perspectives and to explore as many of these different contexts as possible in the pursuit of a complex perception of the whole.

Context is multi-dimensional

What this all means is that Context is multi-dimensional. We come to understand context by approaching the same question or idea from many different perspectives, vantage points and experiences. This relates to the original meanings of the word we wrote about above, where curiosity is related to cycles of exploration, or never being satisfied. Curiosity is a continual exploration of all the dimensions that relate to our question.

Context is relative

The idea of context is a *paradoxical conundrum.* One could argue that the answer to this question is a question of context. Sometimes it's useful to understand the network to understanding the meaning; at other times it is useful to understand the meaning in order to fathom the network of associations.

Context is not only its literal meaning '*with text.*' Context has to be explored for all new situations and things we are curious about. Sometimes that knowledge is only found in a given situation or even goes unwritten amongst a group of people. Sometimes the only way to understand a new context is to live it. This is why we are interested in investigative journalists. Investigative journalists have to get deep into a context, while at the same time remaining critically distant from all they are experiencing.

Anthropologists have at the centre of their discipline this paradox of understanding context. The difficulty of both being an outsider and needing to overcome being an outsider in order to understanding things from within context. At the same time they try not to be changed by the context and also not to change context in turn. An impossible task. We will always be changed by new context and in turn change that context whatever we do.

Margaret Mead spent time on a Polynesian island and discovered practices scandalous to Western society at the time. Her research was criticised after the fact because it was clear that her presence would have changed the society she was researching. It's a conundrum.

Does context exist or is it created?

Here we come to another one of the curious paradoxes of context and curiosity. Curiosity can be understood as both an exploration of an existing context (where a body of knowledge has been laid down), or the creation of an entirely new context (it is created by the action of your exploration). Let's take a moment to understand this important distinction because the exploration of context is different for the types of curiosity—general and specific.

Creativity and new context

When we engage in a creative process we are effectively creating context where none existed. The action of creativity may take place within a context, but as soon as we innovate something from scratch, or invent something, or create something new—perhaps a building, or a business, or an architecture of ideas, or creative writing, or pottery, or a website, presentation or composition—we are creating a new context. Laying down new pathways, making new connections, creating new architectures of the mind—from scratch. Learning from childhood is focused on achieving this feat—of embodying as much contextual information as possible. The same is true for all the concepts linked to, say, learning a language or telling the time.

Contemporary artists live their lives within the creative process. Those engaged with conceptual art, performance art, performative art and installation art create new contextual realities as a direct result of their artistic work. Marcel Duchamp was the master of this idea. He specifically created new frames of reference and new contexts, which gave rise to his art. For example, his famous character Rrose Sélavy was a fictional character whom Duchamp brought to life—she engaged with his art and critical practice, she published, she attended parties, and her story gave rise to his masterpiece *Étant Donnés*. She was an evocation of Eros, which was the life force Duchamp was exploring, as well as his *alter ego*. This character allowed Marcel Duchamp to explore worlds and say things he felt he could not. Rrose was Marcel's vehicle for curiosity.

A set of connections that don't yet exist are created through our exploration and new context is made. We essentially are making the map and creating a new world at the same time.

Curiosity and existing context

Curiosity can explore existing context—an accepted architecture of ideas within the minds or texts of others. For example, to study to become a doctor is an exploration of everything that is accepted within the medical profession.

In this form of Curiosity, we are embodying an existing understanding. A set of connections that exist externally to us become internalised through the process of exploration. That is, we recreate a representation of the context we are learning about within our brains. We essentially are redrawing the existing map of an existing world.

Why is context important for curiosity?

Context exists in every situation. When you move into unchartered territory you are going somewhere where you have no pre-existing map. It's a problem for sailors and explorers just as much as it is a challenge for the curious. Sailors and explorers have invented tools for solving this specific problem.

Exploring and mapping context

Over the past five hundred years, the age of exploration has brought a level of sophistication and documentation to navigation, unheard of in recorded history. Institutions and societies have been established that progressed the navigation tools and knowledge that have enabled sailors to traverse the world, emerge with new knowledge, establish trade routes and minimise loss of life. Satellites and GPS have meant that exploration of the unknown is safer than ever before.

What has evolved is tools for measuring latitude and longitude, the use of highly accurate timepieces to do so, charting and surveying in three dimensions. All of these skills instrumentalise principles that are useful for the curious.

Interestingly, the tools for navigation also include documentation of narrative or storytelling. This became recognised as being as important as numerical observation. The captain and his logbook became a vital thing. Throughout his voyage into the unknown the captain kept regular and detailed records of every notable event and experience encountered. These were often highly detailed documents, complete with illustrations and even input from the local inhabitants that the sailors met along their way. If things were complicated, the narrative of the voyage was logged every ten minutes. Geography and time were as important as the narrative or the story of everything that was unfolding, and all the connections and new knowledge that were being made.

Captain Bligh, famous for the Mutiny on the Bounty, is revealed to be very different from the character portrayed in the movies. Here is an extract from his actual log—

> **February 2, 1789.** Position 18°52'3' S, 129°27'45' W. Winds light, W by WSW. Seas 2–4 feet. Am much vexed on account of Mr. Christian. His mood-compass vacillates sharply between Hysterical Agitation and Sullen Lethargy. I had so wanted this Voyage to be special for him.
>
> Last night upon seeing him brooding, I told him I would stand his Watch and to go below and curl up in his bunke with a saucy book and a tot of grog. Whereupon he expostulated at me with such Violence that all I could do was mutter, 'I keenly regret that you should feel so, dear man,' and retreat to my own cabin.
>
> Calmed myself by re-drawing the Admiralty charts of the North and South Atlantick, which I found to be rife with Errors.
>
> **Febr. 10.** Upon examining the Log, I found that Fletcher, who of late hath taken to addressing me as 'Captain Bilge,' had put us on a course not for Otaheite but for the Greate Barrier Reefe—named by myself on my Voyage with the late Captain Cook, God rest his fine soul.
>
> Not wanting to embarrass him in front of the other Officers, I quietly ordered the helm up 2 1/2 points. Whereupon he appeared on the quarterdeck, wearing no Breeches but only a nightshirt and a most fierce look in his eyes, and proceeded to accost me in a manner alarming and disrespectful, calling me Names which Decency prevents me from here enumerating.

> I could only reply abashedly, 'But your course, good man, though indubitably well intentioned, would have set us upon Sharke Rocke!'
>
> But he would hear none of it, and called me the sharke.
>
> 'Fletcher, Fletcher, Fletcher,' I said to him with a soothing aspect, 'pray lie down, and I shall send Surgeon to bleed you of this unbecoming Humour.'
>
> Thereat he threw his grog cup at my feet and stormed off, beating an angry quadrille with his boot-heels upon the deck.

It was this log that was thoroughly examined when the Mutiny on the Bounty was investigated. The reason the logs were created was not only to record the technical data, where they were, the weather, the time, but also to record and create the narrative data of the voyage. It was their mechanism for creating and mapping context.

Going where no one has been before

The areas of the brain that fire when we explore an existing context are different areas from those which fire if we are creating context ourselves.

Curiosity is a means by which we are able to explore the context shared by others as well as share the contexts we have discovered. It is interesting to note that dopamine is required to lay down the neural paths. This is why stories are vital to the reproduction of culture and shared understanding. In many ways music and dance are at the heart of reinforcing the meanings associated with them. Music and dance flood our brains with endorphins and dopamine.

At some point within any curious exploration or curious learning experience we should be able to answer the question—what is the context of the area we are interested in?

Leading into the unknown

Edwin Hutchins book *Cognition in the Wild* is an exploration of the tools required for successfully navigating uncharted territory. It provides tools required to understand any endeavour that requires charting the uncharted—from sailing, to exploring land, space, new territory.

Imagine that we are exploring context and we define this as the exploration of a set of ideas that are to be found in the shared understanding of a group of other peoples. We could be said to be exploring an architecture that exists within the minds of others—coming to share an architecture of minds.

The tools that Hutchins identifies all relate to mechanisms for understanding where we want to go, our vision, understanding where we are, documenting these facts and establishing a feedback loop between them.

He defines three important roles that exist within all exploration—the Plotter, who defines where we want to go; the Bearing Taker, who tells us where we are; and the Recorder, who ensures our records are accurate. These roles are backed up by tools and technology that are appropriate to the context. Whether it be maps, or compasses, GPS or depth-sounding pieces of rope. In any situation of exploration, it is these three roles that ensure we can sail into the unknown with safety and certainty.

The risks

For leaders of fast-moving organisations, exploring new contexts is clearly a risk but is also a necessity. The ability to read and map context as it changes and see the blind spots is paramount for a leader in to provide strategic direction. However, now that we all have access to such a broad context being able to filter and focus on what is important becomes ever more important. Leaders need to support their people in a VUCA world, providing clear direction and vision. Leaders also need to provide the tools and technical systems that support the plotting, bearing and documenting that are required for enabling curiosity.

Context and community

Being curious and being surrounded by a community of people who inhabit that context is one way to tackle this. If you have ever walked in nature at night and been surrounded by fireflies, you will have experienced a similar sensation. Even in the pitch black of night, those thousands of small flies act as independent sensors, exploring and giving you a sense of the terrain around you. (If you are curious to see a world-class display of fireflies in action, head to the Elkmont area of the Great Smoky Mountains National Park between late May and early June.)

The flies are simply being curious—looking for food or for a mate—but in their act of exploring and establishing their environment, they provide us with the bigger context—where there is water, where is danger, where is the safe path ahead?

The community is a sensory organism

The people working in the community can play a similar role to these fireflies. They can provide huge amounts of data about the context and landscape the organisation is operating in, sensing danger or identifying areas of opportunity, but only if they are empowered to speak up. As fiction author William Gibson famously wrote, 'The future is already here—it's just not very evenly distributed.' An organisation full of curious explorers will find the pockets where future opportunities and value lie far faster than a single research team or a set of innovation experts ever will.

Context is a social construct. A definition of insanity can be linked to an understanding of shared context. People who are considered insane may live in a world that makes perfect sense to them, but because it's not shared with others it appears as insanity.

Understanding and sharing the architecture of a context in the minds of others are what creates a culture, and a sharing culture is what creates a civilisation. To be outside of a shared context is to be alien.

Leading in unknown territory

How can leaders take their people safely into the unknown? Here are some ideas for how to use and work with context as a starting point for leading curiosity.

Chart the course

Establishing the North Star. The great polar star was historically the primary means for navigators to identify where north was. Establishing a contextual mechanism by which to steer by is a tool that a leader can use to enable everyone to explore a context from many different perspectives without getting lost. Establishing questions may be the best way to do so. For example, 'How do we stop babies crying?'—one question to steer an enormous amount of research.

The North Star for the Disney Corporation is to 'entertain, inform and inspire people around the globe.' For Novartis, their North Star is to 'improve and extend people's lives'—this provides a single clear purpose to all associates across the company and can be used for orientation and guiding decision-making.

Visualise context

The knowledge, concepts and relationships that constitute the context of an idea can be mapped. Mapping context is a useful tool and it can be done in many ways. For example, we can draw a relationship diagram, draw a network diagram, list all the books that consist of the canon associated with the idea, name a concept, describe the narrative, draw a picture, build a model, write a text—all of these tools help describe the context. Leonardo da Vinci would devote a notebook to a single idea—but explore it from every possible angle—and in doing so both understand existing context and create additions to it. A context that is mapped through its relationships is called *rhizomatic*, because it looks like the rhizome (rootstalks) of a tuber.

What this means is that visual representation is one of the most powerful mechanisms for reflecting on the context we are exploring. Creating one, and updating one in a systematic way, creates the ability to achieve a stable point while in a world of exploration—a world that is becoming known—a world that is essentially unstable.

Inventor Thomas Edison was a copious note-taker. He was responsible for more than 1,000 patents and inventions that still impact our lives today. In the course of his creativity his notebooks were ever present. A treasure trove of data and findings that eventually spanned more than five million pages. Every experiment was documented, and not just the successes. Edison saw it just as important to document when things went wrong and why. The process of note-taking helped him and his teams as they synthesised what they had learned and to problem-solve. He became one of the most influential and productive inventors in modern history, able to work on multiple projects in parallel.

Inventors keep notes as a matter of course, not only to learn from their mistakes and reference what has been tried and built so far, but also to provide evidence of their work. Patent offices around the world specifically recommend keeping a dated notebook to validate progress and to protect ideas from theft.

Curious leaders can see themselves as inventors, charting a course into the unknown and motivating their teams to join them on the journey. Visualising context helps people understand where they are and where they are going.

Define the organising metaphors and symbols

Another role of the leader is to introduce people to a context, to help shape the shared understanding of context, to ensure clarity of language throughout the contextual system and to help choose the visual metaphors or symbols that can promote the ideas necessary to communicate the context.

Metaphors of context that we use to define our identities as human beings on the planet today include things such as—

- The solar system
- The earth from space
- The globe (as distinct from the flat earth)
- The tree of life
- Contemporary art
- Modes of music
- The sporting arena
- The gods
- The Mappa Mundi

When Novartis started the journey to move to an inspired, curious and unbossed culture, symbols were seen as vital to creating a new shared context. Senior leaders moved out of private offices into open spaces, executive limousines were no longer permitted on the HQ campus site, and the previous formal dress code was relaxed to casual dress. Individually these could be considered small changes, but collectively they symbolised a more significant change, that the new cultural aspiration was real.

What symbols, images or metaphors can we as leaders use to communicate the shared context?

Take soundings from reality

Delusions may exist in organisations that are linked to all manner of complex histories, developments, languages and experiences.

The Space Shuttle disaster was attributed to the O-ring problem technically. However, there was a delusional culture within NASA that meant that problems could not be talked about. The pressures within the NASA culture led to a delusion of invincibility, which led to the *Challenger* disaster.

Ongoing delusion is about updating the wrong map.

Leaders need to constantly take soundings from reality and feed that back into the system—ensuring they are updating their map of the context with soundings from reality.

Create safe spaces

One of the interesting things about the human brain is that when our map of the world begins to differ from our experience of the world, we begin to suffer anxiety.

Changing our internal representation of the world leads to the release of cortisol. This is a hormone that is linked to our fight-and-flight reflexes. Anxiety can be pathological, especially if our map of ourselves cannot accommodate the alternative, or if it is associated with feelings of loss of control or power. When our internal representation of ourselves or the context we inhabit is different from what we perceive or are experiencing, we become anxious—and anxiety causes us to stop. It's a self-preservation mechanism.

Successfully negotiating the external reality in a way that makes us feel safe is a way to remap the context and our identity within it.

Amy Edmondson, a professor at Harvard Business School, writes about the need to create psychological safety. This is vital to give people permission to be curious as well as to create the safety required for people to give accurate soundings, even if the news is difficult to hear.

The role of the leader is to create a safe space in which we are all able to successfully explore new context, new ideas, solve problems, voice problems and ensure the architecture of the mind shared by all is an accurate representation of our shared reality.

Summary

We have delved deeply into an exploration of context because establishing context is the basis for successfully being curious. Learning about what something is, how it is done and what all the associations are that lead to understanding and knowledge, is how we begin to be curious. Curiosity is about asking the right questions and knowing which questions to ask. The difference between wandering around randomly in the dark and growing new knowledge is about understanding the tools that can be used to define the context. These tools include language, concepts, texts, psychological safety and openness. Exploration of a new context is about ensuring the three roles are in play, the Plotter, the BearingTaker and the Recorder.

The curious can only be so if we are free of anxiety and equipped to go safely into territories we have never been before.

The next chapter is about how communities are vital to being curious and understanding context.

References

Calvino, I. (1972), *Invisible Cities*, Vintage Classics
Edmondson, A. (2018), *The Fearless Organization: Creating Psychological Safety in the Workplace for Learning, Innovation, and Growth*, John Wiley & Sons
Hutchings, E. (1995), *Cognition in the Wild*, MIT Press
Wittgenstein, L. (1922), *Tractatus Logico-Philosophicus*, Kegan-Paul

7.
COMMUNITY

'If you want to go quickly, go alone. If you want to go far, go together.'

– African proverb

If you're curious and want to know something, you can try to figure it out by yourself. This will always be supposition. 'How does this work?' you might ask. Then very quickly you will have to ask, 'What if I…?' of the situation. You might figure something out, you might create a new way of doing something, but in order to know you have to verify and validate your ideas. This requires others. Other context, other knowledge, other expertise. In order to come to a solid conclusion you have to explore context, learn the language in play but fundamentally find the people who can help you. Curiosity requires a community.

This chapter is focused on the Curious Community. This chapter explores why and with whom we should share our voyage of curiosity? What kinds of people can we seek out as companions and who can help us get to where we want to go?

Curiosity is powered by the community

Curiosity is powered by a community. It's never the lone genius—particularly today. It requires multiple disciplines. Curiosity takes off through social interactions, when learners engage with one another to collaborate and share knowledge. These connections can be planned or happen organically, by creating engaged communities, building collaboration and creating strong and supportive networks.

Escaping the echo chamber

The community we create around us as curious learners, at every level, no matter how small the question or how large, will have an impact on the quality of what we learn.

One of the wonders of curiosity is that it enables us to escape the echo chamber of our own thoughts. How many times have you thought things were one way, only to discover that they were another thing completely when you did some exploration? Perhaps a lone object you found in the kitchen? 'I wonder what this does?' you ask. It's a strange knife, you think, based on all your previous experience of things called knife, only for someone to come in and tell you that it's a tool for opening shellfish.

How many misrepresentations do you think you harbour? How can you escape the echo chamber of the mind as it seeks to make sense of the world? Our brains are hardwired to work this way, to make sense of the world as best we can. Our most useful information is usually the information that is created from relationships with others.

JS Bach's incredible output

If you ask any musician to rank composers in history in order of importance—there are very few lists that will not have JS Bach at the top. If you ask a music historian to show you Bach's output on a timeline there are two periods that stand out. The first was when he lived in Köthen from 1717 to 1723 where he was working for Prince Leopold von Anhalt-Köthen. He produced most of his secular work during this period, including the *Brandenburg Concertos* and *The Well-Tempered Clavier*. There were about five hundred works produced during this period.

The second period stands out above all others. Bach moved to Leipzig to become the Kapellmeister in 1723. Philippe and Gérard Zwang have created a list of all Bach's religious work in chronological order. The level of productivity whether writing cantatas, organ music, choral music, chamber music or music for pupils is unsurpassed—as is the quality of his creativity. There must be something curious about how JS Bach was organised during this time? What did he have around him to help him cope with the demands and the productivity? Which frameworks was he using that enabled him to create such highly structured, mathematically coherent yet exquisite music? How was he motivated? What caused this astonishing level of output?

What we know is that Bach was in the midst of family life. His first wife had died suddenly and he was now married to Anna Magdalena, his second wife. He had children running around and a family to support. Six from his first marriage and eventually thirteen from the second. They in turn supported him in his daily life. He had the safety of his job as the Kantor (the church musician) at the Thomas Kirche. But this came with significant responsibilities. He had to train and prepare the boys' choir. He was responsible for their daily education, as well as preparing them for three services on a Sunday. Each service required the composition of a new cantata (a piece of music for voice with instrumental accompaniment) thematically in line with the themes of the Lutheran religious year.

In addition, resources were tight for musicians, orchestras and performers—and necessity was often the mother of Bach's invention. Usually a cantata was written for at least four voices, and a choir, and an orchestra; however, sometimes financial constraints led to him create a cantata for one voice and two instruments. Some of his most creative work was born out of constraint. He created an incredible dialogue between only two voices in his Cantata BWV32—where the two could have been singing a love song to each other but were expressing a profound sense of spiritual love implicit in the text.

In addition to these duties he had to support the large community choir that met for rehearsals on Wednesdays and continually write new material for them. His correspondence shows he had to appeal for funds and resources from the church and city fathers—which were not often forthcoming. In addition to his church and civil responsibilities, he had to compose great celebratory cantatas for the full orchestra for high days associated with the city. It seems to have been a time in his life that any modern-day working parent could sympathise with.

Baroque shorthand

We know that at the time Bach had certain arrangements around him that enabled him to satisfy these incredibly strenuous requirements. He had a group of students to whom he could hand broad compositional brush strokes and tutor them to fill in the parts.

He used a pattern language of baroque music that was generative. The baroque patterns of scales, chords and the relationships between them, now known as the cycle of fifths, was a powerful tool. When chord structures are clear, the pattern rules would enable an assistant to fill out the parts required to be detailed.

The chord structures and baroque rules, once taught, would enable someone to enter the context of the composition and flesh out and copy the parts according to the embellishment ideas that were prefigured. In this way Bach could write the primary composition and others could help him create the parts that had to be sung or performed. This doesn't make it easier, but it does mean it could be shared, because the pattern language of the composition was shared. This is not unlike the way that large teams create online games or digital films today.

Bach was up against the clock in terms of requirements; however, there was nothing pedestrian about his output. He generated a huge amount of work. There were occasions where he would use themes and introductions written for a different situation in another context—for example, the organ introduction for Cantata 29 is used as a violin sonata and solo elsewhere—however, in the main mostly everything was a newly composed.

Bach's community

Bach was also a member of the civic society of gentlemen who led the city of Leipzig. These were clubs for socialising, but in the Protestant tradition they were focused around specific edifying interests. These groups would get together regularly. There are occasions where they would challenge him to go further in terms of his composition. For example, could he create a cantata that featured radical discordance? He did so in Cantata 46 and the result is shocking, and meaningful to the text, and works musically.

Bach could not have achieved all this without groups around him who challenged him, had requirements of him, perhaps helped him laugh, pushing him to greater creativity and innovation, which helped him achieve the documentation requirements of the truly enabled curious learner.

Bach's curious confidence

Within the frameworks of baroque music, and within the frameworks of the religious music of the time, Bach went further than anyone. He was certainly curious. That is well documented. When he was a young man, Bach was curious about the work and performance of the most famous organist of his time—Buxtehude. As a young man, Bach walked from Arnstadt to Lübeck, some 280 miles, to hear, and perform and meet with Buxtehude. He had the confidence to do so. He came from a line of musicians. His father died when Bach was ten, and his brother taught him the organ. He had a profound singing voice as a young man and was placed in a choir from a very young age. He was immersed in the world, languages, practices, society of music. Perhaps all of this provided him with the confidence and context to enable him to want to explore further—and winning the admiration of the masters around him sufficiently for them to open up to him.

It was the community around Bach, many people playing many roles, who enabled him to chart his course to places undreamt of before.

The community you need around you

In order to sail in the good ship curiosity, we require different people around us as sailing companions—each of whom provides us with a particular form of specialist knowledge that enables us to be Curious Learners. Who are some of the people we would want in our boat as we explore new worlds?

> *The Guides*
>
> These are the people who show us the way, pointing us in the right direction. From the moment we ask a question that goes beyond us, we become attractive to people who have the knowledge about where some of the answers may be found. Pay attention to these people, allow them to show the way and make sure to acknowledge their generosity. One note of caution—be aware of false guides—those who are pretending to know, or who are deliberately obfuscatory, for reasons of their own. Who do we have as our local guide and have we acknowledged their generosity recently for sharing their wisdom?
>
> *The Gatekeepers*
>
> Gatekeepers are there to open the door to the next level. A good gatekeeper will only allow us to progress when we have reached a level of mastery or they have a recognition that we are able to operate in a new context. They might do this to protect the integrity of the system—think of pass marks for an examination that permit you to enter a university

or society. Or possibly for our own safety—in martial arts a good sensei will only permit students to attempt a grading when they feel they can already perform at the higher grade, because the opponents they will face become progressively harder.

The role of the gatekeepers is also to send us in new directions to enable us to achieve the wisdom, experience or language required to take us through the gates we want to open. These are the gatekeepers—they push us to learn the things we need to enter the areas where the knowledge we're really after is to be found.

In our context, we should be clear about who the gatekeepers are and the role that they are playing for us. Sometimes they offer direction and sometimes they may seek to hold us back for our own safety.

The Wise

These are the people who have trodden the path before us. They possess broad wisdom. Sometimes they will open the books and take us through them, sometimes they will direct us to the relevant texts, sometimes they will offer us words of wisdom for the journey of discovery. Listen to the wise, they might save us a lot of time and wasted energy but also help us to exercise critical thinking. Though the ways of the wise may change with time, and they may not be aware of a newly available path, the wise are the keepers of the knowledge bases that frame a particular world or discipline.

The Provocateurs

Provocateurs are annoying. The reason is that they usually inhabit a reality different from our own. They see things that we don't see. As such, when we encounter them, they destabilise our view of the world. They may jolt us out of our comfort zone or introduce us to ideas that may indeed satisfy our curiosity. We need them, they keep us questioning and moving in new directions. When provoked, we should seriously consider what is going on before we react. When we feel a reaction we should ask ourselves why?

Provocations help us to be more curious, but applying curiosity will also make provocateurs less daunting—for example, seeking to understand the ideas behind the provocation with a 'tell me more,' rather than a more emotional reaction.

The Experts

The experts are those who have deep technical knowledge and provide us with the deep expert knowledge we seek. We work with our experts by either building something with them, or joining their team and learning from them. Note, we may have to pay a price to do so. We show them our work and get feedback from them. They teach us the skills we need to complete our journey.

The Audience

Everyone needs an audience. An audience of people who are somehow interested in our topic. Find an audience and prepare to perform for them—whether speaking, showing and telling, or presenting our narrative in an art form, or a documentary video. Somehow, present each step of the journey. We grow support, obtain feedback about the veracity of our experience, and may even find the people who can join us or lead us on in our quest.

The Technicians

These are the people who help us build the vehicles or concepts that carry us forward, as well as the tools we require to answer our questions. The technicians are vital for their skills which enable us to go further and to return safely.

The Synthesizers

There are people whom we can tell our story to, who are able to hear what we say and help us summarise and model, or map what it is we are coming to understand. We find these people and they help us synthesise our ideas.

The Motivators

These people love us in some way and remind us why we are putting our energy into solving riddles and persisting in our aims. We will need their encouragement. Their care and interest enable us to continue when we feel lost or overwhelmed part way through the journey.

The Companions

These are those who travel the path with us. They may be answering similar questions, or simply travelling

> along the journey for a time. These are the people who share our ups and downs and keep us company. Value them and appreciate them, as we provide the same role for them in turn. We travel together.
>
> *The Storytellers*
>
> These are those who are able to transmit the knowledge about something through its stories. They promote a particular world view. Malcolm Gladwell calls these the salespeople as they're trying to get people to buy into their view of the world. However, not all of these keepers of the frames, or world view, seek to persuade others to buy into their way of seeing things. What they transmit through these stories is technical skills and language that may save you a great deal of time. We all, in time, become the storyteller.

What this means is that we need to be conscious about curating our curious network.

Who is in the field we wish to explore? We think it's important to be intentional about the people we have around us. We need to find the community, both physically and virtually that enables our curiosity.

Putting community into practice

Over the summer of 2019 a curious community was created in Novartis with the goal of promoting and championing learning for the company's second enterprise-wide Learning Month. The Learning Month was first launched in 2018, as four weeks dedicated to promoting the various learning opportunities available across the company, through local events and global webinars. In 2018, more than 10,000 people were involved in over 100 events, resulting in over 50,000 hours of learning. In 2019 the goal was to move it up a level, expanding it to more people and building more awareness, increasing curiosity and ultimately developing greater skills.

The creation of the community started with the motivators and the technicians. Motivators, in the form of the learning leaders, creating the momentum and excitement of what could come, painting a picture of an exciting four-week programme of valuable learning experiences from internal and Experts.

Technicians, the project managers, created the framework for how the month would pan out—the model for people to suggest and deliver the global webinars, the branding for the local events and the communications templates that could be adapted.

Next came the Guides, approximately one hundred volunteers from across the business and across the world. They understood their local environment, the paths that needed to be taken and the things that would be of most interest.

Amongst the guides, ideas were generated, others played the role of Synthesizer to collate and distil these ideas. Then the Gatekeepers helped to step things up a level, adding new ideas or building on ways to make things bigger or better—for example, unlocking access to communications channels or new audiences. What started as a bold plan for two webinars every day for four weeks (40 in total) was stepped up to become 130 webinars, many with between 500 and 1,000 participants!

Other people joined in along the way—the Companions supported, the Wise promoted, steered and role-modelled, and of course, the most important group of all—the Audience—participated.

These people all came together to orchestrate four weeks of intense curiosity—130 global webinars, plus 250 local events in locations all around the world—topics ranged from scientific to digital to soft skills to product overviews. 'Curiosity walls' were created around the world for people to share what makes them curious, which then evolved digitally to over 1,000 conversations on internal social media using the hashtag #IamCurious.

Over the four-week period over 100,000 learning hours were invested, there were over 34,000 registrations for webinars, and over 30,000 people in 95 countries demonstrated their curiosity.

It was only a little over two years before that we had considered having the first Novartis Learning day, then pushed ourselves to consider a week, and finally decided to be bold and settled on a learning month.

Through mobilising the players in the curious community, a global movement was created that continues to grow and inspire curious learning across the Novartis organisation.

Working with our Curious Community

The most important thing we know about the way adults learn is that deep memory is acquired through experiences. Whether it is learning to drive a car or becoming a surgeon. It's our experiences that reinforce our understanding and it is our experiences in community that significantly reinforce our learning.

People and communities

We may have many learning communities that we are members of. One of the key things about curious learning is that it is driven by activity. Curious learners are people who have projects. Curious learners are people who have activities. It's the activities that we have and the things that we do that drive the questions that we ask. By having great questions we generate great answers.

Whether those questions are coming from people, generated by machines, a search engine or other online service, they generate a constructed learning journey. Nothing drives our motivation as much as answering great questions and then showing our findings or our newly gained skills to our community.

These ideas about the activity, and the community, are very important points that drive context, and that drive our ability to learn fast, quickly, and in context. Think about if we are learning to throw a pot, in pottery. We start with the clay. Perhaps we've never done it before. The first thing that we have to do is learn how to throw a pot, how to spin it on the wheel, how to create the shape. There are many processes we need to learn. Things like, How do we create the shape? How do we glaze it? How do we put it into the oven, so that it becomes cured? How do we then use it? Do we show it to people? Do we give it to our friends? Do we take it home?

This is a simple example about being curious to do something, learning to do something, and then doing something, and then showing it to our friends—it is the complete cycle that a curious learner inhabits. Being a curious learner and having radically personalised learning is all about having friends who can help us, and having a project that we want to get right. Whether it's learning to be a surgeon, whether it's learning to play the guitar, or learning another language or anything related to the workplace.

Social communities

Curiosity takes off through social interactions, when learners engage with one another to collaborate and share knowledge. These connections can be planned or happen organically, by creating engaged communities, building collaboration and creating strong and supportive networks.

Through online learning experiences in communities we can easily communicate with one another to connect, collaborate and share knowledge around topics both broad or highly specialised. Through rating, commenting on, and sharing content, people power a strong community of learners.

Within organisations, dedicated platforms are appearing. Learning experience platforms (LXPs) are already enabling communities to form quickly for resource-sharing, curation, comments and group learning activities.

Colleagues as coaches

This trend is changing our relationships with people we work with, as well as with the communities we join. Colleagues at work are more and more becoming learning buddies or people in our curiosity network. Our co-workers become active advisors and coaches, helping each other on our continuous learning journeys.

In a survey by Mercer in 2019, 74% of employees who felt empowered to drive their own career said that their manager provided coaching and supported their development. As the organisational structures continue to change and become flatter, coaching and mentoring will become an activity that happens between colleagues in a non-hierarchical way.

Learners as creators and curators

We see a trend in peer-to-peer learning, where employees are empowered to create their own online content and share learning resources. Through learning apps, employees can already curate, publish and share content to keep peers, teammates and managers updated with the latest and most relevant content. Crowd-sourcing means content is constantly refreshed, removing the barrier of irrelevant information which can deter time-poor learners. We can already see users creating content through blogs (WordPress) or videos (YouTube, Vimeo). Google, for example, leverages YouTube for their 'G-to-G' peer-learning program.

This concept stretches beyond organisation boundaries through platforms like LinkedIn and Twitter that create communities on common interests globally.

Summary

The ability to engage and connect with a wide network of peers and experts is important for curiosity. Social learning and experimentation are at the heart of creating a culture of curiosity.

We require a community of people playing different roles as we explore the context, content and languages of a question that we have. Our curious community not only guides us through, they provide the confidence we require to learn new things and to explore new worlds. They assist with our questions and they help us check our biases. Finding our community is vital when being curious, either in our immediate circle or organisation, or outside it. Once we identify the questions and start being curious, the law of attraction suggests that our community will gravitate towards us as we gravitate towards it.

References

Unger, M.P. (1996), *Handbook to Bach's Sacred Cantata Texts: An Interlinear Translation with Reference Guide to Biblical Quotations and Allusions: An Interlinear Translation with Reference Guide to Scriptural Allusions*, Scarecrow Press

Curious Conversations

On Curiosity and Community

Theo Anagnostopoulos is a Scientist and social entrepreneur, a science communicator and a public speaker. He runs the Athens Science Festival and is the Founder and General Manager of SciCo, an international social enterprise aiming to make science simple and understandable to the public.

On communities and change

I am interested in how to get communities of people to engage with science. The most important principle is that the citizens need to get an understanding of some basic science and how this connects to their everyday lives. Examples are climate change and its anthropogenic causes, health issues such as vaccination, healthy eating and exercise, the future of technology plus more.

Everybody is born a 'scientist' as everybody is born curious. Somehow this is frequently programmed out of us by our environment—our family, our education system and our society in general. A more interactive, empathetic and biomatic way of teaching is needed.

With regards to communicating science it has frequently been done in a wrong way. It is not the lack of information or convincing data that people are missing. For example, *An Inconvenient Truth* by Al Gore has been out since 2007, and it was giving all the facts about the destruction of the climate, and eventually the planet, with all this data and facts. This, instead of convincing, it was scaring people off hence they were just rejecting it. So, the mechanism is to create engaging, fun, educational methods that will not necessarily seem as teaching, but it would feel more like an entertainment if possible.

As an example, we created the first science festival here in Greece, back in 2014, and now we're running about six of them all around the country. We have around 60,000 visitors collectively every year.

When people go to that fair, they don't necessarily go to learn science, but they go to have fun. Now, learning a little bit of science as a positive consequence, it's something which comes out of this experience. We use gamification, and by not having a lecture type of approach. This is the main answer. What we do, it's edutainment, education and entertainment.

The best result comes out when an educational program is 'phy-gital.' Both physical and digital.

On community intelligence

The collective intelligence of a group increases in very specific ways. One is the way that you allow people to talk and fully express their opinions uninterrupted. Collective intelligence also is meant to increase when there is a higher number of women in the group, because it increases the social perception of the group. In addition, people from different backgrounds increase diversity which is vital for community intelligence.

8.

CURATION

'No idea is so big that you cannot take the first step.'

James Altucher

Being curious moves us from the broad to the specific. We form an end goal in our mind that brings our curiosity into focus. As we move towards an outcome, we curate the things we need around us to progress and 'resolve' curiosity as our understanding develops. We can curate our community, tools, knowledge, experiences and learning to form a personalised compendium centred around a specific curious exploration. It is curation of our experience and knowledge that brings us to our desire.

Why is curation important in the digital age? It helps us deal with the overload of information we are now presented with. To organise and construct pathways through content, to make it relevant to our needs. It's about filtering and focusing the content we learn along the way.

In this chapter we discuss the role of curation in curiosity. Why curation is important—what to keep in and what to leave out as we resolve a curious exploration. Also, we are interested in how technology can help us by personalising our exploration of knowledge and experiences and even creating content for us.

Curating court

Louis XIV, the Sun King, created a highly complicated set of court ritual, designed to reinforce not only his power, but also the control of his aristocracy. He curated an entire system of 'being at court.' It was a world within a world, managed through the physical installations and interactions he designed. His gardener, André Le Nôtre, designed the park of the Palace of Versailles as a curious learning labyrinth. It was an exploration of myths and classical allusions, all to the glory of the Sun King.

The King animated the court by creating complex *bal des fêtes.* The choreography and dance moves that were required of the entire court, within the spectacle of Versailles, served to continuously reinforce the power and principle that Louis ruled. These were embodied by the court literally—through dance. The activity was designed to put these ideas into the brain of the courtiers through the activity of the body.

The advanced language of these movements was known as *sprezzatura,* which dictated not only how one was to talk, and what one had to wear, but also the precise movements that accompanied communication. To enter this world required a lifetime of training from specialised individuals, and served to ensure the barriers to entry of this context were almost impossibly high.

His successor, Louis XV, created the conditions at Versailles for inspiring curiosity. In 1725, a number of Native American Indians were sent to Paris from Illinois. They danced for the King and this inspired Rameau, his composer, to write an opéra-ballet called *Les Sauvages.* Through various additions, such as the section called 'Les Fleurs' in which the lead male arrived dressed as a female, which caused a scandal, and pricked the curiosity of all, the opéra-ballet morphed into what has become known as *Les Indes galantes.* It is full of the silliness we now know as the noble savage, full of romantic inspiration, full of the promises of the new world, crafted from the gossip and titbits that had come to the court by then, full of the suggestion of riches and desire to be had. It was focused in four sections that extolled the desires of the Ottoman Empire, Peru, Persia and North America.

However, through opera, dance and narrative, Louis XV curated the dynamic within his courtly small world that inspired the curiosity of a generation of courtiers who desired fame, money, success and access, and essentially focused his country on its trade connections with the world. Every construction in the making and development of the piece would have been effective in promoting curiosity about the new world—from decisions to be made about the set design, to the music of those cultures, to the clothing.

The interesting thing about creating such an antiquated form as opera, especially in this day and age, is that it synthesises a vast number of technical skills, disciplines and languages to coalesce into a performance—with a cast of thousands and many more backstage.

Louis XIV and XV curated a world of behaviours, activities, customs and spaces designed to create a learning experience that reinforced the values of the court and power of the Kings. It taught their subjects mentally and physically how they should behave and interact. It is interesting that today we are again curating protocols for how to behave and interact—this time, when we are online.

These were sophisticated baroque mechanisms for curating culture, reinforcing culture, transferring knowledge, promoting power, and also inspiring curiosity. The Kings wanted to encourage adventurers to explore the new world and hopefully secure land and gold.

Exploring a new world with curiosity is a process of curating our choices and actively inhabiting the world we discover. It is an adventure. We tell our own stories. In the past this activity was the preserve of kings. Today, we all possess the ability to curate our own kingdoms online.

Making choices

As anybody faced with an overwhelming amount of content and choices, too much information is not a good thing. Try searching online for 'hotels in London' for ideas of where to stay. We're not sure the 1.2 billion search results are going to be of much help, especially when there are some 1,500 hotels in the city. To make any sense of the data we need to narrow down our options. Fortunately for us search engines do this by prioritising based on perceived relevance.

In the workplace we face a similar problem. With an increasingly vast amount of content and information available, we are faced with the challenge of finding and accessing the knowledge and learning activities that are relevant for us at any given time. Organisations large and small struggle with how to manage and maintain this ever-increasing volume of information. Our learning tools are not yet as effective as our search engines in curating and recommending learning and knowledge, at the time we need it, and taking into account the detailed context we are each in.

Curation is about synthesis and making choices. What's in and what's out. Whilst it is important to remain as open as 'necessary,' we need to continually bring information into focus to make decisions and progress.

A place for everything, and everything in its place

The Doge's Palace in Venice, the official residence of the leaders of the Republic of Venice, is a remarkable building and was operational as a place of government for several centuries. It contains multiple rooms, each room having a specific purpose. For example, in the judicial chambers, the Senate of the day would meet to assess financial matters and deliberate over criminal cases. The Scrigno Room housed a Golden Book that listed all members of the city's patrician class.

Within the palace, the *Sala dei Filosofi* (Philosophers' Hall) leads to the *Sala dello Scudo* (the Map Room). It is filled with enormous maps from the 16th century. They depicted the known world at the time, showing the economic and political power of the Republic of Venice.

The Doge would curate the experience of those who visited. He brought his guests to the appropriate room to discuss the matters of the day. They would go to the Map Room to plot voyages, the War Room to plan war. Each room was curated with the knowledge and decoration to allow for decision-making and exploration of a particular topic within a particular context.

Another example of these rooms designed for a specific purpose was seen during the Second World War, deep below the Treasury building in Whitehall, London. These were the series of rooms from which Winston Churchill and his teams would direct the Allies' war. There were four main rooms in the complex: Churchill's bedroom and study, the Map Room, the Cabinet Room, and the Telephone Room. They were in operation twenty-four hours per day throughout from 27 August 1939 until August 1945. Within the Cabinet Room, senior politicians met with military chiefs to direct the war. When he first visited the room, Churchill declared, 'This is the room from which I will direct the war.' The Map Room—covered wall to wall, floor to ceiling, with maps—was used to produce the daily intelligence briefings for the King, Prime Minister and Chiefs of Staff of the military. Each room was specifically curated for a purpose. They contained the necessary people and information required for the work of that room to be done.

However, how we curate depends on our context. There is a story that when Maori people came to visit the British Museum, they found objects from their culture that were mislabelled with incorrect descriptions. The Maori's saw these objects as they related to their everyday lives. The museum curators were blind to their uses, symbolic meaning and practical application. The Maori people immediately understood what they were, how they were used and where they fitted into the context.

As we curate, our context might change, and we need to be aware of this. For example, if we are curious about a certain way of cooking, we might suddenly discover an entirely different approach to making a dish, which requires different ingredients, spices, even different pans and utensils. To be successful with this new context in mind, we need to adapt and edit our kitchen accordingly.

Radical personalisation

In the past we curated rooms and exhibitions. Now we are curating our digital lives. For those with a smartphone or tablet, there is a constant process of curating even just the apps we use. We need those that we use most commonly to be at our fingertips.

We are seeing a shift towards a radical personalisation of our digital tools and content in all aspects of digital media. The digital music platforms we use provide tailored playlists based on our listening history. Movie and TV platforms serve up shows they calculate to be most appropriate for our age, geography and viewing preferences. Even our online supermarket recommends food to buy based on the other items in our basket. The more curated the experience the platform provides, the more we buy or engage with its products.

We imagine that these platforms will become smarter and smarter in curating their services and content to our needs. A media platform serving video content could suggest the two or three shows that it thinks most suit our needs, given the time of day, how much time we have available, what we are doing, even what mood we are in. Imagine if our smartwatch could tell our media platform that we are travelling on a train, on our regular thirty-minute commute to work. In this situation, a two-hour film is unlikely to be required and so the media platform could present a selection of twenty-five-minute programmes, on topics that help inform our day ahead.

Digital learning is going through a similar curation revolution. We are rapidly moving beyond the days of 'mass eLearning' to highly personalised learning experiences. Personalisation will revolutionise learning by creating customised experiences for all employees, which are based on their individual learning preferences, the challenges they are facing in their current role, and their career goals.

Artificial intelligence and machine learning are being incorporated into corporate learning platforms to provide improved recommendations, but we still miss the detailed understanding of individual context. As the available data and the sophistication of the algorithms improve this will come. When commuting into the office and accessing learning via a smartphone, we might want audio book or podcast content that can be completed by the time we reach the office. When in the office, though, we may want video content, articles, courses or resources relevant to the work we are doing at that time. If we're trying to address a specific or new challenge, we may need something targeted and specific. Our context has changed in each of these situations and at the moment our systems have not yet reached a maturity level to realise it. When this 'contextual curation' arrives, we will see a new level of relevance and engagement.

There is now an expectation to be forever refreshing skills, to learn, and to be ready for whatever shape our roles take as we move forward. However, the roles change, and what we need to learn changes, almost as quickly as we can learn what to do next. Not only is the amount of information that is available overwhelming, but also the way that we filter that, and make it relevant to us, and determine what we need to do next. We see it's becoming more and more critical to curate and recommend in a coherent way, for people in organisations.

Getting to a 'contextual curation' approach to learning would allow employees to unlock knowledge in a way that is best for them, at their own pace, using media that is optimally suited for their learning preference, situation and work environment. This curation will also need to take into account a user's general and specific curiosity. As we have discussed, *general* covers a broad interest in a topic area, and *specific* covers a particular need they have or chosen focus area.

Content will also need to be curated based on what is required for given roles or organisational requirements (including also what is mandatory) as much as by personal preferences and goals.

Artificial intelligence and machine learning power are already delivering sophisticated levels of personalisation at enormous scale. By understanding what the learner requires, these systems can provide smart recommendations on what to learn next. By adding the understanding of curation, the learning can then better relate to 'in the moment' skill building—'how do I do that?'—or longer-term capability building—'what do I need to know next?'

Personal learning clouds

It can be helpful to think of the series of rooms in the Doge's Palace when curating the information and community we need for our various curious experiments. Working digitally means we can curate and organise content, people, tools and methods to create multiple 'rooms' of exploration. We can change the outcomes we require by curating a different contextual environment. The modern equivalent is a 'personal learning cloud.'

In a world with an overwhelming amount and access to information, the role of learning development professionals partnering with subject-matter experts is to curate the technology and information that form relevant content clouds for the needs of their organisations. They will also be the guides for learners in their decision-making about where to focus their learning, complementing the AI recommendations with human curation, so they progress in their work and their careers. They will be creating the learning solutions and resources that help our people find the right information and at the right time.

At Novartis, subject experts and influencers have access to create their own learning playlists, that promote content and resources in the Up4Growth learning system. These playlists can include formal learning, but also articles, website links etc, to point curious associates to the content that best supports their area of curiosity. Playlists range from summer reading compilations, to learning digitally, diversity and inclusion, and (in rapid response to the COVID-19 pandemic) remote working.

We will be able to access our personal learning cloud from anywhere. Whether it's our laptop, mobile phone, television, in-car system. Today's knowledge platforms are starting to provide easy access to learning, everywhere, feeding us information that is useful and which is changing constantly as we move around.

Could you write a hit song?

With the right algorithm, yes you probably could. There are music algorithms that can predict if a song will be a hit with 60% accuracy. For years, hit songs today follow a formula—whether it's using a single note melody (for example Taylor Swift), or repetition of the same three chords (for example, Oasis or The Beatles). Making music is essentially the combination of different mathematical relationships between tones sequenced in time. Computers are really good at this.

Technology firms have already developed artificial intelligence that can compose music. At jukedeck.com one can now press a button and have software write a song. All you need to do is input the song length, preferred genre, tempo and select some instruments and let the magic do its work. TikTok is a social media video platform for users to make and publish lip-sync videos. It bought Jukedeck in 2019—hungry for the ability to provide royalty-free automatically generated music for its users. We are likely to see more convergence and collaborations between AI algorithms for content creation and platforms to provide the content.

Automated content

The same is true in learning. There are tools, such as Udemy for Business's Smart Recommendations engine that powers personalised learning using the data of 30-plus million learners on Udemy worldwide. By analysing billions of learning interactions, the company can deliver smarter, personalised learning recommendations for each individual, surfacing more powerful and intelligent content to learners. Not just, 'This is the thing you should learn,' but, 'I understand the level you're starting from, the way you learn, and what is now relevant to you in your role, and what you need to do next.'

We imagine within a few years, much like with music, learners will be able to compile their own learning courses and learning journeys at the push of a button. Algorithms will source the most relevant, most respected content and even add interactive elements such as games, questions and tests to the learning. We would no longer subscribe to a content library of pre-existing content, but instead to a set of algorithms that author content on demand.

For such automated (or user-generated) content and programmes to become mainstream, the quality will need to be validated to ensure it is appropriate, relevant and up to date.

Companies such as Area 9 and Sana Labs are already demonstrating some of these concepts with AI-powered *adaptive learning*. Using their approach and platforms, learning content is broken down into small units, and then served up based on what we demonstrate that we already know and are learning over time. In pilots at Novartis, this adaptive approach, which is personalised to every user, considerably increased retention and reduced learning times.

Regarding artificial intelligence, yes, we believe in ensuring friendly AI, and yes, we believe in making sure that we code machines and robots, to make sure that humans are not optimised out of the situation. Undoubtably, AI will play a huge role in helping us to curate digitally. How much power and control we allow it to have remains to be seen.

Individual learning journeys

As organisations recognise the importance of providing learning experiences that match individual preferences and development paths, there is an increasing request from associates to move away from a 'one-size-fits-all' approach towards delivering learning. In addition to 'in the moment' learning, there will continue to be a place for structured learning programmes. However, these learning journeys will be highly personalised, to cater for role, location, time available, learning styles, past experience and more. Already today, we can ask Alexa to 'play some jazz in the sitting room'—and music will start suited to the time or day and your usual listen preferences. We will soon see this level of personalisation for learning journeys. Learning journeys and experiences will be uniquely tailored to their needs. AI and machine learning will also help to curate content and learning journeys that make it easier to navigate information and organise paths of exploration.

These tools can start to predict if we do a certain set of learning, or we're at a certain point in our career, 'If we do this next, then this will help us make leaps forward into other roles, or into other areas.' Research shows that within two, three years, almost three quarters of organisations are going to be investing in their machine learning capability.

Lifelong curation

We also think that the curation of lifelong learning will be supported by a repository, or validation piece of technology, like blockchain, a distributed piece of software that enables your learning to be validated from great sources, and to be available to people to whom we want to prove that we have the skills. Also, useful for the system to be serving us the kind of learning information that we need.

Individuals will have a personalised learning index that records and certifies all of their soft skills and formal learning. Learning journeys and experiences will be uniquely tailored to their needs. We think it will be a combination of technology that allows the radical personalisation of learning journeys and technology like blockchain that allows us to keep an index of everything that we've learned in a trusted way.

This will also mean you can bring the learning we do from outside of our organisation into our everyday working life, and vice versa. If we study a new language and get a qualification or certificate, this will enter our personal learning record. If we learn a new skill within the workplace, this joins as part of our learning record, and if we then go to a new organisation, we can take all of that with us. The learning record is owned privately by us and continues to grow and stay with us throughout our life. The learning record could also inform learning engines that use it to serve us updates and relevant learning experiences throughout our lives.

Curated people networks

As we explore our curiosity, we need to curate not only the tools and information we find, but also the people around us. Who are the companions (friends and colleagues) who are exploring similar topics, the local guides or experts to guide us, the gatekeepers who unlock knowledge, the wise who know who or what to know? How do we find and connect with these individuals? How do we curate this network to aid us in our curiosity?

Clearly, technology can help curate our curious community as we progress with our discovery. Imagine we are curious to learn how to play the guitar, so we join an online guitar platform. A system tells us, 'There are a number of people who live near you who can play the guitar,' and if we enable it, we could meet up with them. Then the system recommends a set of teachers suitable for beginners. After some time of studying and we want to have fun with it, the system recommends a list of bands who get together and play the guitar at the weekends.

Curious companions

Curation is an ongoing dynamic activity. The people, information or tools we need around us will adapt as we progress deeper and discover more.

We imagine digital companions will make our curious curation become as easy as wearing a pair of spectacles. Spectacles were radical technology, a thousand years ago, when the Chinese invented them. Now they are taken for granted. Soon, digital companions will construct curated experiences, so that all learning is genuinely the kind of learning tools and content that their users need. Provided along with the colleagues, friends and experts they need to nurture their curiosity.

Jacob Collier

We think the Grammy Award-winning musician Jacob Collier is an amazing individual and provides an example of the power of curation.

Jacob is an incredible talented young man who shot to fame when he started to put a cappella recordings of himself singing all the parts to songs he had harmonised online. His mother, Susan Collier is a professional musician (currently a Professor of Violin at the Royal Academy of Music). Susan encouraged Jacob to feel and understand tone and pitch from the earliest age. She told us that she would ask him to associate the tones with colours and smells and emotions. Through this he developed near-perfect pitch When Jacob was two years old and there was a vacuum cleaner in the room, his mother would ask, 'What note do you feel that is, Jacob?' and he would reply, 'It's a 'G' or 'A.''

The other thing that Susan did was to provide Jacob with a place to make music and, as she says, she worked hard not to stifle any creative impulse in her children. Jacob filled his room with a range of musical instruments and eventually computers. His mother had encouraged him to make music from the simplest things, just using rhythm and found objects. He started making music with just a microphone and his voice. He started harmonising and putting some of these amazing pieces on YouTube. His arrangements were so impressive that he captured the attention of Quincy Jones and Herbie Hancock. Both were overwhelmed by his talent and he was signed to Quincy's label.

Jacob has now been on a world tour for three years. The tour is called 'In My Room.' There are hundreds of thousands of people who have been overwhelmed and moved by Jacob. Jacob's curiosity and his attitude to learning are inspiring. He has the ability, like his mother, to communicate extremely complex ideas in simple ways. He inspires the people he comes into contact with. For Susan Collier, it was about feeding curiosity and enquiry, nurturing experimentation, providing the thinking tools to make the most out of very little and learning by finding out and doing.

Billie Eilish and her brother Finneas have composed many of the top hits of the moment from their bedroom in their small house in Los Angeles. In an interview with Billie Eilish and her mother they describe the curation processes at work in their house. Billie said that her mum's rule at home was that the two children didn't have to go to bed as long as they were making music. Also, the definition of making music was fiddling around and doing anything. There wasn't any judgement or boundaries around what the definition of making music was. They could be twiddling around doing anything vaguely musical, such as on a ukulele or figuring something out on a piano or drumming on a box. All of that was defined as making music. So, Finneas and Billie Eilish did that all the time. That is a wonderful indication of how we can create the conditions for people to feel totally free to create and curate amazing outcomes. They have become two of the most successful musicians on the planet in three years.

The point is that curation of one's environment is not about having access to the latest technology, but it's about having access to the support and the encouragement to find the universe in whatever we may be doing. Curation is as much about our psychology as it is about editing, making choices and having access to resources.

Linking curation to organisation strategy

In the chapter on context we discussed the need for a North Star to navigate towards. At Novartis, the North Star is to improve and extend people's lives. It provides a purpose that the whole company can navigate towards. The company strategy defined five strategic priorities to get there. The skills and capabilities required needed to be developed across the company in line with this strategy. So during 2019, Novartis changed the learning organisation model to have the divisional learning heads move into the strategy teams (while being part of one overall enterprise learning model). With the learning teams driving the activity to build and curate the learning solutions and curricula, this strong alignment with strategy enabled the organisation to use learning as a lever to achieve the strategy.

Under this new model, the creation and curation of learning content can be clearly aligned to the skills needed in specific roles. These in turn can align the capabilities needed to deliver the divisional goals in line with the overall strategy. This provided a better line of sight between any individual learning solution and the overall company strategy. This alignment is already demonstrating strong results in the Global Drug Development division where this approach was first established.

How to curate

Here are some ideas for how to curate the content, tools and people around us to feed our curiosity—

1. Create categories and collections - What are the different areas of knowledge, tools, people to discover?
2. Make a place for everything - Just like the rooms in the Doge's Palace—make a physical or virtual space only for those things that relate to this exploration—even if it's just a shelf in a cupboard. The digital equivalent is tagging and folder structures or bookmarked links.
3. Select your sources - Research can be time-consuming—especially with the thousands of journals, magazines, books, reference and videos libraries to choose from to find people and information. Our suggestion is to make a short list—it can change or grow over time but start with the most reputable sources that are the easiest to navigate.
4. Make it visual - Bring curiosity to life—make it interesting for yourself and others. It will encourage further exploration and the connection of ideas.
5. Ask questions - Form specific questions to drive the exploration and curation. By asking a question—the broad immediately becomes specific.
6. Make tough decisions - What's most helpful, what's not relevant? The process of curation is about decision-making—

choosing what to keep in and what to ignore. Be ruthless with the analysis to focus on what's most helpful.

7. Exhibit - There is little that is as powerful as having to tell a story, or perform for a presentation, in helping curate what is most powerful. Do this as often as possible.
8. Archive - Don't lose anything—storage (at least digital storage is cheap)—we never know when we might need to come back to it!

Summary

Curating means making choices as we learn more through our curiosity. Without curation, we quickly become lost in a labyrinth of disconnected ever-expanding ideas and information. The process of curation is the synthesis and filtering that we do to remain focused on our objective.

When curating we need to maintain a big enough system of information and people that is useful for our exploration. It needs to be open enough so these new worlds become clearer and better defined as we focus.

Next, we look at how to power our curiosity forward through constructing our curiosity engine—creativity and construction.

References

Herremans, D. (2019), 'Data science for hit song prediction,' https://towardsdatascience.com/data-science-for-hit-song-prediction-32370f0759c1
Jacob Collier website, https://www.jacobcollier.com
Norwich, J.J. (1989), *A History of Venice*, Vintage
Spaworth, T. (2010), *Versailles: A biography of a palace,* St Martin's Griffin

Curious Conversations

Attention with Stefan Van der Stigchel

Stefan Van der Stigchel is Professor of Cognitive Psychology at Utrecht University and the author of *How Attention Works* (MIT Press).

On attention and curiosity

As a researcher I study the visual domain, what we pick up from the world around us. I think the brain is inherently curious, because it has to pick up information around us. It has to sample the environment. And we sample by a process called attention. We focus our attention on the things that we want to explore, the things that we want to know more about, the things that are relevant to us. The way attention works is that we can only sample a part of the external world at one time, and this forces on us a decision about where to focus. We can all be in the same room, and because we all have different views about the world, we all focus our attention on different things.

If you're curious about the world around you, you will focus your attention differently, given what you're curious about. Meaning that the way we sample the world is determined by what we want to pick up from the world around us.

On using knowledge

If two people are looking at a painting and you study at where people look, just look at the eye movement patterns, you will see that we sample that painting differently.

Then if you're quiet and after a period you talk to each other, you'll immediately notice that both of have picked up on much different information and that will also influence how you interpret the painting. I've had lovely experiences with people who know a lot about art telling me and informing me about where to look on a specific painting. I would never have been able to pick up on that information if I had not had that knowledge. Without that knowledge I would not have picked up on that information, and I would have perceived the world differently.

On focus

From an evolutionary point of view, we have to pay attention to certain things. If something starts to move abruptly, we will all pay attention to that piece of information. We have to. It's one aspect of our behaviour that has led us to survive, because someone might cross the road in front of our car, or enter the room, and it might actually constitute a threat. A lot of people complain about this, right? 'I'm reading, but I'm being distracted all the time.' But we don't say, 'I tried to go to work, but every time I crossed a busy road, I am distracted by all these moving cars!' It's the same evolutionary process at work. The brain doesn't know whether the thing that's flashing on the screen in your periphery is evolutionarily important, whether it's actually a threat or it's completely irrelevant. The brain doesn't know it. The brain only has one modus. If something flashes, if something's moving, we should automatically move our attention towards that information.

The good news is you can make this work for you rather than against you. You can instruct yourself to pick up on certain information by giving yourself a specific assignment to focus on. For example, if you enter a room you could instruct yourself to look at architecture of that room, your attention will be guided by the task in hand.

On your attentional window

An attentional window is the size of your spotlight. As a spotlight in the theatre, your attentional spotlight can also change in size. When you're reading something, you have a small attentional spotlight. You're focusing on the letters, on the individual words. However, when you're in a new supermarket for the first time and you're looking for your favourite pack of milk, you have a large spotlight. We're constantly zooming in and zooming out, given the task that we have.

There are some very interesting individual differences between people who are more able to look at a world with a smaller spotlight, and other people who tend to look at the world with a large spotlight. You need both.

On concentration

What is the difference between attention and concentration? Attention is the filtering process, what are you pick up from the world around you right now? Concentration is sustained attention.

Concentration is like a muscle, you need to train it. Meditation is a very good concentration exercise, it's like hyper-concentration. It is concentration boiled down to its essence. Focus on something and ignore all the external and internal distractions.

On bias

As everyone, I generally believe that I'm right! And so, what I try to do when I'm making a statement, like for instance about climate change, I really try to take one step back and think, 'What's the evidence? What's my evidence? Where do I get this information from?' I try to be conscious of my own bubble and see if I am perhaps incorrect.

One piece of advice

Remember that your perception of the world is limited, but that's not a problem. It's actually a solution to a huge problem, because we cannot deal with all the incoming information. But that means that our attention is something that's very precious. Try to think of your attention as a resource that is very valuable and use it wisely.

9.

CREATIVITY AND CONSTRUCTION THE CURIOSITY ENGINE

'The noblest pleasure is the joy of understanding. For once you have tasted flight you will walk the earth with your eyes turned skywards, for there you have been and there you will long to return. I have been impressed with the urgency of doing. Knowing is not enough; we must apply.'

Leonardo da Vinci

Whenever curiosity has been sparked. What happens next? Curiosity is not just wondering, it is about being engaged in making, testing and exploring in the world. Curiosity (like innovation) is to act. To 'wonder' is to just keep it in our head. Curiosity is finding, building, doing—if we want to know something, we must 'have a go.'

This chapter is about putting our curiosity into action. We describe how creativity and construction bring our curiosity to life, by exploring, doing and making. We cover both creativity and construction in this chapter, as whilst they are different the two must work together for us to progress our curiosity.

Creativity and construction combine to form a powerful curiosity engine, providing the momentum that moves the exploration forward.

We stopped before we started

All too often our curiosity stops at 'I wonder if.' Our smartphones are full of apps we download but never use. Our cupboards full of food we do not eat, and shelves full of books that remain unread. Just having access to resources—however well curated—is not enough.

Like the piano in the house that is never played, our curiosity lies dormant. Perhaps since childhood. It is waiting for us to take the leap to put it into action. To fire up our own curiosity engine and bring it to life.

What is the curiosity engine?

An engine converts energy into motion. Your curiosity engine converts our energy—our passion, our wonder, our intrigue—into innovation, learning, connections and new opportunities. Just as a mechanical engine has fuel and a spark. Our curiosity engine is sparked with a new idea or thought and then fuelled by connecting with others, finding resources and learning and exploring. Going deep into new areas, constructing and exploring a personal labyrinth of discovery. The engine creates motion—when it has a project to work on, something to apply our findings to. Through such projects, we may create something entirely new or discover something we hadn't known before.

For example, imagine we are considering a new role at work. A career path change, from a researcher to a salesperson, a musician to a producer, an actor to a data scientist. Or perhaps we are thinking of moving to another country, or even inventing a new business or product. Something sparks our curiosity, through something we've read, or seen, or by someone we have met. We start to explore the context of this new world—who's involved, what's involved, what skills are required. We might join a new club or community or subscribe to a new journal. We start to gather information and resources about the new role, or this new place and curate and organise this knowledge base to synthesise and document your learning.

Now, we start putting our knowledge into practice, to experience it in the real world. In the case of a new role, perhaps we try out a position on secondment, or outside of work. Making a move to a new country usually starts with trying to live there for longer periods, perhaps an extended summer vacation. As we put our curiosity into action, we also understand the context more widely and thoroughly, make new friends and contacts—further extending our community, as well as learning and curating more information. Our curiosity engine is at work!

Something that appeared unachievable or unfathomable to start with suddenly becomes clear and doable. Our curiosity engine takes the fear out of the unknown, because we can go into it prepared, one step at a time. Before we know it, we are putting our wonder into action. Exploring. Creating. Building. Growing in confidence. Scratching that itch.

Da Vinci's Codex

One of our favourite examples of an individual putting their curiosity into action is Leonardo da Vinci. At the time of writing, it has been exactly five hundred years since his death. His ideas and work still captivate and inspire us today. He was intensely curious about the world around him. Artist, scientist, mathematician, he used his visual and analytic skills to build and curate his own exploration of every aspect of the physical world from the ratio of steam to water, to the flight of birds and the brightness of the moon. He produced a vast volume of work—diagrams, paintings and experiments. His writing and drawings interlinked as he visualised and iterated his thinking. He explored and wandered through many different domains, dealing with messy, ambiguous concepts through drawing and visualisation, and connecting ideas from places previously unlinked.

He approached his art just as he did his science—as experiments. Some failed, some succeeded, but no matter the outcome, everything he did involved detailed planning and design, for which he took copious notes. His notes, running to several thousand pages, have been compiled into multiple codices. They contain his sketches, experiments, engineering diagrams, studies of the anatomy, even short stories inspired by literary works from Florence. Reading his stories (with the help of a mirror—he usually wrote in 'mirror writing' from right to left on the page) is like looking through a window into da Vinci's studio and his mind.

Da Vinci perfectly demonstrates a curiosity engine at work. Throughout his life exploring, combining and recombining ideas, and discovering through documentation and experimenting in the real world.

Creativity

The role of creativity in curiosity

'The world is changed by your example, not by your opinion.'

Paulo Coelho

Why are artists annoying?

Artists are disruptive. They deliberately seek to challenge existing norms and ideas. They often provoke a reaction—whether it's intense dislike, intrigue or joy. These reactions are often the starting point for our curiosity—whether in the world of art, science or business. We ask ourselves, 'Why is this like that?' or 'I wonder if…'

The process of exploring this 'wonder' is often a creative process. Creativity, of course, is from the verb 'to create.' We tend to think of being creative as someone who draws well or who has imaginative ideas. However, being creative is simply the act of creating—making something. Discovering and combining existing ideas to form new ideas that challenge conventional thinking. How 'creative' those ideas are relates to how diverse and ambiguous the original stimulation has been. Being creative is not just about how good you are at drawing or, in a musical context, playing the notes. Of course, the realisation of these ideas into a new something usually requires a level of expertise in the tools and skills of that craft—but that's not about creativity, that's about production, or '*construction*.'

By being curious, we give ourselves permission to be disrupted and to be open to something new. The moment we move from wondering to acting we start to become *creative*.

General or specific curiosity

One recent research study looked to understand how creativity and problem-solving is impacted by two types of curiosity—general and specific. In the study, participants were asked to design a marketing strategy to increase sales of a particular company's product. They were provided with a large set of background materials and given as much time as they wanted to review the content. They were then asked to create a list of ideas for the marketing plan. The researchers equated the time spent on reviewing the background materials as a measure of 'information-seeking.' They also measured the quality of their 'idea generation.' Doctoral students assessed the quality and originality of each participant's proposed marketing strategy, to provide a measure of creative problem-solving.

The study found that general curiosity—information-seeking—led directly to enhanced creativity. Those who spent more time being 'generally curious were more creative.' The new information found sparked better idea generation, which indirectly increased creativity. By contrast, specific curiosity, pre-selecting areas to focus on, had less impact on idea generation. Information-seeking matters. We need to allow the time for broad exploration and discovery before diving in to problem-solve—it leads to much more powerful outcomes.

Find the unfamiliar

One idea to stimulate new thinking is a *dérive*. A *dérive* (which means literally to drift) is one of the main tools of psychogeography to understand the effects of the environment around us. In the *Theory of the Dérive* (1956), Guy Debord defines the *dérive* as 'a mode of experimental behaviour linked to the conditions of urban society.' The purpose is to disrupt our traditional patterns and behaviours that become common in everyday life.

A *dérive* involved stopping all of one's normal activities for a period of time and following a previously undiscovered path. It is quite different from a stroll or meander. With a *dérive* the participant takes a specific stimulus—such as follow a blue car. Debord also suggests taking a *dérive* with one or two others to allow for objective analysis of the experience.

To stimulate our creativity, we can also take a mental *dérive*, meandering through information not usually explored.

The Mnemosyne Atlas

An incredible example of a theoretical or mental *dérive* was undertaken by Aby M. Warburg (1866–1929). His unfinished *Mnemosyne Atlas* meanders throughout art history and cosmology, joining and weaving images and concepts together in 'pathways' of exploration. In total, it forms a picture atlas of thought, containing almost a thousand images, brought together and arranged across large panels. The panels cover topics such as the language of gesture, representations of Mars and ancient cosmology with pictures, cuttings and artworks from the Renaissance, antiquity and from the 20th century.

Warburg intended to bring to life for viewers of his *Atlas* the 'polarities' that exist across these different domains. He combines opposing visual ideas and uses the pictures to curate stories that would otherwise take thousands of words to describe. They were like our modern-day mood boards of inspiration.

Putting creativity back into curiosity

Here are some ideas for how to bring creativity to the forefront of our curiosity—

- Explore broadly. Extend the types and sources of information to uncover before starting to ideate and problem-solve.
- Allow time for curiosity to meander—explore different paths and directions.
- Keep it open. Don't curate, close or frame too soon. Give curiosity some slack.
- Ask 'What else could it be?' and 'Could there be something more?' Use questions as prompts to find something new.

Constructing

The next part of the curiosity engine is construction. It is through the act of making and experimenting that we learn and progress with our ideas.

How to turn out a ship every four hours?

In the golden age of Venice, at their dockyard, the Arsenale, the workers and merchants wondered how to build ships bigger and faster than had been seen before. There was a mercantile impulse to do so—the more ships Venice could build, the more trade it could finance, the wealthier all would become. To do so required bringing together communities from across the city and to experiment to find better and better ways of combining these trades to develop these huge ships. At the time, in other dockyards of Europe, large, ocean-going vessels would take months to build. At the Arsenale, the Venetians created a modular building process and the first moving production line on water. At any one time up to a hundred galleys could be in various stages of construction. By bringing these galleys and the materials to the workers in an assembly line, the Venetians could turn out an ocean-ready ship every four hours.

Galileo Galilei was instrumental in the problem-solving and innovations required to build ships in this new way, in particular his research on the strength and use of the materials required for these large galleys and his study of accelerated motion. Galileo put his curiosity into practice by experimenting and problem-solving in real-life—to aid construction at the dockyard. Like da Vinci, he was an avid documenter. His subsequent publication of his documentation in his book *Discorsi* detailed his experiments, his failings and his findings.

The Arsenale is a wonderful example of the application of curiosity through constructing, bringing diverse minds and skills together to work collaboratively to define and create new ways of doing things.

What would be your equivalent of the four-hour ocean-ready ship, if you apply the same degree of creativity and construction?

Putting the Engine to Work

'Experiment is the interpreter of nature. Experiments never deceive. It is our judgement which sometimes deceives itself because it expects results which experiment refuses. We must consult experiment, varying the circumstances, until we have deduced general rules, for experiment alone can furnish reliable rules.'

Leonardo da Vinci

What are the components of our curiosity engine? If you were a chemist in a laboratory, or an engineer in a workshop, what tools would you have around you?

Building our curiosity engine is to put ourselves at the centre of a network of technology and people and making. It needs access to the fuel that feeds our curiosity—interesting people from diverse backgrounds and approaches, frameworks to explore and combine knowledge and tools and technology to prototype, build and document.

Here's how to put a curiosity engine to work—

Surround yourself with many different types of people

When it comes to stimulating curiosity, being surrounded by diverse thinkers is vital. Take a look at the network of people you regularly bounce ideas off. Do they tend to think like you? Do they have a similar age or background? Whilst it can be uncomfortable, make the effort to connect with people who are different from you and as different from other people in your network as possible.

Gather the fuel

As humans, our ability to continuously learn will become more and more vital to differentiate ourselves, as technology encroaches into our world. Along with the ideas and knowledge in the heads of the people you know, build and curate your personal library of content and experience. Gather the fuel that will feed your curiosity.

Start the engine

To start the engine requires the lightning strike of desire. What do you want to know or discover? What problem has to be solved? Without impetus there's no need to use the resources. These sparks of wonder can often come several times per day, if you pay attention to them.

Create a project

As da Vinci or Galileo knew, as soon as you have a project, things start to happen. Projects force you to learn, to make and unfold. To find the rabbit holes and the solutions until your curiosity is sated. Curiosity sparks the building blocks for what we want to achieve. Learning a language is best done in the country. Nothing accelerates that process than falling in love with someone and wanting to communicate with them. Or owning a house and having to negotiate everything practical and legal that comes with that in another language. Turn your wonder into a project—define an outcome, build a team—give your curiosity a purpose.

Make a show

Make an exhibition, a presentation, a performance, a show and tell—it drives curiosity and forces us to create outcomes—a real product that synthesises our progress so far. It also is great for providing feedback and moving us forwards. Creating a visual storyboard is a good starting point. Creating and telling stories is a fantastic way of not only bringing your ideas to life for others, but also helping you become clearer about what you are doing, and why. Nothing focuses the mind quite like having to give a performance.

Choose your frameworks

Constructing with others requires frameworks. For example, perhaps you want to compose a piece of music—you could sing it, but the moment you want to share it, harmonise it, perform it and get others involved you need frameworks. Sharing frameworks is like sharing a common language. We would go faster and further if we shared a common understanding of rhythm and harmony. This is easily understood as soon as musicians from Eastern and Western traditions try to work together. They inhabit very different systems of music. Frameworks have to be shared or invented together in order to collaborate. If we learn the rudiments of music writing, we can document our tunes. Understanding the cycle of fifths in music enables us to harmonise and create chord structures.

What are the thinking tools you can use or frameworks you can apply to structure and accelerate your work?

Curate your tools and technology

The right technology tools can accelerate your curious engine. Technology that enables curiosity and includes automated workflow tools is really helpful. For example, the Ludic Group couldn't find a platform on the market that did what was necessary to enable online collaboration so they built it themselves. After ten years of research and development in the school of hard knocks and testing in many real-life situations it matured and evolved into Ludic's SmartLab platform. SmartLab makes sense of the overwhelming complexity of connections we face online and provides structured, curated experiences for people and groups online. It is unique because it was built out of a legitimate need.

Track the journey

Any curious exploration requires documentation of where we've been and where we're going. Just as the sailors and explorers of old created logbooks and maps, and scientists today record their experiments, we also must track our journey. Technology can help us to create a timeline of our experiences, the information we gather and our progress towards our goals, such as Instagram or Google Maps to give two of many examples of such tracking technologies.

It works both ways

In *Harvard Business Review*'s November 2019 Special Edition 'How to Learn Faster and Better,' Erika Andersen tells a story to explain how making a conscious effort to apply curiosity can help, whether it is a specific project or the need to adapt to an organisational change. Andersen shares how a corporate lawyer faced the challenge of taking onboard knowledge of employment law that she considered as the 'most boring aspect of the legal profession.' By applying 'curious language' and curious questions—for example, 'I wonder how… anyone could find it interesting?' and 'How might knowing about this make me a better lawyer?'—the curiosity added intrigue, led her to connect with the curious community (an experienced colleague) and ultimately motivated her to achieve her goal.

Organisations as a curiosity engine

In the world of IT development, *devops* has emerged as a leading process that uses elements of Agile to bring together the different teams involved in developing and operating new systems, to reduce timescales and improve collaboration across the organisational areas involved. Essentially in a devops approach users are working with the new technology as it is being built, providing feedback and improving it as they go—rather than it being delivered in a staggered, waterfall-like approach.

A recent Deloitte report into the future trends in learning, they describe a similar concept in the context of learning. Deloitte call this *devwork*. The idea is that learning and work are completely interconnected—we need to continually learn as we deliver our work. In the past, learning was presented as something to 'go and do'—separately from the day to day. Expressions such as, 'I don't have the time for training' and, 'Most of this course isn't relevant to me,' were (and in many organisations still are) commonplace.

In devwork there is no specific distinction between work and learning. As an individual is undertaking a task, they access the learning and resources they need to complete the work as they go. In our personal lives, many people already do this automatically. For example, when faced with assembling a complex piece of furniture or having to mend a piece of equipment, we most likely will find a step-by-step video tutorial on YouTube and watch it—pausing at each step—whilst completing the task at hand.

In work, this should be no different. Let's imagine we need to use a new feature of a software system and are struggling to understand how to do so. The software could detect our difficulties and provide an onscreen automated guide that takes us through the task step by step. Is this learning or work? Or both? Tools such as WalkMe are starting to target this need in an ever more sophisticated way.

According to Deloitte's research, for organisations implementing a devwork approach to learning, learning and knowledge management need to be integrated into individuals' workflows. As with the example above, the right information needs to be available at the point of need. Tailoring the learning experience and providing the appropriate access to learning also mean that individuals can learn when it suits them.

Channels for everyone

There are multiple digital channels to deliver learning now emerging. For example, the researcher working in a sterile lab cannot access a laptop during an experiment—however, their safety goggles could provide an augmented information layer, activated by voice or eye movement—enabling them to access the information they need. For remote workers, or those continually on the move, a companion on a digital tablet can access their learning platform and connect them with experts. There are in-ear companions that can listen to our interactions and give us timely feedback. Other wearables, such as a digital watch, enable us to receive instant nudges—notifications and reminders of what we need to do, or key tips for our day.

Creating the ecosystem for curiosity

How, then, do we create the infrastructure for enabling a curious ecosystem? When, in 2019, Novartis made the decision to 'Go Big on Learning,' it involved building a new learning organisation and model in order to ensure that learning outcomes are achieved.

The ecosystem approach put the learner experience at the centre of the model and considered four main elements—

- Learning culture
- Content
- Channels
- Infrastructure

Let's take a look at the case in more detail.

1. Learning culture
    - Learning strategy - What they decided as an organisation to be the key skills, behaviours and knowledge that were needed to focus on, as well as the relevant channels, experiences and initiatives that they need to invest in.
    - Performance development - Considering how learning integrates with performance development activities.
    - Leading learning - Enabling leaders to drive learning in their teams, providing the tools and processes they require to do so, as well as encouraging leadership development activities.
    - Time and recognition - Creating and assigning time for associates to participate and engage in learning activities, as well as identifying ways of recognising their learning and development.
    - Key measures and tracking - Setting strong measures that allow them to track the success of their learning initia-

tives.
- Team and capabilities - What is the model for the team, centralised or local, and which locations and what capabilities are going to be needed now and in the future?

2. Content
   - Relevant - Content that they provide to associates must be relevant—it needs to adapt to their learning needs and requirements. This is an important characteristic to keep in mind when creating or curating learning, but also as an element that might be achieved by leveraging technology that filters and shares relevant information to associates based on their personal profiles.
   - Engaging - Creating engaging content. This can be accomplished in different ways, including making it relevant for associates and using diverse media types.
   - Bite-sized - Creating content that is easily digestible in bite-sized pieces. While these smaller pieces came together to support a larger learning objective, they could be completed as standalone bites of content.
   - Diverse media - Using diverse types of media to convey messages and deliver content.
   - Multiple sources - Gathering content from diverse sources, including new sources of content, such as user-generated, external platforms, and internal knowledge areas.

3. Channels
   - Immersive experiences - Learning delivered through virtual or physical immersive experiences, such as VR/AR, mixed reality, simulations, virtual and physical classrooms.
   - On-the-job learning - Learning happens on the job, when actively completing assignments and participating in challenging projects. Novartis is working to enable associates to find space to learn on the job, as well as pro-

viding support for them to take on new roles and challenges. Other key experiences they consider are projects, focused sabbaticals, secondments, rotations and gigs.
- Self-learning - Learning activities that are completed by oneself, without connecting with other learners.
- Learning network - Learning from others and connecting learners with a network that brings peer-to-peer learning, as well as connecting with SMEs.
- Coaching and mentoring - Supporting associates with coaching and mentoring is a key channel for learning.
- Central Hub - Providing a single platform or portals where content can be accessed.

4. Infrastructure
   - A single learning platform - A learning platform that provides access to all learning content and activities and supports the learning journey for all our associates.
   - Integration - Providing dashboards and interfaces that bring together multiple tools, platforms and data into one easy-to-use place.
   - Multi-device access - Learning platform, content, activities can be accessed through multiple devices, such as desktop, mobile and tablet, or wearable devices (e.g. smartwatches, goggles).
   - Learning assistant - Learning can be supported through the use of digital learning assistants, such as chatbots or voice assistants (e.g. Siri, Alexa).
   - Data analytics - A strong data and analytics machine that provides critical inputs and outputs and informs AI/ML functions.

Essentially, the goal of the learning ecosystem being created at Novartis is to find ways to better connect people with knowledge by linking people to knowledge, linking people to learning and linking people to people.

It should be noted that while some of these elements may sound straight forward, at Novartis it took over five years with a sizeable team and significant efforts from across the company to consolidate to a single learning platform. It was the foundations laid by this team and their efforts that paved the way for the move to 'Go Big on Learning.'

The best restaurant in the world

Ferran Adrià is legendary. He created the best restaurant in the world called *El Bulli,* in Spain. It reigned as such for ten years until he closed it to focus on teaching his methods. There were many unique things about the *El Bulli* ecosystem, but one of the most curious was that he would close the restaurant every year for six months, despite the clamour for bookings, and retire to a lab with his team. He established a laboratory for exploring every aspect of food, technology, science, art, molecules, taste, smell, experience. They would brainstorm and explore in minute detail. They would question and seek answers through failure, discovery and serendipity. They would document everything and produced exquisite books that photographed their discoveries, laid out their methods and presented new foods and menus. Ferran Adrià created an ecosystem for curiosity. He understood the power of creativity and construction, and it propelled him to the top of his world.

An unexpected nudge

When in March 2020 most of the world went into isolation, being moved to curiosity wouldn't have been the first thing expected under those circumstances. Interestingly, though, the data from within Novartis shows that there was a huge surge in the amount of learning that was undertaken across the company—an increase of over 300% in a single month for the total amount of learning registrations. It would appear that our curiosity is always there, just looking for the time and space or opportunity to be put into action.

Changing people's routines and providing time seem to have provided the nudge people needed.

Summary

Using our curiosity engine is a powerful way to put our wonder into action. Continually look for new stimulus, from the people and knowledge around us. Take a *dérive* to explore the familiar in an unfamiliar way. Stand on the shoulders of giants by combining old ideas with something not tried before. Creativity enables us to approach idea exploration in completely new ways. Construction enables us to learn by doing—the combination is the fuel for our curiosity engines. Organisations can be configured as giant curiosity engines by encouraging individuals to be curious and by building the ecosystem required to satisfy the big questions such as, 'I wonder if…?'

And when we get stuck and don't know what to try next, put pen on the paper as da Vinci did and start to draw. The answer will most likely appear in front of our eyes.

The next chapter asks the question, how do we know if we are pursuing the right things, and when we learn new things how can we trust our new knowledge?

References

Adria, F., Soler, J. (2005), *El Bulli 1983-1993*, Rba Libros

Andersen, E., 'How to Learn Faster and Better,' November 2019, *Harvard Business Review*

Da Vinci, L. (1478), *Codex Atlanticus*, http://www.codex-atlanticus.it/#/

Debord, G. (1977), *Theory of the Dérive*, Atlantic Books

Deloitte Research Report (2019), *Future of Learning and Development*

Hardy, J.H., Ness, M.N., Mecca, J. (2017), 'Outside the box: Epistemic curiosity as a predictor of creative problem solving and creative performance,' *Personality and Individual Differences*, 104, 230-237

Curious Conversations

Curious people and their curiosity engines

Professor Bill Sherman is the Director of the Warburg Institute, sometimes called the home of curiosity. Previously, he was Director of Research and Collections at the Victoria and Albert Museum.

John Dee and his library

Curiosity for me is simply the pursuit of things that we don't know, we tend to do that in places, let's call it a library, or a university, or an information economy setting. What is problematic is that our tools are very much focused on taking us, in a way, to what we already know, or to provide methods for us to show that we already know something. That's not necessarily helpful in being curious.

John Dee is often thought of as the kind of Merlin figure at the court of Queen Elizabeth I. He was heavily associated with magic, with alchemy, with all kinds of prognostication, but also crucially the creator of the biggest library in Renaissance England. What I tried to focus on is what that library empowered or enabled him to do. To open it up really as a different kind of institution and to think about what that kind of cutting edge, universal, magically inflected library would allow an individual who owned it to do.

In my doctoral thesis, I called it a kind of think tank, but that was not necessarily the best choice. It could be a laboratory. It could be an alchemical site, it could be a magical site or a place of curiosity.

I think the other thing to just say very crucially about Dee, and about Aby Warburg is that curiosity hasn't always been a good thing. I think it's important to look at the history of concepts, and the history of words, and if we were having this conversation in 1600 rather than in 2020, if you had asked me about curiosity I would almost certainly have a negative answer because it's risky, it's dangerous, it's in some ways looking at what you weren't supposed to look at. I think with Dee he was really pushing the envelope and paid the price in some ways because he was very *avant garde*. He was very much on the edge of things.

On Aby Warburg

The library of Aby Warburg starts as a personnel collection of books. It's a private library. It's funded by capital. It's the result of his family having become one of the great banking families in Germany. He becomes very curious about learning, and about books in particular, and so at 13, as the oldest of five brothers at the age of 13, he says to Max, his youngest brother, 'Max, I know I'm the eldest son, and I've inherited the birthright to the great family bank, but actually I'm not interested in banks, I'm interested in books. I'm interested in scholarship, and a particular in art history, and so I will give you the family birthright. You can become the great leader of the bank if you buy me any book I ever ask for.'

When his house became too small to hold all of his books and all of the activities that he wanted to host he bought the lot next to his house and built a research library. In 1929, his brothers endowed it and became the trustees, but that same year Aby himself dies. Then four years later, in 1933, the Nazis come to power. The entire thing is evacuated, and after some discussion it is sent over to London. So, from 1933 to the present the Warburg Institute has been in London.

The library created by Aby Warburg has a very unique classification system, and it's probably the thing he's most famous for today along with his Magnum Opus, the Bilderatlas, or Image Atlas. The library structure is unique in that it is structured according to four general categories, so each floor is devoted to one of these four general concepts, and they are image, word, orientation, and action. That is because, and he's very famous for this phrase, that his library was built around the principle, or the law of the good neighbour. That is, the information we need is often not in the book we are looking for but rather in the one next to it!

It forces you to look for things that are beyond what you know already.

Alongside the library of books he also creates what we now call the photo collection. It's a photo library, and it's an image archive that is also classified according to a unique system of classification. In this case it's what we call iconographic.

It basically takes you to subjects of meaning, so instead of taking you to Titian, and to a specific painting by Titian, it will take you to the god or goddess represented, or even the concept embodied in a particular image.

Instagram today is similar but it is much more individual. It's based on individual patterns, and it's also a very limited range in general of tags. All of our visual classification systems in the digital age tend to use a very, very limited range of tags. The Warburg has over 20,000 categories in our photo collection.

I sometimes say that Aby Warburg was digital before there was digital. I think he is one of those people.

On creating tools

Walter Benjamin's got this great essay that everybody likes to quote, but very few people read, which is about the work of art in the age of mechanical reproduction. That essay has an incredibly interesting section where he says that some people seem to call forth a technology that doesn't yet exist. They seem to need a tool, or even a medium that doesn't yet exist.

Shakespeare in some ways invented films and the moving image. It's just an interesting and provocative way of putting it. The kinds of sequential narrative, the kinds of jumps that the cuts, the kinds of things that as a technology cinema allows don't yet exist in the Renaissance where you're really talking about words on paper, and people moving around on stage. You've really got a set of narrative, and visual, or dramaturgical techniques that we actually associate with much, much later periods, and much, much later technologies.

It's a visual map through time and space of these move types, or gesture types, that actually structure, and preserve memory.

We know so much more now from neuroscience, and neuro behaviour about how memory is laid down. Not only through the use of hormones and neurotransmitters but also the way that images, and connections are made in the brain. They are much more febrile and have a network. In some respects, he is mimicking what is going on in our brain at some level. The collage of the moods, the general links between things, which are very fuzzy in some respects, all lead up to an impression of something which is more profound.

Digital tools are actually operating in a very narrow bandwidth—the idea of the Warburg is to keep the bandwidth large and open. It forces you to ask questions.

Aby Warburg's approach gives us a way into that in terms of how to be curious. If you look at his own work you see two clear examples of the kind of move to curiosity, or prompt to curiosity that you're talking about.

One is he continually draws on the language, and method of other fields. He's primarily working in art history, but almost all of his language comes from the mechanical, natural, earth, human sciences, so what can we learn by drawing on these adjacent, or even opposing disciplines

The second thing he does is move through time. He'll say, 'What can you learn about the ancient world by looking at modern advertising?' Or vice versa, 'What can you learn about the Renaissance, Botticelli, by looking at Ovid?' He's continually asking how one period can speak to, destabilise, energise another period.

In summary, continue to look for questions as much as, or rather than, answers. Browse as much as search. Finally, put things in association with each other rather than in some kind of causal, limited, linear line.

Keep asking questions. We have to keep being open to the haunting of the past. We have to keep being open to the puzzles posed by people who know other things than us, and who speak other kinds of languages than us. I think that is the definition of curiosity, continuing to be open to what we can learn from what we do not know even from what we do not understand. I think that's where it all starts.

10.

CRITICALITY

The key to meaningful curiosity

'I think unconscious bias is one of the hardest things to get at.'

Ruth Bader Ginsburg

Being curious will always lead us into interesting territories and experiences. We will continually be faced with decisions to make, directions to choose and a need to evaluate whether what we are learning is the real deal. How are we to know we haven't stumbled into a hall of mirrors as Alice did in the *Through the Looking Glass*?

In many cultures there exists the idea of the 'trickster.' In Native American culture he is represented by the coyote. He leads, he acts as a guide, but he may also present us with false information, or send us in dubious directions, in order to teach us something. The trickster has integrity, but how are we to be wise and avoid his games?

We think two things are the key—criticality and awareness of bias. In this chapter we will explore these concepts together. What is critical thinking? How is it related to curiosity? Why is criticality vital for making meaning? What is the relationship between curiosity, criticality and bias? Why is awareness of bias vital for curiosity? How is criticality related to failing fast?

Who does it best?

Investigative journalists are really good at using critical thinking as well as dealing with bias. We think there is a great deal to learn from their discipline in getting at unbiased understanding. Their objective is to understand something, how it was made, who is involved, their meaning, to overcome the obstacles of obfuscation or bias and to get to the fundamental answer of how do we know this to be true within its context?

Living in the post-truth world

As the Internet provided us with more and more access to information, and as its use became a tool for politicians and others who were invested in skewing data, we are coming to understand how important the idea of veracity of knowledge is. Truth is a big topic to go into here, but to keep it light, we have come to the understanding that we no longer live in a world that is governed by absolutes.

There is an increasing understanding that the world is made up of interest groups and power blocks. These interest groups have their own version of the truth and some seek to impose it on others for political, power or financial purposes. Truth has become accepted to be relative. Truth is contextually dependent. In a post-truth world, information presented as truth can't be trusted. However, we may know something to be true for a given context. Being curious in a meaningful way requires us to fact-check as a discipline and a mindset, and not to just accept something to be true.

Multidisciplinary exploration

Multidisciplinary teamwork (working with people with different skill and knowledge areas) always reveals multiple perspectives. This is one reason why multidisciplinary working is a growing trend. It is half of the reason why this book was written with three authors and not one—the diversity of backgrounds, expertise and opinions from the corporate, academic and entrepreneurial worlds, brings a greater ability to understand the topic from multiple dimensions and viewpoints. Multidisciplinary exploration creates new, powerful debates, a need to expand individual understanding, and brings an open mind to new and varied opinions.

The ability to understand a particular question by enquiring about it using many different perspectives provides a richer understanding of the subject.

(In case you are curious as to the other half of the reason for writing together, it was the significantly accelerated time to write a book that is provided by three brains rather than one, plus the benefits that social pressure and commitment of having shared deadlines provide to actually get things written!)

The multiverse view of the brain

By sharing different perspectives from different disciplines about the brain, for example, we grow our collective understanding of the brain in all its complexity. Neuroscientists, behavioural scientists, psychiatrists, computational scientists, artificial intelligence scientists all view the brain using their own models of the brain. Imaging technology is advancing in so many ways. Neural imaging falls into two main categories—structural imaging and functional imaging.

Electroencephalography (EEG) shows the brain activity under different psychological states (awake or drowsy). Positron emission tomography (PET) shows brain activity by showing glucose use in the brain which reveals where neutrons are firing. Magnetic Resonance Imaging (MRI) uses echo waves to distinguish between the different matter in the brain which contains different amounts of water. Functional MRI takes multiple scans a second apart and uses a computer to animate them—showing shifts in the structures, densities or pathologies. Each version of the brain produced by these different technologies is truth within its own context, but relative to our universal understanding of the brain. Each is a vantage point.

We have already mentioned how curiosity causes the brain to operate in a different modality, firing neurons and laying down memories in different ways. Joy and pleasure in experimentation and curiosity are also as impactful.

Criticality doesn't mean being critical or negative. It means being determined to discover an unbiased understanding of a situation.

A curious trajectory

The trajectory of curiosity is a spiral down from the broad to the specific. Our curiosity is sparked by open questions, and explorations are defined by decisions that cause branches in our journey. Some routes may be short, others long. Some may be parallel, others linear. Psychologists suggest that we are mostly driven by the psychological need for safety, the need to know something. The perception of a gap in our knowledge becomes something that we yearn to fill.

In turn, curiosity destabilises our existing view of the world—answering a curious question may slightly increase our knowledge or it may smash apart our existing view of the way the world is organised.

Abjection

Consider the word 'abjection.' It means something which is cast off or separate from us, and in psychoanalytic theory it relates to our concepts of the Other, and things we are horrified by. Julia Kristeva considered this in her 1980 book, *Powers of Horror: An Essay on Abjection*. Here's an example—your own blood. Blood is something that is meant to be inside the body. Anytime it is found outside of the body it becomes abject. Consider the horror we may experience in any situation where blood is not where it's supposed to be. Yet blood is in itself mostly water, minerals and various cells. It is inherently inert and without meaning. Doctors and technicians learn critical distance as they understand the professional context of what blood is, what the pathology of blood can be, and how it can tell us so much about the condition of the body. Context and criticality go hand in hand.

Horror movies

Here is the dark side of curiosity. Firstly, we are bound to encounter things that go beyond our conceptions of the world, and our safe model of it. Secondly, we tend to possess a bias against the things that horrify us. Horror movies exploit exactly this. Curiosity will always take us to places that unsettle us.

This is a problem because in order to understand the truth, or be meaningfully curious, we may be required to engage with the abject or simply unknown and put ourselves in a position of insecurity—the opposite of what a curious mind desires.

Criticality is a big part of the process of being curious. Being curious, we go beyond our normal expertise, experience and knowledge. It's about disrupting our understanding, being unafraid of 'The Other.'

Psychological safety and confidence (as we will see in the next chapter) are vital for curiosity because they allow us to venture into places of ambiguity. They enable us to function when our assumptions are blown away, and they provide us with the ability to rewire our brain (they release hormones that keep us safe such as dopamine, serotonin, oxytocin and endorphins) to do that.

We need to balance the degree to which we explore outside of our comfort zone, pushing those boundaries without becoming terrified or paralysed—which is a function of too many of the stress hormones being released.

These basic hormonal responses are triggered by the amygdala in the brain. It responds immediately to triggers in our environment and prepares us for fight or flight.

Higher order functions of the brain, which are constantly evaluating the complexity of the context we are inhabiting, provide feedback to our systems as to whether we are okay to relax or not.

Critical thinking gives us the tools to make sense of what we know and don't know, to calm anxiety and to permit us to progress further.

Snakes and scorpions

Children who are brought up in Africa are taught a particular way of picking up stones and looking under rocks. They must never put their fingers directly under any stone. Rocks and stones must be moved with a stick or by lifting it from above. This rule saves children from any nasty surprises that may be living under the rocks. It's better to teach children this rule, rather than hiding them indoors and not allowing them out. Children are free to play in what may be considered dangerous terrain, if they know some basic rules that will keep them safe as they explore. It's not unlike putting the address of a child in their shoes in an urban context or teaching road safety.

Criticality and critical thinking are like that. A sophisticated process that enables us to explore safely in unknown territory. They also enable us to consider dispassionately new information we may find.

What is critical thinking?

Critical thinking is essentially not accepting anything at face value. It's about asking the question, 'How do we know that?' Curiosity can be about considering everything that allows us to answer that question alongside the question, 'I wonder if…?'

How is it related to curiosity?

The foremost exponent of critical thinking was John Dewey (1910) who was an educator working in Chicago. He helped make the link between children's development through play, wonder, curiosity and the love of experimentation with the scientific method. One of Dewey's main insights was that people develop through doing things that are *meaningful* to them.

We know now from neuroscience that *meaningful* curious experimentation is the most powerful way to lay down memories and enable deep learning.

Question everything

We should question everything. In particular what is claimed as 'fact.' It's also important to try and not be emotionally involved in the information.

Criticality is also about being aware of our biases. We all carry inherent biases—through being personally reflective and critical we can challenge these and become more aware of our own limiting beliefs. Our biases may lead us down paths that don't serve the unbiased ability to learn new things.

Why is criticality vital for making meaning?

The brain is a meaning-making machine. It is relentlessly striving to understand the world we inhabit and to internalise it. We experience new things, we attempt to make sense of these experiences, and we create language to explain it and store it. Neuroscience imaging shows us that whenever a single word is fired, so is every connection, visual image and memory associated with that word. We know, too, that if we have not formulated a concept for something and it doesn't relate to something we already know, we cannot perceive it. In order to do so, our brains have to work hard to lay that concept down. We chunk it into groups of concepts, we attach it to concepts that may be similar, and we begin associating it with every other thing we can relate to it. This takes work, it costs glucose. Glucose is the fuel energy that is used by the brain.

This ability is powerful and makes us human. Meaning, all these associations, is what drives our motivation. Curiosity is essentially the drive for making connections and laying down new electron pathways in the brain. Meaning causes us to move forward. If making meaning is at the heart of our brain activity, then the faster we can make accurate meaning, the faster information becomes useful to us.

It's curious, but apparently the heavy glucose requirement of the brain and all its activity has a downside—that is the need for sleep.

As a species we have to become inert and vulnerable to allow the brain to recover and prepare for the next bout of meaning-making.

We are not going to go deeper into the benefits of sleep here, but the growing evidence on the value of a good night's sleep is worthy of further reading.

Why is awareness of bias vital for curiosity?

Another downside of all this associative energy is that we may become prone to bias. If we're constantly laying down information that connects with existing information, we may fall into the trap of only exploring things that we know something about already, or assumptions we may have, or things that make us feel safe.

Assumption is the mother of f*-ups**

As Robert Ludlum wrote, assumption is that we know the answer or understand the context about something, unaware that we may not. The burden of our experience allows us to go very fast in situations where we have been before, through making the necessary assumptions. The problem is that context changes and what is appropriate in one situation may be utterly wrong in another. Even if the situation appears readable.

We know from Quantum Theory that something can be changed just by the action of our looking at it. How do we overcome this, if we are always an actor in everything we are curious about? How can we remain unbiased if our biases are always acting upon us? How do you check your assumptions at the door and reflect on your biases.

How many biases are there?

The first step to knowing something is to name it. We found a very useful tool—the Bias Codex—which is a powerful starting point and can be downloaded at https://curiousadvantage.com/codex.png.

Being aware of bias is a valuable filter for critical thinking. It is a great starting point for asking where should I go next? What should

I be curious about next? It's a fantastic way to steer our curiosity to answer the question about what we want to experience next.

To highlight a few that have been categorised by Buster Benson in his Codex. Bizarre or funny things stick out more—but this may just be the bizarreness effect. Something bizarre in itself—rather than something being bizarre because it is outside of our existing knowledge—may be a bias. Confirmation bias may lead to us being drawn to things that confirm our own beliefs. The clustering illusion might lead us to find stories and patterns even when looking at very sparse data, making meaning of things that don't exist. We simplify numbers to make them easier to think about. To avoid mistakes, we aim to preserve autonomy or status. We might make assumptions because we have no time. We edit and reinforce some memories after the fact—especially if they are unsettling to others or impact our identity.

Unconscious bias in business

There are many examples of unconscious bias in business. To select a few, orchestras were found to hire less men when auditions were conducted behind a screen and people were hired on musical skill only. More French wine is bought in shops when French music was played. At least these days subliminal programming in advertising is explicitly banned.

Diversity in organisations can be problematic due to affinity bias, or onfirmation bias, labelling bias or selective attention bias. Diversity is one way to help us accept those who are different from us and overcome our bias against difference. As we mentioned previously, research by McKinsey has shown there is positive correlation between profitability and diversity in business.

Unconscious biases in data lead to assumptions that can lead to errors. Unconscious bias in curiosity can lead us down paths that lead nowhere or unleash nothing in terms of knowledge.

How should we overcome bias?

Psychologists distinguish between explicit bias and implicit bias. Explicit being our stated beliefs and implicit being the more difficult internalised biases we may have. Sometimes these are at odds with each other. This causes dissonance and distress. For example, you may find yourself giggling nervously in a situation where what you are involved in is at odds with your idea of yourself. Think about gender stereotypes and how they can be perceived by people uncomfortable with their own sense of self. You may find yourself laughing nervously at a joke that is at odds with your explicit beliefs yet triggers your implicit biases. For example, you may hear a joke that you know to be racist, you might giggle nervously, you might tolerate it as 'lightly' racist, yet it may sit at odds with your self-identity as a tolerant, open individual.

Miranda Fricker, the philosopher, identifies *epistemic injustices.* These are biases that may be implicitly coded within texts, law or language (such as jokes). These hidden biases are hard to decipher, but they can have a huge impact on the lives of people. For example, when some people are believed or not believed because of their race or identity in a situation. Knowing about these forms of injustice and being able to name them is the starting point for spotting them when they exist.

There are known methods that are used to help us be critical and form new knowledge

Inductive thinking

Scientists are very good at this. The scientific method is designed to challenge assumptions and test bias and hypotheses and come to conclusions based on reality. As you may be aware, Francis Bacon invented the scientific method of hypotheses and testing (Novum Organum), in the 1620s. It was referred to as 'The New Method.' This is inductive thinking.

Design thinking

Design Thinking also encourages us to challenge existing thinking by imagining possible alternative futures and working backwards towards the current state. This is deductive thinking. However, the key point is that the ideas are not just accepted—but tested against reality by building prototypes and working models.

Critical making and speculative design

Design thinking is a powerful tool for moving through a process of speculating, coming up with options, testing and deciding. It's a synthesis of the creative process that professional designers employ.

A few years ago, Canadian academic Matt Ratto and his team in Toronto began to add critical theory and critical thinking to design workshops and the results have been impressive. It has led them down a path where they are more likely to find creative solutions to situations that have impact in the real. The approach came to be called *critical making* and it is proving to have real-world application in robotics, algorithmic design and artificial intelligence.

Another approach to design with critical thinking in place is called *speculative design*. This was an approach that took extremely unlikely disciplines and combined their contexts together. Consider the work of designer Joana Seguro who used speculative design principles to manufacture very beautiful glass objects that contained bees. The bees had been trained to walk to chambers within the objects based on their detection of pheromones linked to pregnancy and various pathologies. By blowing into these objects, the bees' behaviour could inform a woman whether she was pregnant or not. It could also test for various ailments.

Kill the company

To question everything is both a mindset and a skill, and a science and an art. Lisa Bodell, bestselling author of *Kill the Company*, advises making it a habit to ask tough, uncomfortable questions that challenge the accepted ways of doing things—challenge convention and even the sacred cows. She promotes curiosity and continuous learning as two of the traits that are necessary to thrive.

Bodell takes this questioning to the extreme, encouraging you to ask the questions that would kill the company—putting yourself in the shoes of a ruthless competitor and asking what would it take to find the weaknesses or areas that can be exploited? In asking these questions they need to be phrased to not appoint blame, and lead to a pre-existing assumption, or stifle creativity, but instead to challenge the status quo and open up a wide range of potential solutions. If asking questions to 'kill the company' is too big a challenge to start off with, or if you are working in government or other organisations, then Bodell suggests starting with 'kill a stupid rule'—providing the same opportunity for great questions and a curiosity to improve the status quo to drive a positive impact.

Driving out bias

There are things that we can build into our everyday exploration that can help us be a curious learner who is aware of bias.

Name it

Understanding bias, naming the various types of bias and reflecting on our own biases is the first step to using the bias filter in our curious adventures.

Check our emotional reaction to something

If our emotions are too comfortable with something and we want to promote it without understanding why we like it—we may be prone to confirmation bias. On the other hand, we may be happy because something has an outcome we are after—if so, we should pursue but we should keep our confirmation bias in check. Happiness is not necessarily the best indicator of veracity.

If we are made uneasy by something, it may be our flight or fight safety psychology kicking in. In which case it might be best to run a mile. Although it might be that what we have discovered sits outside of our frame of reference, our identity or our expectations. In which case try and be objective and emotional about the situation, reflect on why something makes us uneasy or afraid—if it is not harmful, get curious and explore. However, go into a new context armed with information about what is likely to be encountered.

Go to the uncomfortable data first

Making decisions about where next is difficult when data sits outside of our expectations or has difficult implications. Start with the difficult stuff. It's usually where the most insights are to be found.

Support failure

Failure is a tough sell in highly focused, success-orientated cultures. However, the right kind of failure is one of the most important tools in our toolbox. We talk about the need for high-volume, low-impact failure. Lots of little tests and failures lead to rapid understanding of solutions. High-impact, low-volume failure can lead to a one-and-done breaking of the bank. Not good! Encourage testing of reality with low-cost prototypes—failure is the best way to learn and update our understanding quickly.

Bring options to the table

Options enable us to be free of situational paralysis. When we have no options and are challenged, we may experience a form of paralysis—whereas options give us things to consider. The ambiguity leads to creative ways forward. As we explore we need to continuously consider our options. Always consider at least three possible scenarios as a rule, test these scenarios, make decisions based on the results, and look for more options.

Learn from experts

Once we enter a context, we should find the centre, find the motherload of knowledge, find the area of greatest expertise and go there to explore. No matter how uncomfortable that might make us feel. Here's a tip, all experts love people asking them questions about their topic.

Fresh eyes

Find new people who have had nothing to do with our exploration and ask them for their opinion. Fresh eyes are a powerful tool for checking our biases and enabling us to go deeper.

Document the journey

Notebooks that provide tracings of your journey are powerful ways of achieving critical distance from the subject. An idea fills our mind, and yet when we write it down, draw a picture of it or create a mind-map of it—and then return to it—we are immediately able to make a judgement about it that may be free of bias. It may seem smaller to us, more relevant or less relevant, or the focus of further exploration may suddenly become clear.

If we think again about the Codex of Leonardo da Vinci, not many before or since have documented their learning in such an incredible way. It was clear that he would continuously update his notes and practice and further his understanding as he followed it through. Look at all the options for flying machines that he considered until he settled on something that resembled a bird.

The brain fires very differently when we are creating information to when we are reading information. By translating our experiences and reflections into notes—and in particular visual maps of information—we are able to obtain critical distance from the information and keep our biases in check.

Ask killer questions

Be prepared to ask the questions that nobody really wanted to consider—for example the question, 'How could we destroy the company?' will lead to understanding where the weaknesses are.

What we can learn from investigative journalists

UNESCO defines investigative journalism as 'the unveiling of matters that are concealed either deliberately by someone in a position of power, or accidentally, behind a chaotic mass of facts and circumstances—and the analysis and exposure of all relevant facts to the public.'

The idea is to make sense of the chaos and the noise. To get at the backstories and synthesise down to the specific facts that drive a situation. Investigative journalists have a process and they are taught in a specific way. They are asked to consider cases, in order for them to become used to asking questions that get behind the stories.

They are taught to be empathetic in order to establish trust with people, they are also taught to be unemotional about the facts, in order to limit bias and get behind the façade. They are taught to be trustworthy, to never reveal their sources if these are not on the record, and it is this principle that promotes safety for everyone concerned. They are taught to communicate their findings in a way that lays out the context and defines the validity of their investigation. They are taught to tell the story in a way that is compelling and makes the case. Above all, the best investigative journalists tell stories that serve no one but the facts.

Investigative journalists know how to explore critically

Journalists who live on the fringes, in war zones, or exploring different communities have to gain trust and be able to discern that which is of material interest from the stories that people tell. How they do this is a learned skill and process which includes—

Find existing documents

The first thing they do is research existing documents, stories and ephemera as much as possible. These provide the background and historical facts required to approach sources, to be taken seriously and to be able to ask probing and relevant questions.

Identify sources

Discovering who the people are at the centre of a particular context is central to discovering where the reality exists within it. There are always people who know more about something than anyone else—find these people by asking questions.

If you want to find the coolest person in a playground, ask the kids there, 'Who is the coolest person?' They will point you in the direction of others, ask those others, and keep asking until you find the person who says unequivocally, 'I am the coolest person in the playground.' It's at least one way that works for discovering valid sources.

Develop trust

Developing trust between you and your sources is the only way that the door will be opened to often sensitive or hidden information. Research and background knowledge are a vital component to someone taking one seriously enough to share. Humanity and being trustworthy are valuable for establishing trust—both socially—as well as being linked to others who are trusted—or references. It cannot be faked. Trust is active, and requires someone to validate you, or you have to prove that you can be trusted.

Check facts

Once facts emerge, they have to be checked and validated from a secondary or third source—this is vital to curiosity. Fact-checking and reference trails are vital for ensure unbiased reporting. This includes the accumulation, documentation and archiving of evidence—in order to establish what is known and how that knowledge came to be known. Curious learners may not need to defend themselves in a court of law, but evidence-gathering is a vital part of being curious.

Clarity of mind

The psychology of good investigative reporting includes clarity of mind, in order to discern fact from fiction in the moment, recall documentation, and be able to make quick and astute decisions about where to go next, a sense of personal safety and confidence to take risks, the ability to order information, synthesise and develop evidence, and the ability to create a narrative and tell a story that is compelling and frames a perspective or argument.

Create new context

This is the understanding that by entering a new context, and by reporting on it, we become part of the story, and the context. This has to be respected and understood. The experimentation, documentation, reporting and engagement change the context. With this comes responsibility.

Summary

Criticality is an important part of being curious. It helps us to avoid going too far down blind alleys, pursuing only things that reinforce our belief or not being open enough to new possibilities. Critical thinking is a skill that can be learned, just as investigative journalists do. By becoming aware of our biases we can start to keep them in check and ask others to do the same for us. Criticality and awareness of unconscious bias are two of the most powerful tools for ensuring we truly learn new things.

In the next chapter we show how being engaged with curiosity leads to a virtual cycle that builds our confidence, which in turn leads to more ability to be curious.

References

Bacon, F. (1602), *Novum Organum*

Bodell, L. (2012), *Kill the Company: End the Status Quo, Start an Innovation Revolution*, Bibliomotion Inc.

Cognitive Bias Codex (2019), https://www.teachthought.com/critical-thinking/the-cognitive-bias-codex-a-visual-of-180-cognitive-biases/

Dewey, J. (1910), *How we Think?*, Isha Books

Kristeva, J. (1980), *Powers of Horror: An Essay on Abjection*, Columbia University Press

Ratto, M. (2011), *Critical Making: Conceptual and Material Studies in Technology and Social Life*, The Information Society, 27:4, 252-260

Curious Conversations

Investigative Journalism with David Harrison and Sara Moralioglu

David Harrison is an award-winning British investigative journalist and documentary-maker with over 35 years' experience covering major stories in the UK and worldwide. He has worked for leading British national newspapers, including *The Sunday Times*, *The Observer* and *The Sunday Telegraph*, and currently makes television documentaries for Aljazeera's Investigative Unit.

Sara Moralioglu is an award-winning documentary filmmaker and journalist who produces documentary films and content for leading UK and US broadcasters, including BBC *Newsnight* and Channel 4. Sara produced *Grenfell - 21st Floor* (about the tragic tower block fire) which was nominated for the best current affairs film category for the RTS Journalism Awards.

On finding the story

David

Like most journalists, I started off for many years doing news and along the way I was doing investigations. I've probably reported in nearly 100 countries. I've done investigations of a massive range of topics. I think often investigations spring from a news story that you've done and often it comes from a hunch or a feeling that there's more to this. I think what drew me to it was that after a while you just want to get into things a little bit deeper. Then there is also that drive to expose and to reveal wrongdoing, which is the kind of area of investigative journalism that I'm involved in. You need a huge amount of curiosity. You need to want to know. You need that desire, that thirst, to find out and get behind stories that are often covered quite superficially in the news.

Sara

I started off in natural history documentaries and then moved into anthropology programmes like the Bruce Parry documentaries. As I got older, the subject-matter got more serious. I moved into current affairs and programmes like *Newsnight*, *Panorama* and *Dispatches*. I'm currently at Channel 4 News.

In this work, I think you have to be very curious and want to expose things. I think for me, once I start to get an inclination that something's wrong or not going as it should be going, you have to be sort of obsessed, really obsessive, to uncover things. Some people just aren't that interested in things except for what's going on within their own lives, and some people really are curious about what's going on in the world.

On process and principles

David

My work has certainly broadened my perspective. I've covered stories from all over the world. I also run occasional training courses for journalists in developing countries including Sudan, Algeria, Morocco, Syria and Lebanon. And that's really helped me, I think, because it really helps you get inside the mentality of a country and its people.

Sara

In terms of process, usually what happens is either I'll pitch a story about something I'm curious about or I will be approached by the commissioner or an editor. Then it usually starts off with getting access. It's all about making connections with people and speaking to them—ideally meeting them face-to-face. I think my process is really trying to understand what that person would want out of this and why they should want to expose something, so that they want to tell their story.

One of my objectives has always been about holding those in power accountable and trying to expose the truth to get to the bottom of whatever the issue is. For example, with *Grenfell*, my main motivation was to give the survivors, who had gone through the most horrific tragedy, a voice.

David
There are lots of principles of journalism that relate to being curious. You've got to be dogged, determined, you've got to be forensic, curious, sceptical, asking questions all the time. It's about testing your own thoughts, testing your own evidence. Does it stand up? Is it really watertight or is this a bit flaky?

On being curious

David
I would say try to stay open-minded and challenge your own views, but embrace people, don't push them away. I've found that all over the world if you do that, you embrace people, they embrace you back most of the time and you learn from that. I remember in the war in Afghanistan, the refugees everywhere, people suffering everywhere. I remember this poor family lived in a mud hut and they invited us in to share the last of their food. It's acts of kindness like that that blow away your prejudice and your ideas about certain groups of people, certain types of people. I would say, yes, stay open-minded. Be receptive to other people's views and challenge your own views. I think in the end you end up with a broader perspective.

Sara
I think in my work it is really important to listen to people and engage. Try to understand their story and what they're about and put yourself in their shoes. I think empathy and just communicating and being open-minded are really important and enriching.

11.
CONFIDENCE

'Each time we face our fear, we gain strength, courage, and confidence in the doing.'

Theodore Roosevelt

Some people simply exude confidence. What gives them that confidence? Are they confident in every situation? Probably not. The world's best soccer player might dread public speaking. A renowned business executive might be afraid to try speaking a foreign language. Our confidence is usually specific to a particular skill or topic area where we have plenty of past experience.

In this chapter we tackle the final C of the 7 C's. Perhaps the most important C of them all. Confidence is the condition that enables us to go boldly into new curious contexts. It is the state that takes us further down the path, connects us with more people, and allows us to learn faster.

Why confidence?

Confidence is not something we are born with. It's also not 'acting cool,' with bravado or even courage. We can pretend to ourselves and even others that we are supremely confident, whilst at the same time be a mess inside—full of self-doubt.

The origin of the word confidence is based on the Latin 'with trust.' From *con* meaning 'with' and *fide*, meaning 'trust.' Confidence is to have trust in yourself and with others.

It is at the heart of the psychological understanding of self-efficacy. This is defined as our capacity to believe in our own ability to perform certain goals. It is related to our belief in our ability to control our own motivation, behaviour and environment to achieve things.

Thomas and Bandura were the psychologists who defined the sources of confidence as including mastery experiences, vicarious experiences where we see others achieve things, verbal persuasion from those we respect and trust, and physiological and affective states that prepare us for a situation.

In 1952, Bernice Milburn Moore's article, 'Self-Confidence for Competence,' reflected on confidence in teachers. Moore describes self-confidence as 'a trust in self, a faith in one's ability to be able to meet situations as they may arise.' We need both confidence and competence—one without the other is not useful, in fact alone might be dangerous.

Does confidence come from success? Perhaps. However, the confidence that comes from success is a fickle thing. Think of any sports star who one season is at the top of their game and in the next they can't score, land that triple salchow or hit a straight drive no matter what they try. They have developed mastery of their sport—but when the success stops, the confidence disappears. Mastery is not necessarily confidence.

Imagine you want to learn to rock climb. Completing successive climbs of greater and more complex ascents would certainly build your skill.

Failure is key

However, what if, during your training, you forced yourself to regularly fall, from greater and greater heights—ideally onto soft mats below—or at least with a secure rope? You deliberately put yourself into more and more difficult situations, fail and survive them.

That's what overcomes lack of confidence—knowing that you can cope when things go wrong. Your mind and body have already been through the pain and how to respond. It's this experience that gives you confidence.

Confidence requires failure

We think confidence is more closely related to your level of certainty to achieve or deliver something. Which requires knowing both how to do it and what happens when you don't. In many ways, confidence is like respect, it has to be earned. Over and over again.

Confidence is based on repetition, but it is not just repeating success, in fact counterintuitively confidence has been shown to increase as we experience more micro failure. To reduce our lack of confidence so we can be truly confident we have to understand and be able to deal with failure. We believe it is the act of failing, not succeeding, that gives you true confidence.

Curiosity and confidence

In the chapter 'Curiosity and Me,' we described how being curious affects the brain. Being curious primes us for rewards and stimulates dopamine. The chemical response in our brain makes us feel happier, more optimistic and more confident the more comfortable we are with a situation.

There appears to be a virtuous cycle created when we approach something with curiosity. Studies have shown that approaching a task or learning with curiosity—learning by doing, trying and failing—improves memory retention and gives us confidence.

In the book *The Confidence Code*, Katty Kay and Claire Shipman found that 'failing fast' was one of the best ways to build confidence.

As playwright Samuel Beckett said, 'Ever tried. Ever failed. No matter. Try Again. Fail again. Fail better.'

However, failure can hurt. We often say to our teams, 'Don't open on Broadway.' By this we mean don't try out your new idea, skill, product or service on your primary audience first. It's too big a leap, with too much risk. Just as high-board diver wouldn't try out a new move from the highest platform first. We need to build up our 'failures' and our successes gradually to learn and improve at each stage.

We can build these 'single points of failure' into our exploration of anything we are curious about. If we have never baked anything before and want to bake a pie for a special event, bake a series of larger pies, each time deliberately choosing different combinations of ingredients—knowing that some will not work out. If you need to give an important presentation—in your rehearsal—don't just practise it going well—try to make it too short, too long, only visual, without the lights on, without the slides.

By understanding both what does work, and what doesn't work, we become more certain of both. We trust ourselves more by reducing the places where we lack confidence, therefore increasing our confidence overall.

Confidence and curiosity

There is a virtuous cycle that exists between curiosity and confidence. Being prepared to have a go at something and being unafraid of failure or what others may think is a powerful starting point for the curious. Confidence is attractive to other people and it is one of the most powerful means of making new friends and creating your community.

By being confident enough to show others that we don't know much but are passionate about a topic, we will be able to learn from others. Confidence helps us learn by doing, helps us curate the direction we want to go in, enables us to perform in unfamiliar situations, and essentially provides the platform and the guiding light throughout the curious learning process. By doing more of something, we become more confident in doing so, and more able to trust ourselves when we go out of our comfort zones. Curiously confident people are wonderful people to hang out with, we are all attracted to them.

Becoming sure

One of the key tools for becoming sure is to document our journey. A written diary of our experience, or a video diary of our day-to-day learning, has been shown to have a powerful impact on our learning process. Not only do they chart our progress, but they have been shown to have an enormous impact on the anxiety associated with learning completely new things or going into completely new situations. Pre-flight checklists that we compile as we go, along with a narrative of our experiences, provide immediate feedback. They enable us to not only track our progress, especially if we become disheartened or start to lack courage, but also to chart our emotional journey, and as a result obtain critical distance between where we want to be, where we are going, and where we are.

Keeping in flow

Our curiosity attracts us to the unknown even though we may be afraid of the unknown. In an organisation, part of a leaders' job is to create the psychological safety for people to explore, to be curious, test, make mistakes and learn—moving knowledge forward.

When thinking about enabling performance, we are long-term fans of the famous work of Hungarian-American psychologist Mihaly Csikszentmihalyi on *flow*. He describes flow as being a 'state of complete immersion in an activity.' It's when we have the perfect balance of challenge to match the skills required for the task. During his research, Csikszentmihalyi asked people to describe when they felt at their best in their work. They used words such as 'complete clarity,' 'effortless,' 'in control' and 'hours passed like minutes.' The research has shown that being in a state of flow can enhance performance across a number of areas, including learning, creativity and sports.

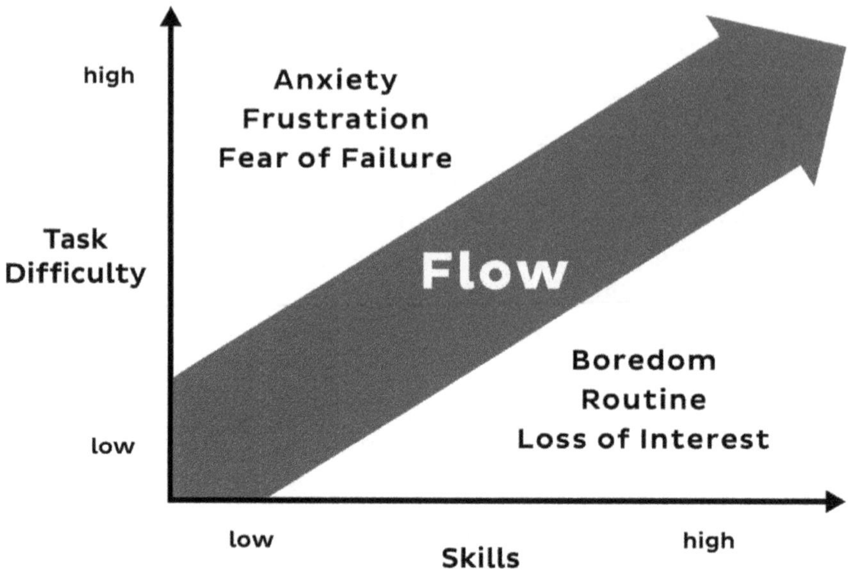

Source: Csikszentmihalyi, M., (2002), Flow: The Psychology of Happiness, Rider

We can apply the principles of flow to our curiosity to feed our confidence and performance. Try or discover progressively more challenging tasks and knowledge areas and at the same time focus on actively developing the skills or knowledge required to accomplish each next level of challenge. With this approach, our confidence will build as our curiosity leads us into new areas.

Keeping it on boil

Forming useful habits is another way to build your confidence whilst being curious. Whether learning a new language, sport or process, if we don't use it, we lose it. There is a concept called the 'forgetting curve.' First described by Hermann Ebbinghaus in 1885, the forgetting curve describes the ability for the brain to remember information over time. He found that whilst memory retention is 100% at the time of learning, if the knowledge learned isn't used, it drops to 40% within the first few days and continues to decline over time.

As adults, many of us have 'forgotten' how to be curious. It has fallen out of our day-to-day practice and we lose confidence in exploring the new. If we stop being curious, we start to be afraid. We can form helpful habits to be curious once more. For example, these could be changing the types of questions we ask, forcing ourselves to approach ideas with an open mind, making time to play and experiment, and putting the right tools around us to map the context with safety.

Our digital tools can clearly help with our habits. We can use technology to establish reminders, prompt us with information, connect us with different people.

Build your confidence by making curiosity an everyday practice.

Putting it into practice

Building confidence through being curious is cemented through the application of knowledge and skills. If people can engage in real work experiences, or through spaces that approximate them, and get to try their new knowledge and skills with real-time feedback, then they will build their skills and confidence. Future learning experiences should include opportunities that allow people to put their knowledge into practice, and that provides accurate and relevant feedback in real time.

On the job

Most people value the opportunity to get professional development on the job, in ways that are directly relevant to their work environment. Through the direct application of skills and knowledge people put theory to practice and ingrain learning into their work lives.

Organisations will need to enable their employees to learn on the job by creating opportunities for employees to take on new roles and challenges, be a part of new and interesting projects and gigs, take focused sabbaticals and secondments, and participate in job rotation programmes. This can be facilitated through a marketplace that allows users to easily find the relevant opportunities and experiences.

Immersive experiences

Through immersive experiences organisations such as Novartis are crafting learning experiences that allow people to test their knowledge and skills in a simulated space. Immersive experiences include learning delivered through virtual or physical spaces, such as augmented reality (AR) and virtual reality (VR), mixed reality, simulations, virtual and physical classrooms.

The use of VR and AR can already be seen in spaces such as manufacturing, where learners can learn, test and apply their skills in a VR simulation. An example of this was in Kundl, Austria, where Novartis created a virtual reality training simulation to address 'manufacturing line clearance'—the process of clearing down a production line of pills and packaging between production of one medicine and the next. Traditionally this training was done 'live' on the machines, which meant taking a production line out of action for the duration of the training. Moving this learning into virtual reality proved highly effective, allowing users to learn in the safety and with the convenience of VR. The simulation was a success, both from achieving the desired training outcomes, but also the cost savings—paying for itself in approximately five weeks.

How to become curiously confident

1. Develop a growth mindset

We certainly believe that we can build confidence by being curious. It starts with approaching things with what psychologist Carol Dweck called a 'growth mindset.' We wrote in chapter four how Microsoft have adopted this concept. Carol Dweck and her team at Columbia (Dweck is now at Stanford) researched the impact of praise on students in schools in New York. In the experiment, the children were given two rounds of tests. After the first round of tests, some children were praised for their *intelligence*. The researchers told them, 'You be must be really smart at this.' Other students were praised for their *effort*. They were told, 'You've worked really hard on this.'

In the second round, the children were given a choice between two tests. They were told they could choose one test that would be more difficult than the first, but they would learn more from it. Or they could choose to do another easy test like the one they had just done.

The team found that of those children who were complimented on their effort, 90% chose the more difficult test. For those who were complimented on their intelligence, the majority chose the easy test. The 'clever' students took the easy route.

Dweck describes these two states as having either a fixed or a growth mindset. Those with a fixed mindset believe that their intelligence, abilities and talents are fixed and that effort is not required for success. Those with a growth mindset believe that their intelligence and knowledge can be expanded over time with effort and that they can improve any of their abilities if they try.

Dweck describes a growth mindset being vital to being successful in any aspect of life. It's certainly fundamental to being curious and building confidence.

How to develop a growth mindset? When you try something new, ask yourself—

1. What did I do that worked well there?
2. What could I do better next time?

2. Try again, fail again, fail better

Find a project. Deliberately build 'high-volume, low-impact' failure into your curiosity. Allow yourself to try and fail. Reflect on how that made you feel and document what happened to learn from the result. The experience will build your confidence to try more advanced experiments and develop your skills and knowledge fast.

3. Make curiosity a habit

The opposite of being curious is indifference, apathy, being afraid. To become confident with your curiosity, it's vital to make curiosity part of your everyday life. Here are some ideas for how to make curiosity a habit—

- Ask questions constantly
- Get used to being wrong
- Don't judge, just listen
- Say, 'Tell me more'
- Get lots of feedback
- Make time to explore something new
- Don't become bored; find something that surprises you

4. Connect with real people

Not only is it vital to test our thinking in reality—by doing the research to validate our work it massively builds confidence. Learning is social; if we connect with experts as well as a diverse community who are interested in what we are doing it will challenge us and help our progress.

5. Keep a notebook or diary

Whether we keep a visual diary or a narrative of our experience, a diary will enable us to chart our journey, show us where we have come from, and provide us with the tracking that's required to remind us where we want to get to. A notebook or diary is a hugely powerful tool for reinforcing our confidence as we learn and curiously explore.

Summary

Confidence is the key to meaningful curiosity. The good news is that the more we actually take the first step and embark on answering a curious question, rather than debating it, but actually attempting to do something, understanding something, and explore context, the more confident we become. We become curiously fit from putting curiosity in practice, by sailing the 7 C's, and by living a life infused with curiosity.

The digital world provides us with the platform, as never before, to connect and learn. To find others who are interested in similar things to us and to enable us to explore and share with them. Curiosity is a team sport, and like all games, we need the confidence in order to play. Small steps and micro failures provide us with the psychological safety required to get there. The tools are available digitally, for streaming new information, for documenting our experiments, for living a curious life, enabling us to go further than any other point in history.

The future belongs to the confident. The future belongs to the curious.

In Part 3, we look at what it takes to realise or manifest curiosity in our lives from three perspectives—the learner, the leader, and in culture.

References

Bandura, A. Jourden, F. J. (1991). Self-regulatory mechanisms governing the impact of social comparison on complex decision making. *Journal of Personality and Social Psychology*, 60(6), 941-951

Csikszentmihalyi, M., (2002),*Flow: The Psychology of Happiness*, Rider

Dweck, C., (2012) *Mindset*, Robinson

Kay, K., Shipman, C., (2014) *The Confidence Code: The Science and Art of Self-Assurance - What Women Should Know*, Harper Business

Moore, B.M., (1952) Self-Confidence for Competence, *Educational Leadership*, 10:3, 140

Murre J.M.J., Dros J. (2015) 'Replication and Analysis of Ebbinghaus' Forgetting Curve,' PLOS ONE 10:7

Thomas, O., Lane, A., & Kingston, K. (2011), 'Defining and contextualizing robust sport-confidence,' *Journal of Applied Sport Psychology*, 23, 189-208.

Curious Conversations

Jacqui Brassey on Curiosity and Emotional Flexibility

Jacqui Brassey is Director of Enduring Priorities Learning and Global Learning Leadership Team member at McKinsey & Company, Adjunct Professor at IE University and Research Fellow at VU Amsterdam. She is the co-author of *Advancing Authentic Confidence Through Emotional Flexibility* with Prof. Dr. Nick van Dam and Prof. Dr. Arjen van Witteloostuijn.

Curiosity regulates our emotions

I'm a researcher of neuroscience in organizations. I'm a confidence researcher. I study emotional flexibility. I study the brain. Curiosity is a way or a technique to regulate emotions, because if you observe something with curiosity, if you open up and you explore different possibilities, you become less defensive, you can actually accept that there are different possibilities at the end of a process. You go from a tunnel vision to an open mind.

You also have the opportunity to take a pause if you use curiosity. When you take a pause, you can actually make different decisions. So, that's how I use it in the work and also in the research that we do.

The opposite of curiosity can actually cause you stress because then you think there's only one possible way, then you likely set yourself up for failure. Often, there's a judgement coming up, and you think, 'Well, if I don't get that done perfectly, then I fail.' If you use curiosity, you stay open, and you think, 'Well, I can choose this path. I can explore, and whatever outcome, it's fine because I can learn from it. Maybe what I initially thought was the best path is not. Maybe there's a better path.'

I can share an example from my own experience. I used to set myself up for failure in business meetings. Actually, I also talk about my own confidence crisis at a TED Talk a few years ago. My habit was basically that I had to be perfect for a meeting. If I had to meet with senior leadership, I had to prepare perfectly. When I then got in the meeting, I had to have everything, all the answers to all the questions that possibly came up. So, I always felt like the spotlight was on me, and every move I made was seen. Then on top of it, if I was asked a question that I didn't know, I would completely feel like I failed because I told myself that I hadn't prepared well enough.

What I started to do in moments that I felt I would get stuck (and freeze), is use curiosity in those moments to observe what was around me and also what problems we were really solving. I would use curiosity for example to see what colours of shirts people were wearing or what was happening in the room. I would connect with what matters most in the moment (which was not me but the problem we were solving). That took the spotlight off me, and actually puts more of my attention in the room. You engage also part of the brain that helps you then down regulate your emotions and your stress.

Curiosity is an emotion regulation technique and also closely related to a tool in our book called reframing. You engage your executive thinking part of your brain, so that the part of your brain that helps you stay in control, but also helps you stay present and helps you to think calmly, and being in control of the situation, and logically, explore what's going on in the moment. If you explore more options and allow these options to be there, you feel safer, when you feel safer, your stress levels go down.

Being authentic gives us confidence

True confidence or authentic confidence is all about becoming comfortable with discomfort. Connecting with what's really important to you, and then taking clear decisions, taking conscious decisions that you want to move towards what is important to you. The authenticity is all about being okay with being uncomfortable in the moment.

Self-authoring

An important principle is self-authoring and co-authoring with others. Central to using curiosity is postponing your own judgements and postponing your own way of looking at the world and thinking there's only one way that is right. The beauty of collaborating with so many other people and teams and organisations is that there's a lot of rich information and rich insights that can be leveraged. Using the curiosity to see what is really happening in the moment and say, 'That's interesting, let's explore this a bit further. Let's postpone judgement and let's create the space to see what happens.' That's when the magic can happen.

At the individual level, of course, you need to allow yourself the curiosity to not know the answer. If we want this to happen, then we also need to give people the space to make mistakes, and sometimes go down a rabbit hole and actually encourage that it is better to make a few mistakes and never get through the answer at all. It has everything to do with creating safety for people. That's at the core of neuroscience as well. I won't go into technical detail, but there's a well-known concept called Polyvagal theory (which explains the central role of the Vagus nerve) that talks about the importance of feeling safe for well-being and performance. Till recently it has not been applied to organisations yet, but I started to introduce this more broadly in my work. Safety is very important for this to work. The moment you don't feel safe, your brain and body lock down, and curiosity is not so easy anymore. Curiosity, however, can be a technique to avoid total lockdown and contribute to staying calm and feeling safe.

Harness acceptance

The big eye opener for me in my work, which is at the core of all of the practises we describe in our book, is about openness. An important part of openness is 'acceptance,' it's almost about how you can go with whatever life gives you and how can you let it be and find a way to accept that.

Another big eye opener for me was about facing difficult situations. We have this saying in Dutch which roughly translates as 'the soup is never eaten as hot as it is served.' It means when you face difficult things, actually, it's never as challenging as you thought it would be.

Curiosity is at the heart of emotion regulation and acceptance and commitment training, which at its turn has been shown to actually lead to better well-being and performance.

Often our first response to something that makes us feel discomfort is to want the pain or discomfort to go away. That's just how we deal with it. It's an understandable reaction. We just ignore it, or we keep stressing about it.

However, by being authentic and curious about it, we can learn to embrace it. This will help us to reduce the pain or discomfort and it will help us to continue to live our life and focus on the things that truly matter. It can be magic if you're authentically interested in it.

Part 3
Realising the Curious Advantage

12.

A CURIOUS LEARNER

'One must learn by doing the thing; for though you think you know it, you have no certainty, until you try.'

Sophocles

'Always go a little further into the water than you feel you are capable of being in. Go a little bit out of your depth. When you don't feel that your feet are quite touching the bottom, you're just about in the right place to do something exciting.'

David Bowie

The skills and experience that we all have will determine how successful we are—in our current role, or in any future role. But which skills are going to be most valuable to personally invest in?

What if there was a way to determine which of those skills would be in most demand? Which are the ones that will be most beneficial to us? Which are the ones that will help us to get that next promotion or which are the ones that will help us most on our next project or assignment?

This chapter focuses on the skills of the curious learner. How we think we can all give ourselves a boost using *power skills* to have even more impact!

Got to keep up

The world is getting faster—and we all have the challenge of keeping up or risk falling behind, or worse, risk becoming a liability.

While reflecting on our time in organisational learning, we started to realise that some of our earlier perceptions about skills, from years ago, may no longer be true. That maybe if we continue to think in the same way as before, then we're going to be wrong or maybe we've been wrong all the time and it's just taken us a while to realise it! We're talking about the perception of soft skills, perhaps they aren't so soft, and maybe what we think of as soft skills should actually be considered our superpowers for the future.

Astro Teller of Google X talks about how the rate of human adaptability has been overtaken by the rate of change of technology. The solution, he proposes, is to learn faster and govern smarter. This is helpful for us to understand why it feels like things are moving so fast, and it offers a solution—learning faster. But where to focus and what to learn?

In this accelerating world, we see that the skills that we have relied upon are changing. In chapter three, we looked at Gartner research that shows that 19% of the skills that we have today will be obsolete in just three years' time.

This is a long way from the days of our grandparents, or even our parents, who, in many instances, could learn a trade, with a set of skills and rely on those for their entire lives.

We only have to go back 50 years. For women in the 70s, the top jobs were secretaries, teachers, bookkeepers, waitresses and nurses. For men, that list included managers, truck drivers, production workers, carpenters and farmers. Compare that to predictions today for the top jobs of the future—solar or wind energy technician, software developer or data analyst, and you can see a much more rapidly evolving skills profile.

Soft or hard?

We are seeing that 'soft' skills are increasingly being considered more critical.

LinkedIn research in 2020 shows the five most in-demand soft skills and hard skills. At the top of the soft skills list we see creativity and persuasion. For the top of the hard skills list we see blockchain and cloud computing.

Top Five Hard Skills	Top Five Soft Skills
1. Blockchain (new)	1. Creativity (-)
2. Cloud Computing (-1)	2. Persuasion (-)
3. Analytical Reasoning (-)	3. Collaboration (-)
4. Artificial Intelligence (-2)	4. Adaptability (-)
5. UX Design (-)	5. Emotional Intelligence (new in 2020)

Source: LinkedIn Learning: The Most In-Demand Hard and Soft Skills of 2020

Taking a short-term view, we could treat these all the same. But taking a medium-to-long-term view, which of these skills will last the longest? In their 2011 book *A New Culture of Learning*, John Seely Brown and Douglas Thomas suggested that the half-life of a learned skill is five years. Something you learned ten years ago is now obsolete. After five years, half of what you learned is irrelevant. IBM research this year shows that those timescales for technical skills are even shorter.

Let's look at those skills again—creativity and persuasion for the soft skills, blockchain and cloud computing for the hard skills. If we look at them from the perspective of durability, how long they will last, we think that we will start to see that hard and soft skills are not so equal. If we invest in building our creativity—we would expect that to last. It is not dependent on a specific programming language that might expire, it isn't based on a methodology that will be replaced by the next generation. Creativity was the number one skill in 2019 and remains so in 2020.

What about blockchain

Blockchain did not feature in the top five in 2019 and now it is the number one hard skill. If we were looking to take a blockchain course today, could we use a course from three years ago, safe in the knowledge that the content is still valid? Even if one existed before, the content will have to have changed dramatically to still be relevant today. In May 2018, Gartner found that only 1% of CIOs indicated any kind of blockchain adoption and two years later it is the number one in-demand hard skill—this is how fast hard skills are evolving!

A recent *Harvard Business Review* survey of 1,000 business leaders revealed that the difference between those organisations who were most successful in filling their requirements for digital talent was not because of the amount they spent on pay or on training. Instead they had four main characteristics in common—

1. **They focused on potential, not past experience.** The survey found that, given the short shelf life of technical skills, stronger candidates were those who were curious, adaptable and willing to learn.
2. **They focused on soft skills as much as technical skills.** In the survey, they found that the most desired skills were teamwork (74%), leadership (70%), and communication (67%).

   They focused on how teams will work and fit together, not the ability of individuals.

   Successful organisations need a wide range of skills to implement digital strategies. They don't try to find all the skills they need in individuals, they look to build teams that together contain the mix they need. It's more a robust model and more secure than banking on one superstar

3. **They focused on incentivising growth in their people.** Leading companies reward employees who proactively develop their skills. They make courses and training available online so individuals can work on their education as it fits their schedule, and rewards those with higher skills with better compensation (67% to 41%), benefits (64% to 23%) and responsibility (78% to 58%).

We think the time invested in building soft skills will pay-out long after our hard skills are redundant. Maybe it's the soft skills that will be most powerful for longest. Maybe these soft skills are not so soft—maybe these soft skills are really our 'power skills.'

If we also look at the broader trend over the last few years we see a shift towards soft skills. IBM's research in 2016 and 2018 shows that the most critical skills for their workforce have changed from computer/software skills and technical skills (hard skills), to be 'adaptability to change,' team working and prioritisation.

It's time for power skills

Ginni Rometty, CEO of IBM, expects AI to change 100% of jobs over the next 5 to 10 years. What can we do to future-proof ourselves?

We saw earlier that AI is one of the top five hard skills. What is the impact of all these people using AI to build bots and automate processes? We think it will have a huge impact on the roles that humans will be doing.

As we referred to in chapter three, the notion of us being fully replaced by machines is a long way off; the reality will be that more and more of our work and our lives will be augmented by machines—taking away complex, repetitive tasks. This, of course, will have an impact on the skills required of these new tech-augmented roles.

So how do we set ourselves up for success in the automated world? In a 2018 World Economic Forum article, Jeff Desjardins wrote about the impact of automation in the workplace and he offers up soft skills (our power skills) as the answer.

Desjardins sees the primary competencies that organisations will need in their workforce as communicating and working well with others, solving problems, thinking creatively, and using emotional intelligence. Three of the power skills that he highlights as top priorities are complex problem-solving, critical thinking and creativity.

It looks as though investing time in power skills will pay off over a much longer period of time than hard skills. Not only are those power skills more in demand by companies, but also those power skills may even protect us from being replaced by robots. They really are starting to look powerful!

What if there was a way to boost those power skills to superpower proportions?

Curiosity as a superpower

Enter the ultimate superpower of curiosity. Why curiosity? Because it can supercharge and power up all the other skills!

Being curious provides *the motivation to learn* other skills; curiosity fuels learning.

As we have described previously, curiosity actually *makes us learn better*. A study from the University of California found that test subjects could better recall information when their curiosity was invoked. Remember, curiosity sparks the reward part of our brain. When we pair curiosity and learning it perks up the hippocampus, which is the part of the brain that forms new memories.

We have also seen how being curious improves our ability to make decisions (by reducing decision-making errors). It reduces conflict, encouraging us to better understand others' points of view and be more open to others' ideas. Curiosity boosts our communication skills and leads to better team performance through sharing information more openly and listening more carefully. Finally, INSEAD research found that curiosity also drives greater innovation. The more curious people are, the more creative people become.

Google recognised the power of curiosity, demonstrated by one of their recruitment campaigns. In 2004, they posted an anonymous billboard advert on Highway 101 in Silicon Valley, attracting the curious with a single puzzle—

{first 10-digit prime found in consecutive digits of *e*}.com

Answering the question led you to a website, that then led you to further maths problems and then for the most curious, a job with Google.

Google have seen the value of hiring curious people. If you are recruiting talent to your team or organisation, do you have curiosity as something you are specifically looking for in your hiring strategy? Are you looking at hiring employees that bring this superpower with them?

Learner experience

As users, we expect to access learning anytime, from anywhere, on any device. Learning will increasingly become mobile, giving employees the ability to easily access when most convenient. Waiting in line? Pull up a simulation on your phone and review. In a lull between meetings? Fire up your computer and work through an interactive learning guide.

Creating bite-sized chunks of learning content that can be completed in short time frames or use bursts of information has the power to make learning increasingly accessible and easily digestible, as well as increase retention. With cloud-connected mobile and wearable devices becoming almost omnipresent, and with the introduction of VR/AR devices into our lives, organisations will start to explore new approaches to virtual learning in which learning occurs in small doses, almost invisibly, through the workday.

We are seeing different disciplines and methods for creating engaging content for learners. Gamification and nudge theory will inform the way we build and deliver learning and allow us to create more engaging and impactful learning experiences that bring content together in new ways. Using combinations of different types of media will continue to be relevant to deliver engaging content to learners, ensuring different learning preferences are taken into account.

Learning and learning departments will have a huge role to play in infusing learning into work that is not automated and enabling curious learners. In fact, perhaps they will not be seen as learning departments at all—rather just infused within the day-to-day running of the organisation.

Curious learners at Novartis

We have heard how Novartis has curiosity as a core part of its culture. During 2019, significant efforts went into supporting the culture aspiration and specifically to encourage their people to be curious. They spent three months focused on curiosity and over this time people invested over 100,000 hours in their personal learning. They developed their skills in key areas that were beneficial both to themselves and to the company. For three years, Novartis had seen a decline in the amount of time spent on learning. In 2018 the average was 22.6 hours per associate. Year on year, from 2018 to 2019, associates invested 58% more time in learning, with the amount jumping to 35.8 hours, at least in part in response to the greater emphasis on curiosity. Going forward, the company has set a bold aspiration for associates to be spending 100 hours a year on learning.

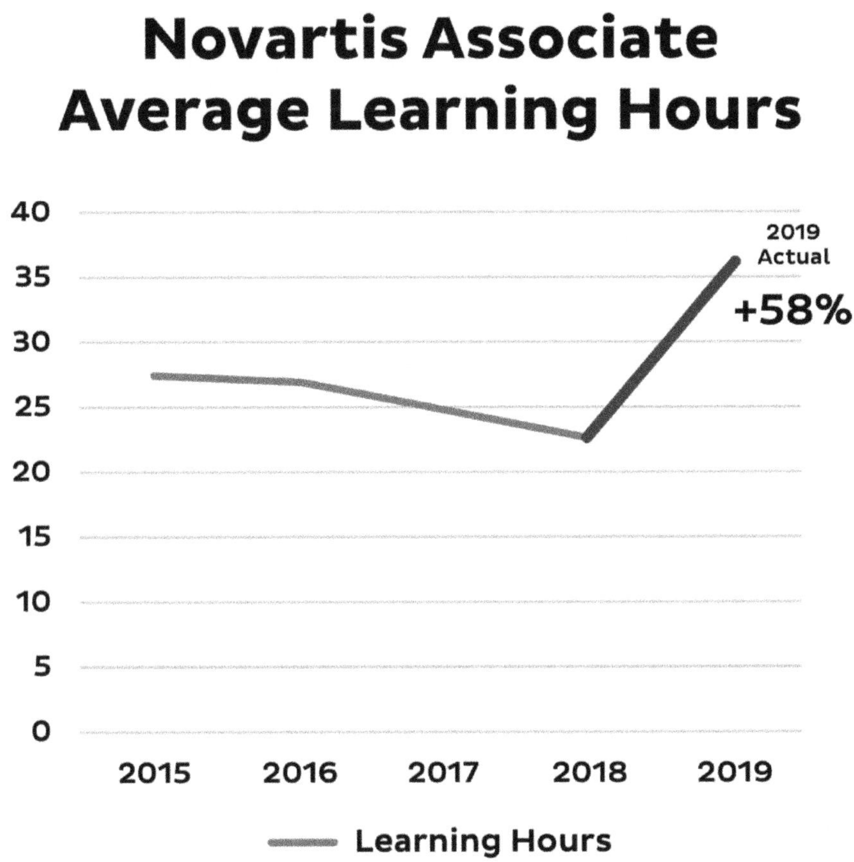

Our challenge to every learner is how can you best invest your learning time to develop your power skills, and most importantly, how will you inspire your curiosity to supercharge all your learning?!

Curious kids

To turn for the moment to the workforce of the future. One question we are asked more than any when speaking with young people is, 'What skills should I learn?'

For many parents thinking about their children's futures, the question of which subjects to study, and which skills to build often surfaces. How can we give them the best possible start for their entry into a future world of work? In this accelerating world, predicting which technical skills may be valuable 5 or 10 years from now is an impossible task, but in a world of rapidly changing technical skills, we think it will be safer to invest in softer skills, and in particular their curiosity, as valuable skills to nurture. These 'super-skills' will power up their learning of other skills.

As we have seen, being curious will make us more successful at building relationships, at forming friendships, at going to new places and discovering new things—powering communication, service and collaboration. When we inadvertently stifle their natural curiosity, maybe we want to check ourselves. In this aspect, the role of the parent becomes encouraging curiosity by creating a safe space in which to learn without causing damage to themselves or others. Creating the opportunity for the brain to develop and evolve to foster curiosity.

Learners are made, not born

In November 2019, *Harvard Business Review* published a special edition entitled 'How to Learn Faster and Better,' focusing entirely on learning and with many references to curiosity. It included an article from Ulrich Boser, 'Learning Is a Learned Behaviour: Here's How to Get Better at It,' that refers to a growing body of research that 'learners are made, not born.' Boser suggests three practical ways to become better at learning, and essentially managing yourself to be more curious—

- *Organise your g*oals - Learning requires effective project management with clear goals and milestones and supporting strategies.
- Think about thinking - Keep questioning yourself, whether you are really getting it, and could you explain it to someone else?
- Reflect on your learning - Take the time away from learning for quiet reflection, including sleeping on it.

Get help from a tomato

Barbara Oakley has focused her career on helping people learn how to learn. One of the techniques that she promotes is called the Pomodoro Technique, named after the Italian word for 'tomato,' and specifically a tomato-shaped kitchen timer that its inventor Francesco Cirillo used in his time management techniques. Barbara promotes the power of using the Pomodoro Technique for learning, breaking learning down into 25-minute chunks (the duration of the kitchen timer) for optimum attention and recall. Then using the brief reward of a break at the end (a short walk, a song etc), which also allows some time to reflect. Oakley is author of the most popular course on the Coursera platform, entitled 'Learning How to Learn,' which has had millions of students from over 200 countries.

Becoming a curious learner

Here are some further ideas for how to stay relevant by becoming a curious learner—

1. Prioritise being curious at work—and find organisations that value curiosity
2. Focus on your building soft skills, not just your technical skills
3. Pay attention to your daily activity—how are you reinforcing curious habits?
4. Plan in structured time to learn and be curious—ideally in 25-minute chunks
5. Find curious communities to work and learn with
6. Ask curious questions
7. Curate your technology that provides relevant information and supports your goals
8. Make a project that puts your curiosity in practice

Summary

For our hard or technical skills to rapidly evolve, our ability and capacity to learn quickly and adapt become more important. The skills that become most important for recruiters are those traits relating to curiosity, such as asking good questions, listening, willingness to learn, and building strong relationships.

Being curious is a power skill that supercharges your learning and therefore supercharges your other skills.

In the next chapter, we take a look at realising curiosity in our lives from a leadership perspective.

References

Boser, U. (2018), *Learning Is a Learned Behaviour: Here's How to Get Better at It*, Harvard Press

Brown, J.S., Thomas, D. (2011), *A New Culture of Learning: Cultivating the Imagination for a World of Constant Change*, Createspace Independent Publishing Platform

Desjardin, J. (2018), 'The 8 major forces shaping the future of the global economy,' World Economic Forum https://www.weforum.org/agenda/2018/10/the-8-major-forces-shaping-the-future-of-the-global-economy/

IBM Study, 'The skills gap is not a myth but can be addressed with real solutions,' https://newsroom.ibm.com/2019-09-06-IBM-Study-The-Skills-Gap-is-Not-a-Myth-But-Can-Be-Addressed-with-Real-Solutions

Kavanaugh, J., Kumar, R. (2019), 'How to Develop a Talent Pipeline for Your Digital Transformation,' *Harvard Business Review*

Curious Conversations

Suzie Collier on Nurturing Curiosity

Suzie Collier is a professor at the Royal Academy of Music in the Junior Department and the mother of Jacob Collier, the Grammy Award-winning musician, and two daughters, Sophie and Ella.

How do we nurture and enable curiosity?

Well, I love the word curiosity. I think it's one that a lot of people are frightened of really, because curiosity means that you're willing to move around within your mind and within the world. It's quite hard to define it, but I would say it's about delving deeper, it's not seeing something just at face value. It's a will to understand something rather than to just know it.

On curiosity and fear

If you allow curiosity to be at the head of what you're doing, then you're not going to be fearful because curiosity and fear just simply don't go together. If you're frightened to look and see what the deeper meaning is or to look at another way of actually seeing something, then you can't be curious.

When going into a situation, if you are feeling fearful, you may not even want to go into that place at all, so you might just avoid it and say, 'I just don't want to do this today.' And in a sense, that's okay. I don't think I am curious all the time but if I allow the innate energy to flow, I become much more curious.

Enabling curiosity in a child

Many people give advice about bringing up a child. They may say it's all about routine, it's about not listening to them scream, otherwise you're going to indulge that child. But I don't believe that it is indulgent to listen to that person, I think it's indulgent for them to say what they want, and for you to just say okay, here it all is, without thinking. Perhaps in a lot of people's minds, it's a very fine line. I just don't think so. I think you can really listen, but you can have very clear boundaries and you can definitely say how you feel and put that in there, it's not just about listening one-sided. And that's the whole thing about curiosity, isn't it, that it's not a one-sided thing.

And without wishing to ask too many questions of a child, you can actually enable them to be asking questions if you ask the first couple in a very open way. If I asked one of my children about how a note felt, for example, then they might have said, 'Oh, I'm feeling that Db and it's really warm and purple and I feel like it's a cosy blanket!' I always felt that my children could take me along a journey, so that they'd be teaching me something new about what we were listening to and why, and in that sense, we were all curious together.

Encouraging children to be unafraid

I think it's to do with a lack of judgement. When you've got a class of people or an orchestra in front of you, judgment's a funny thing. You can pick it up from body language with just a look and a nod of the head, and you've got to get rid of that completely, so there is space for someone to perhaps say that, 'Listening to this feels like I'm up in a balloon, or I feel frightened and I don't really know why.' And if they can say that and it's left in the air without judgement, then it can be explored and it can be understood.

Within a classroom setup, I really have to consider where students have been in their day. If necessary, I might take them outside for a second, not in order to judge them and tell them off, but in order to just say that I acknowledge that there is something wrong and that I wonder really whether they can just take a moment to just reflect on the day and to see what's happened to make this occur.

In essence, I want to try and take away judgement. I also want to express that we are all equal as human beings in a classroom or in a room together. I'm no better than them because I'm older and bigger. But if we're going to really work together, there needs to be some kind of mutual respect in there and I do always say that I can't ask them to respect me, but I really would like to keep the communication channels open, so that if they have a difficulty with what I'm saying, that they can say something without the fear of being judged.

On motivation

My dear dad wrote a scale book, which is a very fine tome. And the way that he's written it with the fingerings and how they work is quite alternative, there's no other scale tome quite like it and I love it. Within his teaching, he encouraged scales to be practised in 100 different ways. Start from the top, start from the bottom, do it in this rhythm, do it in that rhythm, play it in different modes. In short, it's so important to vary what you play to keep up motivation.

I normally teach older students rather than younger, but some of them still do have a parental input, and I tend to talk to parent and child about the process of becoming independent learners, actually for both of them. The ability to learn independently is a really wonderful gift to be able to give to somebody because if they can motivate themselves within their practise to take the next step, then that's really great. Again, it's about lack of judgement, it's about thinking about what you want to do and making your own choices. You might say, in my practice, I know that I want to run this whole section through because it gives me so much satisfaction, even though it's not accurate. And you might say, I really ought to do these finger exercises because when I do run through this section, I want to make sure that the rhythm is really working for me. So it might be that you say well, okay, I'm going to try and do the thing that I don't really want to do first, in order to strengthen up my fingers and discipline them a little bit to enjoy playing through the section more!

The curious reset

But then you might find that you're really bored and you don't want to do anything, and at that moment, I really do advocate that to keep up motivation, you have to do exactly the opposite of what you're telling yourself to do. You put down the instrument and you shake out a bit, you walk to another room, you drink some water, you use your voice instead of thinking about expressing on an instrument.

And suddenly, you will get the energy. And it might mean that 20 minutes later, having had a frolic around with all sorts of pieces and ideas and things, that that person says, do you know something? I don't mind having a go at those scales now. This is the curious reset.

One tip

It's about overcoming fear, being open, understanding rather than knowing, understanding the boundaries and safety and how you move forward with energy. Also the curious reset, this idea that if you are locked or bored or can't figure it out or don't know, try and come at it from multiple perspectives, multi-dimensionality.

One more tip. Maybe get rid of the word 'try' and use 'allow' instead. Hold curiosity gently in your arms rather than trying to grasp it.

13.
A CURIOUS LEADER

'If you want to build a ship, don't drum up people together to collect wood and don't assign them tasks and work, but rather teach them to long for the endless immensity of the sea.'

Antoine de Saint-Exupéry

Why is curiosity a paramount attribute for leaders today and what does it mean to be a curious leader?

The pace of change in the world within our organisations has never been so fast. Today's leaders need to constantly adapt to new opportunities, new markets, new technologies. There's no denying it, leadership is hard. Often leaders have to make it up as they go, using as much trial and error as past experience allows, but this is fraught with dangers, how much does their own bias, their own anxiety, the desire to have the right answer, affect them in these challenges? Today's leaders need to be truly adaptive to handle the complexity that faces them and not just manage their way through it, now more than ever, leaders need to be leaders and not just managers. They need to set the direction, harness the energy and motivate across a diverse ecosystem of customers, suppliers and employees, they need to challenge an old frame of leadership, this is not about leading from the front, it is not about having all the answers. They truly need to be authentic, open, listen to learn and understand, hold space for dialogue and challenge and maintain the ability to rally teams across digital channels. It's a big ask.

Vas Narasimhan, CEO of Novartis, shared with us how, 'Leaders have a huge influence with the shadow they cast across the organisation,' and that with a curious mind you are able to have a bigger impact on those around you and for your organisation, as well as being ultimately more fulfilled.

When Michael Dell, CEO of Dell Inc., was asked to name an attribute he thought CEOs would most need to succeed, he replied, 'I would place my bet on curiosity.'

We would agree. We propose that leaders can cut through much of this complexity by simply being curious. This chapter is about how to become a curious leader. It's about working on yourself, and your ability to be curious and overcoming fear—and then transmitting this.

Curious leaders

Mughal Emperors were curious about the world. Their religion led them to be curious and to be tolerant. The Mughal Court was famous for its diversity—its scholars, its tolerance of other religions, its institutions that promoted bodies of knowledge like algebra and astronomy—that documented and created libraries and that promoted the collision of ideas. They were sensitive to innovation in the service of the court and society. It was their invention of the stirrup that gave them an army of horseback archers—this single innovation enabled them to overrun a continent and rule the greatest part of Asia for 300 years. They possessed mechanical clocks, fountains and technical computers for algebra long before they were invented in Europe. Their love of poetry, art and architecture led to the building of the Taj Mahal.

A combination of factors is claimed for their decline. Some claim that they had become too settled and too wealthy. Others look at factional fighting and economic challenges as they became less able to gather the taxes required to fund their supporters. However, all accounts suggest that the later rulers of the Empire became less open to new ideas, less tolerant of difference and less progressive. Perhaps it was a failure of curiosity.

Curious leaders in the digital age

Many of the leaders in the organisations we meet today would say they are curious. They consider themselves open-minded to new possibilities and willing to incorporate new thinking into the way their organisation works. This is how many perceive themselves, but the research tells a different story. In one study for *Harvard Business Review* in 2018, of more than 3,000 employees, only '24% reported feeling curious in their jobs on a regular basis, and about 70% said they faced barriers to asking more questions at work.' Therefore, what is going on? Well some of this comes from the fact that as humans we love to compare ourselves to others, to create impressions of how we should be, rather than the reality of who we really are. Our minds often tell us one thing, whilst our bodies and our internal dialogue tell us something else.

The challenge is there is and has been a dramatic shift in the way leaders are required to behave as a result of the rapid shift to digitalisation. The traditional, hierarchical models of leadership, which go back as far as the age of Alexander the Great, are no longer appropriate for organisations today that are more like a fluid ecosystems or hyperconnected networks.

Top-down command and control have been surpassed by new skill requirements such as influencing, role-modelling, recognition, nudging and systems reinforcement. Things have changed—and the skills that are taught in traditional MBAs are not necessarily the skills that are required to lead in today's world. We see curiosity and learning being at the heart of leadership in a digital age.

Working alongside colleagues, the leader is an active contributor, and a humble contributor. Being comfortable with presenting yourself and your own vulnerabilities at times enables the leader to inspire, connect as a human being and engage directly with people—whomever they may be.

A recent MIT Sloan study of CEOs across the globe found that curiosity was consistently considered a critical behaviour of leaders. Curiosity is seen as as enduring a quality in leadership as trust and integrity. According to MIT Sloan, the good news is that curiosity is a skill that can be learned. We can be intentional about becoming curious leaders and putting it into practice.

The new MBA

The traditional MBA has long been the go-to badge for the ambitious leader. Today many business schools are taking a good look at the knowledge, competencies and behaviours they equip their students with to cope with the world they hope to lead in. Of course, leaders still have to be proficient in developing business strategy, interpreting financial models and designing organisational structures fit for their sector to deliver employee, customer and shareholder value. In addition, they are required to have a powerful personal brand—online and in person—navigate changing market forces and dynamics as well as balance the drive for automation with the need to provide a better working experience for every employee. Do all this whilst being authentic and a daily role model to the organisation they lead.

We suggest that being curious is at the heart of being a successful leader in today's fast-moving world. Contemporary MBAs should be providing leaders with not only the tools, but also the inner work of leadership that enables them to be curious and therefore to build organisations that are also continually curious. We conducted a thought experiment and devised a curriculum for an MBA relevant today. Let's explore what some of the tools are that would be in our new MBA.

1. How to read and map context

Today's leaders are leading into the unknown. They need to be able to do so whilst dealing with ambiguity and develop strategies that rapidly adapt and learn. In order to do so, they need to be able to read and map the context as it changes around them. Often this is about understanding *weak signals*. We can do this by sending out probes and then analysing and documenting the findings—

Send out probes

One generative tool that is useful in understanding context is from the field of user experience design. It's called cultural probes technique. It is about researching with people who are experiencing a particular situation, to understand from them what happened in the past, what's happening in the present and what they imagine will happen in the future. The use of language and questions are important to get below the surface to find insight. Consider this model from Elizabeth Sanders's wonderful book *Convivial Toolbox*.

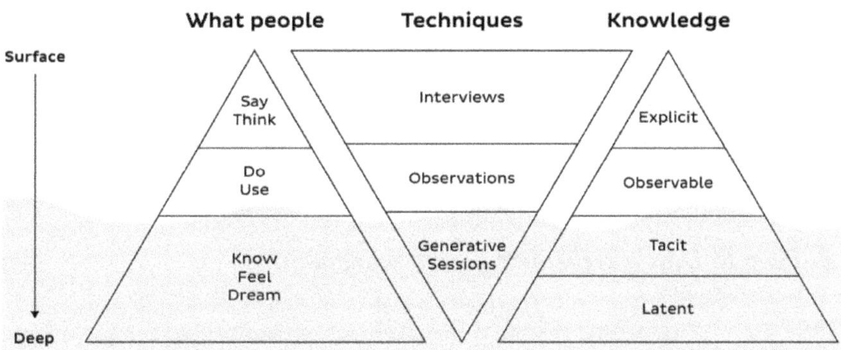

Image source: Convival Toolbox, E. Sanders, P.J. Stappers

We can apply this UX exploration approach to mapping context. For example, who are the customers in your markets that are using your product or a competitor's product for something you didn't expect or asking for something new? What are they trying to achieve? This might give insight into a shift in demand or a new opportunity. Famously in 2007, Apple used this kind of research to great effect by identifying a desire for more visual interfaces for technology devices much faster than the traditional mobile phone companies.

They spotted the context shifting and moved quickly to capture the opportunity.

There are typically three stages to understanding context. Firstly, define the 'probes'—who or what do we want to analyse and how? Specifically, what do we want to know? For example, if we want to understand why the uptake of a medicine is suddenly below expectation when previously the trend has been positive, we have to look at the impact for everyone involved in the chain—from the patient to the healthcare provider and regulator, to understand what's changed for them in their situation.

Next, collect the data. How do people respond to the probes? How do they feel, what do they hope for? Finally, synthesise the data to map the context (preferably using a visual tool) and find new insight and opportunity.

Use analysis and documentation

Making sense of the data is about mapping and documenting. Each experiment or new finding is documented so we can connect ideas and weak signals to form an overall picture of the contextual landscape we inhabit.

2. How to lead a tribe and create movement

One of the primary roles of a leader is attracting great people to work. We think there are a number of indicators and new skills that show how leaders can move and inform the tribe they are seeking to influence.

Providing a purpose

We join communities (or tribes) where we feel we belong—often this is about purpose. A tribe of gym-goers have a common purpose to keep fit; a tribe of scientists may have a common purpose around curing a specific disease. It's the purpose that brings people together. Setting a clear purpose builds a tribe.

Novartis is a great example of an organisation with a clear purpose—or 'big P' as they refer to it. The 'Big P' is a reference from Dan Pink's work, the 'Big P' being the overall purpose such as healing patients, and the 'small p' being an individual's role or purpose within that. Novartis' purpose is *reimagining medicine*. If you go to the company home page, it's front and centre, 'We are reimagining medicine.' It's an exciting and motivating idea. The challenge for the leaders at Novartis, as in any organisation, is to help their people translate this 'big P' into thousands of 'small p's.' What does this mean for every individual in the organisation? How do they contribute? Why should they get up in the morning, fire up their laptops, labs, machines or vehicles and work hard in their particular role? It is because they have defined for themselves, with the help of their leaders, how they are contributing directly to this overall big goal.

Consistency is also important. Nobody ever reached a destination by taking two steps forward and three steps back. Once the community has set a goal, everything needs to be working towards achieving it. Anything acting in a different direction will only destabilise and demotivate those who are working hard to achieve it. For example, if you decide that to achieve your mission, you need to provide a completely personalised customer experience for every customer, everything in the organisation, or the tribe, needs to point in that direction.

Nurturing and nudging

The role of the leader remains consistent—to strategise and define outcomes, to engage the community in the pursuit of those outcomes, and to provide rapid access to skills and resources, including learning resources. However, how do you achieve results if you are no longer leading through command and control, controlling budgets, demanding targets and goals—methods that have not always been successful without burning people out and risking their integrity.

The key to understanding curious leadership of the tribe in the digital realm is to understand that we are nurturing behaviours and outcomes that are developing in a self-organised way.

By providing stimulus and inspiration, and joining up resources, new ideas begin to emerge; however, the role of the curious leader now is to find or spot the weak signals of excellence and goodness, nurture them, provide a safe place for them to mature and grow. Launch many in parallel and then create the mechanisms by which they join up and overwhelm the old system.

We can use nudging as a useful way to encourage the behaviours and ideas that seem beneficial. There are a range of different types of nudge at our disposal. We can amplify great ideas and behaviours across the organisation. We can make it easier for one thing to happen rather than another. We can showcase, reward and incentivise the things we want to see more of. Nudging is a powerful approach when dealing with a complex system, as the impetus for change comes mostly from the people themselves, rather than the leader.

3. How to unboss

Unbossing is about stripping away outdated hierarchies or 'flipping the pyramid,' as Steven Baert, Novartis CHRO, described it in a recent interview. Unbossed leaders are purpose-led, serve and create opportunities for the people around them and empower their teams' success above their own. Professor Amy Edmondson, the Novartis Professor of Leadership and Management at Harvard Business School, describes why unbossing is so powerful, 'So much of the value creation process today is collaborative. No individual person has all the answers anymore.'

The book *Unboss* describes the concept in detail. As one of the authors, Lars Kolind writes, 'The UNBOSSed organization involves everybody instead of the few, it functions through mechanisms instead of structures and it builds on purpose instead of profit.' Organisations are so dynamic that they cannot be controlled by one person. They exist within the levels of complexity that no single person has all the answers. At Novartis, the goal is that all 15,000 leaders around the world will eventually become unbossed.

According to Baert, 'There is no organizational change without individual change. The key to behavioral change is self-awareness.' Novartis have embarked on a programme for every leader to increase self-awareness and build their unboss capabilities. In Novartis, one tip their leaders advise as they move to an unbossed leadership culture is to simply ask 'tell me more.'

4. How to use potent questions

The time of a leader being the expert is dead. It is no longer possible for the leader to be the person with all the answers in a time where there is often no answer. It is now the time of being able to ask the right questions. Narasimhan told us, 'The only way you can navigate complexity is to have a mindset of inquiry, where you're constantly asking questions, navigating, understanding there's not going to be any absolute answers.' The world of education is seeing a similar shift in teaching methods, from 'the sage on the stage' to the 'guide on the side.' Curious leaders are great at articulating the problem and enabling their teams to find the solution or where to find further information.

As we described in the chapter on Criticality, in her book *Kill the Company*, Lisa Bodell refers to asking better questions—killer questions, even—that challenge our biases and our thinking. For example, instead of asking, 'How can we beat the competition?,' ask, 'How can the competition beat us?' This line of questions challenges our beliefs and forces us to address the things holding us back.

By asking more and telling less, leaders can nudge and influence with far greater reach. Leaders must create an environment of curiosity, a safe space to ask questions to find the answers. The team becomes the architects of the answer, not the leader.The leader is the catalyst in allowing the teams to flourish.

Try putting yourself in a situation you would be uncomfortable with and find out what would make you successful. Give up control.

Be comfortable being ignorant. You can't know all the answers but you can be curious to ask great questions. Be inquisitive. Ask the difficult questions. And encourage others to do the same.

5. How to assemble diversity

The power of the curious leader comes from the team and the people they put around themselves. A team of 'yes-men' (or women), or like-minded thinking only tends to reinforce pre-existing biases and stifles innovation. Curious leaders bring together complete diverse opinions, deliberately creating teams that constructively challenge one another from different backgrounds and experiences. We would extend the idea from Michael Dell who says, 'If you are the smartest person in the room, invite smarter people, or find a different room.' We suggest that if everyone you know thinks like you, find someone new to know.

What's the value of diverse teams? Better outcomes. A recent McKinsey report covering hundreds of large companies found that those in the 'top quartile for ethnic and racial diversity in management were 35% more likely to have financial returns above their industry mean, and those in the top quartile for gender diversity were 15% more likely to have returns above the industry mean.' Diversity pays.

6. How to build your brand

Today's leader needs to be media-savvy and articulate across a range of media. In the past, communication media would be most likely used by the CEO and maybe the CFO to speak to the press and to analysts. Now, there is an expectation of leaders throughout the organisation, and indeed employees themselves, to be coherent in communicating through a range of digital and traditional channels. We are even seeing a shift to organisations wanting to publish some of their internal programmes, meetings and discussions in the public domain—at conferences, via LinkedIn, business journals and other channels. Company culture can no longer be 'spun' by a clever marketing or PR agency. If the culture and ways of working are not genuine, then there are a range of communication channels and tools, like Glassdoor, that will very quickly show the realities to anyone who cares to look.

The trend is to be more open and to share. In our media-hungry world the ability to tell stories and turn those stories into compelling multi-media assets wins eyeballs and promotes the brand both externally and to employees.

As many celebrities have discovered, the media is a double-edged sword. It can be a great way to get your message across, to influence your followers and people you want to connect with. On the other hand, social media can be merciless and can destroy careers as quickly as it can make them.

Your personal brand

Whether you want one or not, you have a personal brand. Colleagues, customers, managers, all form their opinion based on the information they find, based on what they read, see and hear about you. He's very passive. They're spikey. She's creative. He's a workaholic. She's only interested in her own progression. They're incredibly innovative.

When working with organisations, brand agencies will tell them to 'take control of the narrative.' The same applies to us as individuals. What do you want to be known for as a leader? What do you want people to say about you? How will you evidence that in the stories you tell, how you perform, how you act?

When Vas Narasimhan became CEO of Novartis he set out very clearly to bring his own personal identity and values into his leadership. He places a high degree of value on humility and kindness, and that is demonstrated through the inspired, curious and unbossed culture he is building within the organisation. His personal role-modelling of the culture is inspiring, including his overwhelming sense of purpose to positively impact humanity and his humility of being open and recognising, like all of us, that not all our decisions are right and sometimes we all get it wrong. In so many interviews with prospective new employees, it is Vas's, or other senior leaders' personal (authentic) brands, that we hear were an important part of attracting the interest of great talent.

Creating your personal leadership brand is about being intentional—by doing the work on yourself to be the brand you want to be, you will become the type of leader you want to be perceived to be.

7. How to create psychological safety

Just as a parent does for their child, one of the primary roles of a leader is to provide safety. To be curious we need to firstly feel safe. We need to be comfortable knowing that we can explore and make mistakes, and this won't be punished but supported. Professor Amy Edmondson, the Novartis Professor of Leadership and Management at Harvard Business School, describes this as *psychological safety*.

What is the key to creating psychological safety? Edmundson says there are three things a leader has to do continuously to create psychological safety at work—setting the stage, inviting people to engage and responding productively. Setting the stage assumes trust and safety in every interaction. Inviting people to engage establishes respect for others' point of view. Responding productively reinforces that we are all working together towards the same purpose.

When things go well and when things don't go well, the response needs to be the same. Leaders who create a supportive, psychologically safe environment for their people—

- **Value resilience.** Be resilient and encourage resilience in others. Demonstrate and be open about times you have found things hard and how you have overcome them. Currently stress and other mental health-related issues are of paramount concern. Too many people are overworked and overwhelmed in their roles. Build and value resilience that people can perform better and are more engaged in their work. Research has demonstrated that a curiosity mindset helps build resilience, as it contributes to optimism and confidence and reduces stress.

- Acknowledge and empathise. Leaders recognise the efforts made and show appreciation for the intention not just the outcome. W. L. Gore, the makers of Gore-Tex, and award-winning for their innovation, have core beliefs that include, 'action is prized; ideas are encouraged; and making mistakes is viewed as part of the creative process.' They celebrate the projects that don't work out, just as they would have had it been a success.
- Reward failure. In his book Work Rules!, Laszlo Bock, Google's Head of People Operations, gives the example of Google Wave, an online platform launched in 2010 and closed a year later. 'They took a massive, calculated risk. And failed. So we rewarded them.' It's not enough just to tell people it's 'okay to fail'—they won't believe it unless they see these behaviours in action.
- Be open. Being a curious leader is fundamentally about being open. This means being open to new ideas and to new connections. Make the effort to see things from others' perspectives and recognise their beliefs and choices. As most of us have found out at some point in our lives, to argue with somebody else's experience is a waste of time, but to add somebody else's experience to your own is hugely valuable.
- Have their back. People will go a long way for you if they believe you will be there for them if things go wrong. Being prepared to stand up for another tends to create a huge amount of loyalty and trust. There are thousands of stories of sports teams, elite military units, extended families who demonstrate time and again the power of 'having each other's back.' Knowing someone is there to back them up means they can go way beyond what they would have otherwise done. How different would your organisation be if you felt everyone working there unquestionably 'had your back?'
- Be aware of your own biases. (fears, assumptions, beliefs). We all have our own biases—conscious and unconscious—as we described in the chapter on Criticality. The starting

point is being aware that it's likely you will bring your own bias in to any and every interaction. Try to catch yourself doing it. A bias usually takes the form of a thought or sentence that expresses your opinion on ability, likelihood or requirement. For example, 'The new system can't be finished in time.' It's a biased statement. Perhaps it's true. Perhaps not. Biases often have the effect of closing down ideas and opportunities too early. Be aware of the biases you have and when you hear them in others.

8. How to role model

Any desired shift in behaviour in others requires influencing. As the McKinsey report on the psychology of change management described, bringing organisation change requires four components, described in their *influence model*—role-modelling, reinforcement/recognition, fostering understanding and conviction, and developing talent and skills. Of all these, *role-modelling* is the most powerful.

The only way to be truly curious is to be truly curious about yourself first. Just think about it for a minute—if I don't understand myself, how am I ever going to be curious about those around me? Therefore, putting curiosity at the heart of your leadership means continually paying attention to yourself and your mindset so you exemplify curiosity to those around you. In addition, demonstrate how you apply the various skills you need to act on, to achieve the outcomes you're looking for. Experiment. Try to make something you have never made before. What did you need to learn? What did you discover? What was hard? How did you do it in the end?

Put your curiosity to work and apply what you have learned to being a role model. At every opportunity, show, don't tell. Demonstrate through your actions the behaviour you expect to see in others. Don't teach or preach, be a model. In UK, in 2018 the government reformed the GCSE curriculum, including tougher grades to achieve. The following year, the headteacher and other members of staff of one of our children's schools sat French alongside their Year 10 students—participating in the lessons and then sitting the exam in the school hall. It was a fantastic example of motivating through role-modelling to students and an opportunity to experience the changes at first hand. How often did you get the chance to 'beat your teacher' in your grades at school?!

In a business context, at Novartis, senior leaders were encouraged to take advantage of the new learning resources and then share with their teams what they experienced and what they had learned. Then they encouraged their leadership teams to do the same. Some of the most positive reactions received were when leaders shared their own personal experiences. For example, admitting that some of the learning was actually really tough, or that in some instances they had even failed the tests and needed to redo them (sometimes more than once!). This seemed to make people much more comfortable with the idea of taking on learning a new area and that it was okay to fail.

Vas Narasimhan described to us why role modelling curiosity is so important for him. 'One of the great joys I have that I've realised over the years of life is to constantly be learning about new things. I find a tremendous amount of energy. I find it's very rewarding in its own right, but it also helps me lead better, see new connections, maybe make a connection that I wouldn't have otherwise made. In an era where it's tempting to become a hyper-specialiser, being curious, learning, building your own range across a range of different areas is tremendously valuable to yourself but also to the organisations you work in...' Steven Baert, Novartis Chief People and Organisation Officer reinforced this, 'Vas is definitely a natural learner. As long as I've known Vas, he comes with curiosity…' But Baert, goes on to share how he found he was not a natural learner and had to relearn it.'Because a job is so demanding and so consuming that it was tempting for me, after a long day of work, to kind of switch off, do a workout, spend some time with my kids, and just read an easy novel. I had to rediscover learning and overcome that initial barrier of it's hard to learn. Now that I'm into it, it's addictive. Now I'm kind of thinking like, 'Wow!' Every time I learn something, a new door opens up and new possibilities emerge.' Baert's authenticity and openness, provides a role-model for others in the company and beyond, who may need to rediscover their own curiosity.

9. How to be authentic as a leader

None of the above leadership traits will endure if they do not come from a place of authenticity. While some may suggest merit in the approach of 'fake it until you make it,' most people can see through a phoney straightaway.

The origins of authentic leadership come all the way from Aristotle's writing on the cardinal or core virtues. He taught that humans should be *prudent* by seeing many courses of action, *temperate*, that is well balanced and in control, *just* or fair-minded and have fortitude or courage in action. Being an authentic leader is not easy. It requires deep self-reflection and selflessness in the pursuit of what is 'right' or 'good' for others, and not just oneself.

The reward is trust by the people you are responsible for.

Authentic leadership combines authenticity with positive psychology. In their 2004 paper, Luthans and Avolio describe authentic leadership as 'a process that draws from both positive psychological capacities and a highly developed organizational context, which results in both greater self-awareness and self-regulated positive behaviours on the part of leaders and associates, fostering positive self-development.' Alongside this definition, four components of authentic leadership have been identified by Walumbwa et al., 2008—

The four components of authentic leadership—

- **Self-awareness (knowing thyself)** - At the heart of authentic leadership is knowing your own strengths, weaknesses and beliefs. It requires developing an understanding of what is most important to you and how you impact on others.
- Internalised moral perspective (doing the right thing) -This is about leading and making decisions based on your own ethics and moral values.

- Balanced processing (being fair) - Authentic leaders take in multiple vantage points and make decisions objectively on the information available, whilst encouraging others to question and challenge their view.
- Relational transparency (being genuine) - This is about being honest and true to your own values. It means being open to sharing with others so people know where they stand.

There are no quick hacks or short cuts to becoming authentic. It's everyday practice in being yourself and in your own body. Start by taking a genuine interest in how you think, feel, act and find somebody you trust you can be open and vulnerable with. Then say what you mean and do what you say.

These are the skills that we think are vital for today's leaders and for nurturing the skills of the leaders of tomorrow.

Applying curiosity as an organisation's culture, having curious leaders and creating an environment of psychological safety is moving towards what Dr. Robert Kegan and Dr. Lisa Lahey (both from the Harvard University Graduate School of Education) describe as a 'deliberately developmental organisation.' They argue that a DDO is organised on the simple but radical conviction that organisations will best prosper when they are more deeply aligned with people's strongest motive, which is to grow.

The impact of curious leaders

The impact of a leader on the curiosity of a team or organisation should not be underestimated. Novartis sought to identify the linkage between a leader and the engagement of their team across different dimensions, and the results were staggering. Through taking data from leadership 360s and regular employee engagement survey data, it was possible to isolate the impact that the leader had.

After anonymising the data, the leadership 360 data was divided into a set of leaders that were considered favourable leaders by their teams, and a set that were considered unfavourable leaders. The engagement scores of the teams of these favourable and unfavourable leaders was then compared against each other and against the results for those that were neutral on their leader.

A leader that was perceived as favourable had an average three points higher score on the engagement of the team, across dimensions such as work-life balance, belonging, collaboration and curiosity. Where there was the greatest impact was on the results for a leader who was perceived to be unfavourable. For the teams that reported their leader as unfavourable their engagement scores plummeted. On average, teams with unfavourable leaders scored 18 points lower across all dimensions. The area where the impact was greatest, with a 22 point difference between a favourable and unfavourable leader, was curiosity. Poor leaders stifle the curiosity of the team. Great leaders not only promote curiosity, they create the culture required for their teams to excel through curiosity.

Summary

Curiosity is vital for leaders in any age. In the digital age it is central to the skills necessary for leading in an uncertain world. Leaders who choose to be curious have a large and positive impact on the culture of their organisation. Curious leadership is something that can be learned. As for any learner, technical skills are not enough; their soft or power skills will be carried with them throughout their career. Curiosity is a mindset that enables leaders to inspire people no matter how complex the environment they may find themselves in.

In the next chapter we look at what it takes to nurture a culture of curiosity.

References

Bhargava, M. (2014), *The Decline Of The Mughal Empire*, Oxford University Press

Gino, F., 'Why Curiosity Matters,' Sept-Oct 2018, Sept-Oct, *Harvard Business Review*, https://hbr.org/2018/09/curiosity

Kegan, R., Laskow Lahey, L. (2016), 'Everyone Culture,' Harvard Business Review Press

Ready, D.A. (2019), 'In Praise of the Incurably Curious Leader,' *Sloane Review* https://sloanreview.mit.edu/article/in-praise-of-the-incurably-curious-leader/

Walumbwa, F., Avolio, B., Gardner, W., Wernsing,T., and Peterson, S. (2008), 'Authentic Leadership: Development and Validation of a Theory-Based Measure,' *Management Department Faculty Publications 24*, https://digitalcommons.unl.edu/managementfacpub/24

Curious Conversations

Vas Narasimhan and Steven Baert on Curiosity and Leadership

Vas Narasimhan, CEO of Novartis and Steven Baert, Novartis's Chief People and Organisation Officer.

What was it that prompted the focus around culture?

Vas
When I reflect back, I think the one thing that had become clear to me over the years is that the most powerful asset that a corporation or an organisation has ultimately is people. If you believe that as a starting point and you believe in the positive side of human nature, that if you give people a sense of purpose, a sense of autonomy, a sense that they can be curious and improve themselves, they'll perform their best.

What led you to choose inspired, curious, and unbossed for the culture?

Vas
When you look at the history of large companies, we go back 100 years and under the world of Frederick Taylor and large-scale manufacturing, we saw that people were treated like cogs in a factory. We kept that way of thinking for probably far too long until relatively recently, and I think now there's been a resurgence in understanding that with knowledge workers, you need to create an environment that enables them to really be at their best. So that's what unboss is all about, servant leaders, inspired people, and hopefully an environment focused on curiosity.

Daniel Pink, in 2009, rekindled an awareness that fundamentally human beings are motivated by purpose, autonomy, and mastery. We thought if those are the motivators, then what is the environment? So purpose relates to inspiration. Autonomy is really around the unbossed mindset. And mastery is really all about curiosity. And if you give people an ability to be curious, they can improve their ultimate mastery and feel fulfilment around that.

I think I was also very influenced by the work of Carol Dweck and her work on how learners, people who have an agile mindset, really can create possibilities for themselves and for organisations. How do you create a learning organisation rather than a knowing organisation, and how powerful that can be for the long-term performance and also the happiness of your people.

Why do you see curiosity as so important?

Steven

I think we live in a world where the digital solutions that we have around us have addressed the obvious but even the complicated. The obvious has been automated. The complicated, artificial intelligence and machine learning can do a lot there. The real added value of people, of humans is how we thrive in complexity. An interesting thing about complexity is that there's no obvious answer; there's no easy right or wrong. Even an expert is less impactful. It is all about exploring possibilities, exploring polarities.

So the strength of curiosity is that you don't immediately jump to the right answer, but that you kind of say, 'Hey, interesting. Let me learn more about this. Let me explore this. Let me look at many options before I narrow it down to one solution.' So it is very enriching, and I think it's also the foundation of then future innovation and forward thinking.

What does it mean in the context of everyday work?

Vas

Our hope is that it creates an environment where people feel like it's not only about what you know today, but also this environment of constant learning. What I like to say is, 'Can you keep learning about those around you and your colleagues, what their thinking is? Learn from the external world, but also learn by looking inward.' So can you really take this kind of 360-degree approach to learning, to be curious about all three of those different spheres? And in doing so, our hope is that again people will come up with more innovative ideas and have bigger impact.

Now, practically how do we do that? I think providing access to a range of tools. We do a lot of work on self-awareness, that kind of self-curiosity as well. And part of creating this unbossed culture, we want to create this environment where people will get curious when they have somebody disagree with them in a meeting or have a different perspective. I think all of that together hopefully builds this kind of environment of curiosity. These nudges hopefully create this different mindset in the company.

Steven
I think if you have a new strategy as a company, there's always an important moment to also evaluate whether your supporting strategies are fit for purpose. So what we quickly realised was that, in order to execute on this ambitious plan that we have for Novartis, we had to have a different culture as a company. And when you think about culture, it is a massive organisational change that starts with individual change. So we had to rethink our entire approach to all of our people processes.

Vas has referred to the industrial revolution. It's interesting that we use the word human resources, it's almost like a reference to cogs in a big machine. We have rediscovered the value of people. They're our most important and our most precious asset in this company, and that's also why we deliberately decided to change the name from human resources to people, and that's where it started.

What have you discovered about the impact of culture on performance?

Steven
I think it's very important that culture is not seen purely in the soft skill sets. What we really believe is that if you create the right environment for your people to thrive and to really bring their full selves

to work, you will get better decision-making, more integrity, stronger performance, and as a result, a better company reputation.

We needed to validate that, and so we've done two things. Externally, we commissioned a piece of work that went through all the culture studies. And what was interesting is that work clearly demonstrated that when you have a fit-for-purpose culture, you link your culture to what it is you want to achieve as a company and you make a sustained, deliberate effort to achieve that - you will get better performance. There was a very strong correlation there.

Internally, we're doing work to look at our best performing leaders and our best performing units, and we're looking at all the culture data we have there. What we're already seeing is a very strong correlation.

How do you know if this culture change has been working and what progress you've been making?

Vas

Steven's team have really taken on measurement and how do you measure a culture? And there's no perfect way to measure, but I think you can get a lot of good markers. We have engagement surveys we pulse quarterly. We have upward feedback on our leaders that is regularly obtained. Then we track that over time, and we see do our interventions make a change? We start to see the numbers really move. The questions are standardised. They link to inspired, curious, unbossed. And it's been really amazing to see.

One of the things that's happened along the way is a significant shift in the mindset of our leaders. We have daily sales and daily financial reports, but our people organisation has also made completely transparent this data around engagement and culture. So now the normal course of conversation for leaders at Novartis is not only to talk about their numbers, but also to talk about their culture numbers and that's been a big shift.

Why was curiosity the hardest aspect of the culture to get traction on?

Vas

There's a few different dimensions to why that initially was a struggle. One, we were a very knowing culture, and when you think about how a company like ours develops, we have experts, a lot of experts in lots of different fields, and they all think, rightfully and understandably, that they know the answers. So it's all about trying to prove you're right and that you look good by knowing answers. So shifting that to a curiosity mindset, a learning mindset, where you're constantly looking for new ideas, challenging your ideas, integrating your new ideas into your current way of looking at the world required one shift.

Second, when you look at how we approached learning inside of Novartis, it was primarily around standard operating procedures and compliance training. It wasn't really about exploring and opening up your mind to new possibilities, even to things far afield from Novartis. So making that shift into learning was also a critical step.

And then the third thing was the behaviour of managers. Managers valued knowers and always knew the answers in meetings. And I see a demonstrable shift to people asking open-ended questions. So now fast forward a few years later. We're making great progress on the curiosity front, but it took shifts in all three of those areas.

What else do you see as part of curiosity beyond learning?

Steven

It has many aspects. Of course, you need to create the environment and the tools and make them user friendly, so people can learn and find information, but what I would also add is you first need psychological safety. There is something intimidating about curiosity in the sense that you first need to admit that there could be different points of views, there could be different answers, or that you may not have the answer. So how safe is the organisation for people to say, 'Interesting. I don't know. Let me look into it'? So is there an expectation that people have the answer, or is there an environment where people say, 'That's fascinating. I have no clue. Let's explore this'? So we have to create that psychological safety.

The second thing it's about is the questions that you ask. So, personally, I've learned to ask different questions. Previously, my questions were definitely always 'listening to fix'. You have a problem. I need a few points of data from you, so I can solve the problem. I'm practising 'listening to learn'. And so how you ask questions and how you open rather than narrow the issue is very influential in how you learn and how you also role model curiosity.

What do you see as the business value and the return from investing in learning or curiosity?

Vas

What I find in this role is whenever we make a move to support our people, show that we care about our people's well-being, how our people grow and expand their horizons, it leads to growth in our company overall across all other performance measures. So if you take that as a starting place, and knowing that a sense of curiosity, learning, and mastery is so important to human motivation, it's almost a no-brainer to invest wherever you can in providing better learning opportunities for your people.

I think in our organisation what it has immediately sent was a symbol that we care and we want to help people grow and learn. We've seen the stats, I think, very impressive in terms of the number of people signing up for courses in a broad range, whether it's language, whether it's digital, whether it's on leadership and being highly engaged to improve themselves, and of course, they'll bring that better self to the office. But I think that the biggest thing is the signal and sentiment you send. You send a signal that you care. You care about knowledge and learning, and you care about creating this environment of curiosity. So I would tell another leader to just do it.

What unleashed that wave of curiosity across the company? A 50% increase in the amount of time people spent on learning.

Steven
I think it's a combination of things. First of all, the symbol, but also the communication. Simon, you were very creative in bringing the 'Netflix of learning' to Novartis, which included the playlist and favourites. The fact that it was transparent to people what Vas's favourite learning topics were, what my favourite learning topics were, it makes it catchy and appealing to others to join it.

Secondly, I think it's about making it easy for people. We've done a lot of work to make it easier to access learning, to find your content. If people need to spend too long to find something, they'll give up and they'll switch to something else. And then I think the learning months and the learning rallies and all of that that we've done, again, it's an invitation for people to join in. We definitely have more work to do.

Why has it been so important for you to role model learning?

Vas
Well, I think one of the great joys I have that I've realised over the years is to constantly be learning about new things. I'm an avid reader, podcast listener, periodical reader. I find it's very rewarding in its own right, but it also helps me lead better, see new connections, maybe make a connection that I wouldn't have otherwise made.

I think role modelling has a huge element. I think people look at leaders, and then leaders have a huge influence with the shadow they cast across the organisation. So I think role modelling is incredibly important. That role modelling is, of course, the behaviour of what do you read and understand and sharing that, but also are you somebody who asks questions or make statements? Are you somebody who values knowing or values understanding and exploring?

Steven
As long as I've known Vas, he comes with curiosity. For me, I am embarrassed to say I had to relearn it because a job is so demanding and so consuming that it was tempting for me, after a long day of work, to kind of switch off, do a workout, spend some time with my kids, and just read an easy novel. I had to rediscover learning and overcome that initial barrier of it's hard to learn.

Now that I'm into it, it's addictive. Now I'm kind of thinking like, 'Wow!' Every time I learn something, a new door opens up and new possibilities emerge. I think our Western Europe education system, school system, has sometimes made curiosity difficult because you were supposed to always know the answer. It was always a test about right and wrong. So we need to make learning and curiosity attractive again, and that's what we're trying to achieve.

Why do you think curiosity is becoming more important in the digital age?

Steven
Over the last few years, in addition to the culture change towards inspired, curious, and unbossed, we've definitely pushed the digital agenda. Now, what we've seen is we're able to predict sales through algorithms with a very high level of accuracy, but in the current pandemic, it's useless because all the algorithms take into account historic trends and analogues, and there is no analogue for the current situation. This is where curiosity, this is where the human brain is the only solution of, hey, this is new; let's explore what's possible. So I think the two go very well hand in hand.

Vas
When you look at the way digital technologies make, in some ways, very obvious things readily knowable, my children can quickly Google about almost anything. The need for building a learning mindset to learn about more complex topics becomes much more important. One of the things at Novartis we're employing is something called

the Cynefin framework, and that looks at the different ways you can categorise problems as simple, complicated, and complex.

I think in the digital age, the simple and the complicated become more and more automated, and so you're left with the complex. And the only way you can navigate complexity is to have a mindset of inquiry where you're constantly asking questions, navigating, understanding there's not going to be any absolute answers, as we're learning now in the age of the pandemic.

You have to almost be an explorer, and to explore you have to be very curious. So I think that shift where human beings are being asked more and more to engage in the world of the complex is going to keep nudging people towards being more curious if they want to be successful.

14.

A CULTURE OF CURIOSITY

'The Universe doesn't care who's going to change the world. It just wants someone who'll seize the idea and run with it.'

Vishen Lakhiani

'Knowing is not enough; we must apply. Being willing is not enough; we must do.'

Leonardo da Vinci

'A person who never made a mistake never tried anything new.'

Albert Einstein

It's all very well having the noble aim of encouraging curiosity and finding ways to formalise curiosity within our societies, education and businesses—but how is this to be done in a way that goes beyond just asking everyone to be curious and defining what that means in conversation?

The network effect is related to the size of the network, how much we contribute to our network, and the quality of what we contribute. This chapter relates to the part about how we can give back and contribute to our communities in order to encourage curiosity within them.

We're looking at what it takes to nurture a culture of curiosity among those around us. Whether in our organisation, communities, villages, groups or family.

In short, how can we encourage the practices that promote a culture of curiosity?

Practices that animate the ideal

If we first look back to our example from history, how did the successfully curious societies create and sustain their culture of curiosity?

The Republic of Venice was a (sort of) proto-democracy that was founded on commerce and curiosity. Venice funded the University of Padua in order to control an Academy that drove scientific knowledge forward. This knowledge was put into the service of the Serene Republic. Ships were built in the most efficient and fastest manner of its day. As we have described, the Venetians could turn out seagoing triremes every four hours. The Arsenale was constructed as the first production line in history. In terms of technical advances, the relationship to the sea, navigation and seamanship were honoured and promoted in every sestiere through their churches, saints, symbols, and scuole—the formal guilds that promoted the development of skills and teaching within a particular area.

Competition, rituals and festivals were associated with saints who represented a particular ideal. The great symbol of Venice is the winged Lion, who is related to the great mysteries of the Sphinx and in turn the patron saint of Venice, St. Mark, who is also associated with navigation, exploration and, as we would say, curiosity.

The digital gift

The Internet is perhaps the most wonderful gift we have given ourselves to be curious. At least based on the experience of it so far. Not only can we create the networks of people we need to find to be curious, but we can also make things using it, and communicate in rich storytelling mechanisms that can be easily accessed by everyone. In some sense the Internet easily enables us to reproduce all the practices that relate to curious cultures as it is so powerfully connected with learning and the synthesis of knowledge.

Perhaps one of the reasons curiosity is trending at this time is because we find ourselves with this great ocean of potential, and in some senses we are all trying to figure out how to make the most of it. There is so much opportunity to be curious that we are quickly overwhelmed with knowing where to start. There are great emergent forces at work, that are accelerating the evolution of new platforms and functionality all the time.

What is a curious culture?

Culture is what we call the environments that we create, the myths and stories that drive us, the rituals that remind us of the cycles to complete, the language that drives the meaning, the access to resources and the rewards and recognition we grant to the things we value.

Culture is dependent on situation and context and it is these things that we must consider, define and shape if we are to change a culture. The context that impacts culture in the physical world is the same for the digital domain. These include values, communication, feedback, humanity, clarity, vulnerability, honesty, integrity, openness, rewards, routines, flexibility, humour, symbols, rituals, language and tools.

The key to a *curious culture* must surely include a community who are biased towards learning, who value experimentation and recognise that this includes failure. A community who somehow formalise the answers and who believe in learning by doing, who take the answers thrown up by curious enquiry and applies them in useful ways, who create safe places in which to be curious, who communicate and establish mechanisms for doing so for others in the community and who have stories and rituals that reinforce these behaviours.

Why do culture changes fail?

Moving to a culture of curiosity or continuous learning is complex and requires collaboration across the whole community. It is like re-organising the basic building blocks or DNA of an organisation.

Changing a corporate culture is hugely difficult. One in three efforts fails according to Gartner in a report in 2018. The most successful and high-profile changes to corporate culture have typically been initiated by existential threats. Microsoft is a great case. The company was known for infighting and losing its innovative edge; it was when Satya Nadella took the helm that a change was desperately needed. Nadella believed in a growth mindset and took the company on the journey from know it all to learn it all.

As we described earlier, in his memoir *Hit Refresh*, Nadella talks of how curiosity must be at the heart of the Microsoft business, writing, 'We need to be insatiable in our desire to learn from the outside and bring that learning into Microsoft, while still innovating to surprise and delight our users.'

Nurturing a curious culture

The seed of an idea that leads to a curious question in turn leads to the purpose for a networked group to come together. To foster a community of interest that *has impact* requires people to join of their own free will, with that belief that being part of that community is somehow beneficial to invest their time and ideas in.

Imagine each community of interest as having fulfilled all the requirements that make it recognisable as the equivalent of a micro-academy, university or technical school.

The group that has within it the fastest cycles for learning and progressing real knowledge—not conjecture or fake news—but knowledge that advances our technical understanding of the world, wins.

Evolution in practice

Chris Meyer, the head of the Nerve Organisation and who designs and runs some of the world's most impactful technology think tanks, applies principles of evolution to the knowledge-generation process. It works.

In essence, evolution, whether applied to biological species, structures like organisations or knowledge generation, requires three things—

- Sufficient diversity within the system to start the process
- Recombination of ideas within the system
- Application of environmental pressure to the new ideas to ensure they can survive and meet the challenges of their context.

These three principles in practice are sufficient to enable new ideas to be generated, tested and disseminated by groups of people. Without them, however, there is only chaos and noise.

Promote digital diversity

Such a wealth of material is instantly available for streaming as digital music, podcasts, audio books and videos these days. There is very little that cannot be consumed digitally as soon as it is thought about. If the answer to a question we have cannot be found somewhere online, we become curious or suspicious, or perhaps even paranoid. Why isn't it available to us the way everything else is? We start to investigate.

Access to this huge source of information serves to keep us attached to ideas beyond us. The Internet, and its platforms for creating like-minded communities—whether family members—or those attracted to a topic—provides us with opportunities like never before to explore new things. It is at the heart of a society where a plethora of ideas, opinions, attitudes bump into each other. They are all being considered and evaluated against their usefulness to us as a great democratic project. It only works, of course, when there exists a rejection of groupthink, or fascist, totalitarian thinking—and where we are all committed to a society where freedom of expression exists. Toleration of the Other, of difference, and an understanding that it is possible to exist together without having to kill each other. When it comes to society and culture, it is not a zero-sum game with winners and losers. It is a place where diversity increases the value of the pot for all.

Digital diversity promotes creativity, creativity promotes evolutionary recombination, and testing and communication lead to the robustness of ideas. We can establish platforms that stream curiosity to people. Actively explore ideas together and create things together.

Shift the language and symbols

The language used within a culture has an impact on what is valued. For example, saying, 'I am curious about…' demonstrates an openness to understand more. The language we use flags the *symbols that matter*. Novartis made an active commitment to 100 hours/5% of learning for each employee that emphasised the value on curious learning. We find words that embody the values we wish to encourage. Novartis have used language specifically to shift to a new culture such as *unbossed*. The term was deliberately introduced to inspire curiosity and encourage people to ask, 'I wonder if….?'

Add the word 'yet' to anything and it opens up possibilities.

'I'm not able to play Chopin's Nocturne in C minor—YET!'

Our language contains the seeds of new thinking and the focus within a culture

Use curious tools

There are times when knowledge needs to be shared, the system hacked and information enabled to flow across the nodes of the system.

Contemporary thinking tools for curiosity include design thinking, experimentation, open innovation, Google Sprints, tiger teams, labs, Hegel's 'zoom in zoom out.'

The more ideas that can be tested in reality, with customers for example, the lower the risk of launching a new product that will fail. Process tools and technical frameworks are the bodies of knowledge that promote the differences and competitive advantages between competing systems. The faster and higher quality that outcomes can be produced, the greater the capacity for achievement of one network over another

Promote synthesis

Synthesis is the practice of combining existing information and creating new knowledge from it. We just have to look back at things we have written or notes we have taken in the past to understanding how much more knowledge we have gained about something. Synthesis formalises this process and updates our knowledge bases. Promoting synthesising behaviours to update models, language and thinking consolidates our communities' understanding about topics and increases the ability of knowledge within the community to evolve.

The word 'synthesis' itself is a powerful word for the lexicon of the culture. It requires us all to evaluate, add new ideas to one another and evolve new ideas.

Design experiences that support curiosity

Focus on the customer experience has been a driving force over the last ten years. it is becoming just as important to focus on the experience of the employee or member of an organisation or community.

Fight for the best people, make it easy for them to find knowledge, obtain new skills and join communities with audacious questions to solve. Resolve frustrations by identifying the pain points in the system and encourage them to be solved involving those most impacted by them.

Keep humanity at the centre of the game. People want to be part of something meaningful and to be inspired by a purpose. Create meaning and reward people in a meaningful way. Promote community and fun—even online.

Enable teams to go on journeys—just as the Venetians had their ships, banking, schools and artefacts that were relatively easy to assemble into a voyage financed by consortia of Venetians, sestieri and families. Ensure the infrastructures are in place, with the resources that they need, to easily promote voyages of discovery focused on the customer.

Creating a continuous learning experience, that allows employees to thrive in their day-to-day jobs, as well as grow and develop professionally and personally, is at the heart of enabling a curious culture.

Create space for learning

Thomas Friedman's book, *Thank You for Being Late: An Optimist's Guide to Thriving in the Age Of Accelerations*, makes the point that learning is essential for survival to cope with our ever-changing world. The pace of change is accelerating and is exceeding organisations' and governments' abilities to keep up. Getting better at learning, and therefore having the right people, leaders, culture and ecosystem in place is no longer optional, it is now essential for organisations to survive.

Enable space for learning, both in terms of time and access. Provide learning that is physical and virtual. Make new knowledge and create new tools and apps. When we consider these experiences, Josh Bersin's framework of micro and macro learning is useful for understanding the different spaces for us to focus on supporting.

Micro learning

Micro learning refers to the spaces of learning that support people in their day-to-day, providing the support when they need it. It is focused on on-the-job or in-the-moment performance, connecting learners with relevant knowledge at point of need.

This learning space is generally accessed through short pieces of content or experiences that function independently and can provide the knowledge, tools and support to the needs of the work.

Macro learning

Macro learning refers to the spaces of learning that support long-term career development or lifelong learning. These formally structured learning activities connect people with the knowledge, tools and support that they need to reach their personal development goals. This learning space is particularly relevant when the learner wants to prepare for a new role or learn something new that will allow them to reach their career objectives.

How Novartis is realising curious advantage

How has Novartis tackled the change to the culture and inspired curiosity? Activity to change the culture started as soon as Vas Narasimhan took over with explanation on why changes to the culture were necessary and what the new culture would look like. We recall asking Narasimhan in June 2018, six months in, which aspect of the culture was proving hardest to solve and his answer was curiosity. That the message wasn't yet resonating strongly with associates.

Novartis chose curiosity as one of three elements of its DNA or corporate culture and placed culture change as the top strategic priority for the company. But what led a traditional Swiss healthcare company to take this bold move?

In 2018, Narasimhan took the helm at the company and described a conversation with one of the institutional investors where they had showed slides from the investor meetings over the years, at which they had consistently been promising that they would unlock the potential that Novartis has. On several occasions, the company had set out how they would maximise the opportunities from a great pipeline and the companies' considerable resources, yet had never fully realised that potential. What could have been holding back the potential of the company? Narasimhan puts it down to culture and has made it his number one priority to change the culture to 'unleash the power of our people.'

A new people strategy

During the summer of 2018 it became clear for the Executive Committee that a greater clarity was needed to make decisions in the context of the new culture aspiration of inspired, curious and unbossed. A major cost drive was underway in the company to free up resources to invest in the largest set of product launches that the company had ever seen. But where should costs be cut and where should investments be made to support the culture initiative?

To support the Executive Committee in making these decisions a people strategy was required. Calling it a *people* strategy and not an HR Strategy was a conscious decision, as it went beyond the areas owned by the HR function. It needed to expand to cover all the aspects of an associate's experience—expressed through the 'moments that matter' in an employee's life. From the day that someone joins the company to the day they leave. It covered the working environment that someone enters into and the IT equipment and support they receive. It included the way the company responds when something happens in your personal life and whether there is the appropriate support. Isabel Matthews, Global Head of Talent, Organization Development and Inclusion, led the development of the people strategy and it took into account a wide range of inputs both internal to the company and external in the marketplace. Focus groups and design thinking sessions were held, the annual employee survey data was reviewed and the company's recent crowdsourcing event on culture provided a rich source of input, with participation for over 30,000 associates.

From all the data, three areas were decided upon as being the most impactful and most important, and these were the ones that the team felt Novartis should use to differentiate. All the moments that matter were important and needed to be supported in a way that was competitive to the industry, but three stood out as being key to focus on. They were categorised as *My Impact, My Growth* and *My Leadership*.

Differentiation

My Impact was about the extent to which an associate is energised to have an impact at an individual level as well as to contribute to the impact of the company overall, in enhancing the lives of patients. *My Growth* was around having the best opportunities to learn and grow. *My Leadership* was having world-class leadership skills, either by personally role-modelling these if in a leadership role, or demonstrating them in creating and being part of high-performing teams. We recall the moment one of the team made the link back to the culture—*My Impact*—that is about being inspired, *My Growth* is all about being curious to grow and develop, and *My Leadership* links to unbossed and the leader role-modelling servant leadership. There was also a parallel made to Dan Pink's work in *Drive*, where he lists purpose (impact-inspired), mastery (growth-curiosity) and autonomy (leadership-unbossed). These links reassured us that the strategy was heading in the right direction.

Investing in learning

The people strategy was agreed in December 2018 and paved the way in 2019 to build momentum in driving the culture aspiration. To build a curious organisation, a working group had already formulated an enterprise learning strategy that had been endorsed by the HR leadership team in April 2018. The strategy had been agreed but no new resources to implement it were available and it relied on borrowing from across existing teams and projects to build momentum. The new people strategy being agreed provided an opportunity to supercharge this work, and in February 2019 we went before the Executive Committee to ask for $100m of new funding to accelerate the strategy in support of the newly agreed people strategy.

The case for investment and support was made on two main drivers—

- Attraction and retention of the best talent
- Building required capabilities to support the delivery of the strategy

It takes more than money

The proposition was to 'Go Big on Learning' to drive curiosity across the company. The Executive Committee agreed to the funding, and from our perspective also agreed to something even more important and symbolic. They agreed to the request that all associates could spend 5% of their time learning—approximately one hundred hours a year. The funding was crucial, but the commitment of time is arguably even more significant.

The support led to the implementation of a multi-year learning transformation programme that had defined three streams of activity—

1. Creating a *culture of curiosity* and defining the future learning experience
2. Ensuring *business alignment* and impact on performance
3. Creating an efficient and *effective learning* organisation

As Novartis looked to foster curiosity through access to new, world-class learning opportunities, internal engagement surveys surfaced that associates felt that they were too busy to commit time to learning and that managers were not always supporting people in making time to learn.

What 'I don't have time' really means

Explicit support from the company to create time for learning moved it higher up the priority list. If someone says they don't have time for something, what they really mean is that something else has a higher priority. Something else is more important. If someone's annual bonus was attributed to spending time learning, one can be fairly certain that it would get a higher prioritisation.

The company drives a lot of that prioritisation by what is measured, what is recognised and what is rewarded. By being explicit that Novartis will support and encourage people to invest one hundred hours a year in their personal development and providing a way of tracking it in the company learning system, it is possible to move it up the priority, at least in many cases, far enough up to get into the area that actually gets attention.

Before we were curious

When Novartis started the culture journey, it was the curiosity message that was resonating least with associates. Narasimhan told us the three reasons why he thought that was—

1. Novartis had historically had a very 'knowing' culture. 'We have experts, a lot of experts in lots of different fields, and they all think, rightfully and understandably, that they know the answers. So it's all about trying to prove you're right and that you look good by knowing answers. So shifting that to a curiosity mindset, a learning mindset, where you're constantly looking for new ideas, challenging your ideas, integrating your new ideas into your current way of looking at the world required one shift.'
2. Learning meant compliance training and standard operating procedures. It wasn't about opening up the mind to new possibilities.
3. The behaviour of managers, in that they valued 'knowers' and were not in the practice of asking open ended questions.

Two years on Narasimhan feels that great progress has been made on the curiosity front, but it took a shift in all three areas. So how was that shift achieved?

The Curiosity chapter

To support the culture change in 2019, Novartis divided the year into culture chapters, Quarter 2 (Q2) was Unbossed, Q3 was Curiosity and Q4 was Inspired. The Curiosity chapter was the most active of the three and utilised a broad range of approaches to encourage curiosity. Curiosity walls sprang up in locations all around the world. The bright orange walls emblazoned with #IamCurious encouraged employees to share what made them curious and became a visible symbol of the culture change. As well as on the walls, people were encouraged to share what they were curious about on the company's internal social media platforms, and over 1,000 conversations sprang up from all around the world, in several languages, using the #IamCurious hashtag.

My holiday reading list

Leaders' role-modelling of being curious was also a key component. Leaders role-modelled curiosity through many channels. Playlists of learning were created for leaders and influencers and posted into the company's learning system. Leaders identified books, articles and courses that made them curious. Many of the executive committee took part including Narasimhan, who shared an extensive list of his personal reading recommendations.

The Learning Month

Throughout the curiosity quarter new features were added to the company's systems to allow curiosity around career paths, exploring fit-for alternative roles across the company. The biggest focus, though, was the 'Learning Month.' Building on something first tried in 2018, the 2019 Learning Month was a huge step up. As we first introduced in chapter seven, over 130 global webinars were scheduled over the month of September, in conjunction with 250 local events to inspire curiosity and continuous learning, organised by a passionate group of volunteers partnering with the local Novartis Learning Institute teams. Bringing both internal and external thought leadership, the events covered all aspects of the business, from understanding the company strategy, to explaining new products and services, the drug development process or new scientific platforms like cell and gene therapy.

There were over 34,000 registrations for the global webinars and over 20,000 people participated across the events. A further 10,000 people took up the new learning offerings that were promoted over the same period—with the most popular focus being on leadership skills and data and digital. These were the areas most heavily promoted and that most aligned with the unbossed aspect of the culture.

Participation in the events was entirely voluntary and relied on people's own desire to learn—their curiosity. Over the period, more than 100,000 hours of learning took place demonstrating the curious nature of Novartis associates. Overall, by the end of 2019, the company had seen a 58% increase in the average amount of time spent learning compared to the previous year. The regular company engagement survey also showed a gradual increase in people's perception on having opportunities to learn and grow, moving ahead of the external benchmark in Q1 2020.

It doesn't have to be expensive

Many of the methods that Novartis adopted here were not expensive and could be used by organisations large and small. Leader role-modelling, access to online learning resources, experts sharing through online webinars or face-to-face sessions, and a common branding and hashtag across the event.

Some clues for how to take an organisation on this journey

How does curiosity map onto this?

There are two perspectives to pay attention to, the *institutional structures* and the *dynamics*. How do we create structures, networks and form within the rhizomatic, hyperconnected world of the digital? How then do we animate those structures in order for them to function together? How can we predict the outcomes of these? What nurtures the curiosity in the culture in a constructive manner? What are simple rules or simple instruction sets that lead to an impact on value generation with the organisation?

Let's return to take another look at the 7 C's and explore how to apply them in our organisations and everyday lives to build and promote a more curious culture.

1. Context

Once we have a question we are curious about, the first thing that we should look for is the people who can help us answer it. Understanding the context of our question must be step one. It involves asking who the networks are, learning the language of the area you want to explore and discovering what technical skills must be learned in order to answer the question.

Getting used to keeping notes, to creating context maps, network diagrams, documenting language and checking your biases are important for getting into the context.

2. Community

Adults learn best when the learning is in a community, based on solving problems not taking in content, linked to something the learner is personally invested in, relevant to our specific context, that is useful within our everyday lives, multi-dimensional and experiential.

Ecosystems and networks are easily created and nurtured through platforms and apps. Organisations need to provide the platforms that enable people to have access to the communities they need for their curious exploration.

All institutions require animation. As we described above, the dynamics, the rituals, the cycles of events, the everyday, the language, the narrative myths told—from the tavern, the liturgical cycles, to the magnificence of the Doge—these are the things that daily brought the entire connected mass of humanity that was the Venetian Republic to life. The same dynamics are to be found in the most successful organisations today. It is the values that are promoted and animated by these activities that characterise the differences and identities that emerge.

3. Curation

Nothing promotes the synthesis and focus of curiosity like curation. Not only do we have to edit, but we also have to make something, we have to communicate those ideas, test them and present them to our community for scrutiny.

We have a friend who is an international curator—he works with the greatest museums around the world. He has a curation lab—he is passionately curious about different models for running the museum, and different models for presenting exhibitions and enabling the public to explore the ideas within it. Within his lab his team are always presenting new ideas for doing so, testing them in live exhibitions and continuously learning about how to take things forward in different ways. They publish their experiences in exhibitions, monologues and books.

Synthesis is a practice that needs to be encouraged. One of the best ways of doing this is asking people to make a presentation, a course, an exhibition, a documentary or some other format about their topic or their work. Something that teaches others about their way of doing things. It is a powerful way for people to reflect on their work and it promotes curiosity as well as synthesis as a practice.

4. Creativity

Supporting a culture that is creative is to create a space where people have permission to dream, to be safe to experiment, share both failures and successes, and be comfortable with ambiguity and diversity.

To take one example, deejaying. It has a relatively low barrier to entry. It provides validation when people enjoy a set of music. Deejays figure out new combinations, beats, rhythms and narrative, ambiguity in beats that lead to new rhythms. All of this can be achieved with a laptop and some software these days. Lowering the barriers to play is important for creativity.

One of the key principles for a creative culture is that of making in order to understand. Promoting understanding through testing and attempting new things will keep the culture open. Be open to new ideas, open to bringing ideas from elsewhere and open to new ways of doing things.

5. Construction

Have a go

Perhaps one of the greatest keys to practising a curious life is to 'have a go,' to learn by doing, and specifically to building something. Though please be safe whilst doing so!

In music this progression could be likened to attempting to play an instrument, learning to play a piece, then learning the frameworks and language related to writing music, composing something and then finally performing it.

Each of these steps requires something to be done. Attempting to play a new instrument will teach us immediately what we don't know and the path we need to take will reveal itself to us.

We promote the idea of 'lo-fi-hi-lo' testing. Lo-fi or low-fidelity testing could be cardboard mock-ups or sketch drawings. Hi-lo means high-volume testing, done as frequently as possible with low impact. Low impact means if things go wrong they don't destabilise the entire system, they take place in safe places.

Not giving up or being disheartened requires a supportive community who can reassure and encourage us each step of the way.

'Have a go' applies whether we are cooking something in the kitchen, building a house or running a business. A culture of construction is one in which many little failures are expected, and successes are rewarded by recognition and positive regard.

Find the verb

If you're curious about something, look for the verb. What can you do that will actively take you down that path? What can be made, what can be constructed, where is the 'doing word?' The purpose of this is two-fold. First, the act of making something will ground your curiosity within the bounds of possibility; and secondly, it will provide you with something to share with others.

Show, don't tell

By having something to show for your exploration, you will provide something outside of yourself and your community to work on together—it's also the most powerful way of communicating. Sometimes we find it difficult to articulate the precise complexity of something we're exploring. If we have something to show, it will have been invested with the complexity of our ideas. It is easier to explain something by showing it, rather than trying to explain it in the abstract to another. In the digital realm, videos, photos, 3-D models are all extremely easy to make and communicate. Having something to show others is the most powerful way to draw your curious community towards you.

6. Criticality

Teach about bias—what it is, what the different types of bias are. Have shorthand for the major biases you might experience.

Use language such as 'check your bias!' and 'where's the evidence?' as a means to explore where you have come from, what you have learned and where you are hoping to go next.

What visible commitments can you make to raise awareness of bias and our ongoing quest to manage it?

7. Confidence

Jacqui Brassey gives us some great clues to enabling confidence in her book *Advancing Authentic Confidence Through Emotional Flexibility*. Her research has led to understanding that emotional flexibility and confidence are key to our development, but that the things that make us unconfident may always be with us. The key is to understand confidence-building as a lifestyle, like fitness. We need to face the things that hold us back and learn to act anyway. Through doing so we build the confidence to continue forward. Accepting and committing to our journey on a daily basis.

Curiosity is a lifestyle. Acting with curiosity will build more confidence and provide us with the emotional fitness to confront our demons and render them ineffective.

Summary

Here are the things we have learned when nurturing a culture of curiosity—

- Continuous learning is core to enabling a culture of curiosity.
- Continuous learning is where people across an organisation are curious to build new skills and knowledge but also experiment to see if there are new or better ways to do things. This must include failure and, crucially, include sharing learnings from failure and being generous with successes.
- The pace of change is accelerating and is exceeding organisations and governments' abilities to keep up. Getting better at learning is essential for survival.
- Investing in learning should be seen to drive both direct benefits such as new skills to deliver strategy, and indirect benefits such as attraction and retention of best people.
- Role-modelling is the most powerful enabler of cultural change.
- Encouraging curiosity in a workforce will achieve openness and faster evolution.
- Moving to a culture of curiosity is complex and will require collaboration across the whole business.
- Visible symbols matter in the change.
- Take a user-centric view of learning and focus on the individual experience
- Don't underestimate the appetite of people to grow and their willingness to share their learning achievements.

The next chapter is the last and is an opportunity for us to reflect on our curious journey.

References

Bersin, J. (2018), 'A new paradigm for corporate training: Learning in the Flow of Work,' https://joshbersin.com/2018/06/a-new-paradigm-for-corporate-training-learning-in-the-flow-of-work/

Brassey, J., van Dam, N. and van Witteloostuijn, A. (2019), *Advancing Authentic Confidence through Emotional Flexibility. An evidence-based playbook of insights, practices and tools to shape your future*, Lulu publishing Lulu.com

Friedman, T. (2016), *Thank you for being late*, Macmillan

Curious Conversations

What keeps us from being curious?

Dr. Diane Hamilton. Author, researcher, speaker and radio show host.

What if you're not curious?

My research focuses on what keeps people from being curious. What I really thought was fascinating was there is a lot of research out there that'll tell you if you're curious or not, but then what if you're not? I wanted to fix that. For example, my students didn't seem to embrace a high level of curiosity at times. They kind of wanted me to just tell them how to do something without trying to figure it out.

Fear, assumptions, technology, environment

I found that there are four factors that keep people from being curious. I came up with the acronym, F.A.T.E. It stands for *fear*, *assumptions*, *technology* and *environment.*

Preventing productivity

When we think about F.A.T.E in organisations, it opens up discussions that no one really has had at work before. This is tied into how engaged people feel with their job. They're not doing things that they feel passionate about.

I've had many guests on my show who are motivation experts and even curiosity experts, and it doesn't matter who I talk to on the show, everyone will agree that curiosity is the spark.

How to go beyond F.A.T.E.?

Go through each of the fear, assumptions, technology and environment as a checklist.

For *fear*, list some of the things that keep you from asking questions in a meeting. Is it failure, is it embarrassment, is it loss of control? Get specific and come up with little ideas of what you can do the next time. For your *assumptions*, think about what it is that is making you disinterested or apathetic or finding something unnecessary? What keeps you from exploring new things? Thinking about *technology*, do you over or under utilise it? Is it because it is just too much trouble? You've not been trained? Are you overwhelmed? And lastly, for *environment*, think of how your education; teachers, family, friends, workers, peers have had an impact on you exploring curiously. If you write those down, anytime you have an answer to some of these things, then you can create an action plan, 'Well, here's what I'm going to do today to overcome that!'

15.

TO QUESTION IS THE ANSWER

The infinite at every scale

The infinite is available to us at every scale. The Latin phrase *multum in parvo* means 'much in a little space.' Finding the universe in a small area is something many have experienced during the lockdowns because of COVID-19.

Sandi Toksvig, the much-loved British/Danish comedienne, has written a book about her life that simply tells that story through every stop on the number 12 bus from Dulwich to Oxford Circus in London. It's called 'Between the Stops.' A route that has plied its way every day for over one hundred years. By stopping and telling the stories of people, the history, the characters and the buildings along the route, Toksvig weaves a story about all of life, including her own—from her perch in her favourite seat, the front right window seat at the top of the double decker bus. Her curiosity is infectious and life-affirming. We encourage everyone to read this book; it is heart-warming, clever and moving.

It demonstrates so powerfully how the infinite exists at every scale. We can be curious about the small things, and find everything we need there, as much as the large things.

Wittgenstein wrote the exquisite line, 'How small a thought it takes to fill a whole life.' Steve Reich, the composer, used this line to create a sung piece that is so sublime in its simplicity it is profoundly moving. Nobukazu Takemura and DJ Spooky remixed Steve Reich's version in 2006 which are again moving in their own way.

Every curious journey starts with a curious question. Indeed, our question for this book was, 'Why is curiosity important for us today?' and our long and winding road of exploration, experience, research and conversation led us to come to understand that curiosity may well be the greatest driver of value in the digital age. It may just hold the key for how we will thrive as a species whilst we figure out how to adapt and make the most of new technology, save our fragile environment and create a more open, kinder society.

On writing together

Collaborative authoring is a wonderful tool for exploration. Authoring with others, in the pursuit of writing a book such as this one, enables us to show and tell every step along the way.

Without realising it, we used our own 7 C's to create this book. Our context for this book was originally about the impact of learning but through conversation became focused on curiosity. The initial idea gained life when we established our curious community of three. We established our notes in the Evernote platform, curated our inputs, and starting the process of creativity and construction through writing notes and ideas. As our notes became complex, we synthesised our ideas into the chapters. Each chapter acted as a chunking mechanism to place similar ideas together that told a story. Our process shifted into writing chapters in Microsoft Word. The structure was constantly fuzzy and evolutionary with further research, interviews and analysis continuing to inform our thinking. We applied the constraints of the chapter headings, time, deadlines, and weekly meetings where we discussed the key findings we had made.

As we devoted ourselves to writing the chapters, we very quickly discovered what we didn't know, but also discovered insights that leapt out from the pages as we reordered the information. We applied criticality as we went and checked each other's biases—this had too much or too little, this was too deep into the details of history etc.

That was exactly how the 7 C's emerged—we knew we had a set of emerging principles. We found that quite a few began with C. We then played a game—could they all begin with C? Then discovered we had 7 C's—and the metaphor had simply suggested itself to us. Curiosity is a curious thing indeed. Continuous and curious learning needs this bias towards construction and making things to enable magic to happen.

We have looked at curiosity from many different perspectives in the hope that each may lend us some insight into what it's all about. We can tell that there are different voices in this book and we wanted to preserve that, as they each provide a fascinating insight into the Curious Advantage. We are sure there is much that is left to explore; we are sure that this experience has been an energetic pursuit by three professional friends who respect deeply one another's perspective. What we have sought to convey is the what, why and how curiosity is the greatest driver of value in the digital age!

We invite you to join us and continue the conversations in our social media channels, and if there is one thing we would like to leave with you to encourage your own curiosity it is...

Remember this

To question is the answer

ACKNOWLEDGEMENTS

Paul, Simon and Garrick would like to thank the following people for their generosity, guidance and curiosity.

All of the amazing Ludic team for their inspiration and involvement in our future of work and learning research programmes—Keisha Ferrell, Gabriela Francke, Clemens Hackl, Jake Holmes, Alex Matthews, Aliki Paolinelis and Georg Seiler. Thanks to our team and participants at the Future Trends Foundation Think Tank - Juan Moreno Bau, Marce Cancho Rosada who help create the context for experimentation and surround us with the most incredible brains on the planet. To Chris Meyer, Antonio Damasio who are infinitely curious, inspiring and supportive.

In particular we want to thank Pasha Adam for his incredible ability to organise us and our ideas, shine a light on our failures in such a way that motivates us to move forward and for helping bring this manuscript to life.

The inspiring work at Novartis to create a culture of curiosity comes from the day to day actions of associates, managers and leaders across the whole company. We would like to specifically acknowledge the following: the whole Novartis learning community and People and Organisation teams, members of the Novartis Learning leadership teams (NLC, NoLI, Regions), the People & Organisation Leadership Team, the People Analytics team, Communications (particularly Matt McCarthy) and Legal (Sanna Maas) and all those in the wider Novartis team for their inspiration and support. For their additional inputs also a big thank you to James Prior, Global Head of Leadership Development, for his help with the 'Curious Leader' chapter, and also Marc Ramos, Global Head of Learning Strategy and Innovation, for his contributions on the learning eco-system parts. Also, credit to Steve Sitek and team for the initial work on the future of learning. We would like to acknowledge Nina Bressler-Murphy and the team that shaped the learning month (and curiosity chapter) initiatives over the last two years - including the volunteers and cultural activators from all around the world that channeled their own curiosity and ideas into creating a curious community—in particular Bhavesh Tanna in 2018 and Natalia Shestakova in 2019. Without your work we would not have some of the stories and examples included. Also, the 'Forever Young' team, who's winning idea from several thousand in a cross-company crowdsourcing event, helped boost curiosity at Novartis. Finally, a big thank you to Vas Narasimhan, Steven Baert and the Executive Committee of Novartis for defining a cultural aspiration that includes curiosity and for the commitment, resources and support to 'go big on learning'. Also, to Vas and Steven for their support in being interviewed for the book and for our writing it in the first place.

This book would not have been the same without the examples, cases and thinking from our curious community, many of whom were also included in the accompanying podcast series. Acknowledgement and thanks to Jacqui Brassey, Josh Bersin, Stefan van der Stigchel, Suzie Collier, Diane Hamilton, Theo Anagnostopoulos, Sara Moralioglu, David Harrison, Gordon Fuller, Edward Oakeley, Bill Sherman and the Warburg Institute. Finally, many thanks to the producers of the podcast John McGinty and Jill Damatec-Futter, the voice of *The Curious Advantage Podcast* series.

ABOUT THE AUTHORS

Paul Ashcroft
Co-founder and partner at Ludic Group, co-author of the book ALIVE: Digital Humans and Their Organizations, *keynote speaker and facilitator*

With a background in mathematics and strategic consulting, Paul is an expert in applying principles of innovation, design thinking and digital tools to accelerate large-scale, sustainable change on a global scale.

During his 20-year career, Paul has been working with the world's leading organisations to design strategy, align leaders and implement, engage and motivate people. As an investor, Paul is successfully establishing and growing innovative and technology-based businesses that deliver global solutions.

Paul has worked with many of the Fortune 500 and works extensively with SMEs. The ground-breaking methods he uses to collaborate, design and deliver solutions enable organisations to transform and make the successful shift to digital. Ludic Group is revolutionising global consulting by delivering services digitally and redefining how transformation is successfully delivered in the hyper-networked reality of today's organisations.

Paul lives in London with his wife Zsanett and their two children Ben and Leanne.

Simon Brown
Chief Learning Officer at Novartis

Simon leads learning at Novartis, a focused medicines company, and one of the leading companies in the world. He is a commercially-minded learning leader with experience across a range of the world's top organisations. In 2000, Simon co-founded Brightwave, one of the UK's leading eLearning companies, which was eventually acquired by Capita Plc. Simon spent seven years working for Accenture, advising companies including BT, BP, Microsoft, Canon, Barclays and HSBC. In 2010, Simon moved to Lloyds Banking Group where he led the award-winning bank-wide learning transformation.

In 2013 Simon moved to Novartis global HQ in Switzerland, where he led various global learning teams. These including being responsible for enhancing effectiveness of learning for the global pharma salesforce, creating the cross-divisional Global Development University, running the Novartis-wide Learning Centre of Expertise and Corporate Universities, and also defining the strategy for how Novartis would develop digital capability across the company.

After leading the development of a new, award-winning learning strategy, he became Novartis's first-ever Chief Learning Officer in February 2019. Since then Novartis has gained several global awards for learning including the award for Learning Strategy Innovation. Simon shares his experiences, speaking at conferences around the world and with an active digital presence on the Linkedin platform.

Simon lives in Switzerland with his wife Rachel, son Oliver, daughter Lucinda, their cat Paddy and a coop of chickens. He can be found most weekends struggling up a Swiss mountain road on his bike.

Garrick Jones
Co-founder and partner at Ludic Group, co-author of the book ALIVE: Digital Humans and Their Organizations, *academic and investor*

Garrick Jones is an entrepreneur, academic and musician based in London. Co-founder and partner of the Ludic Group, he is a renowned expert in digital transformation, digital learning and engagement.

Garrick is a fellow at the London School of Economics and Political Science (LSE) where he has taught Capstone programmes in International Relations and designed the ground-breaking Open Innovation Programme. His research is focused on Creative Economies and large-scale support systems for commerce, culture, education and community development in which innovation is critical. He is particularly focused on the value of the design process, visualisation methods and tools for enabling decision-making and constructive problem-solving. Garrick has been instrumental in the development of purpose-built collaborative learning environments (CLEs). He advises on numerous projects for corporations and governments and state-of-the-art think tanks, including the award-winning Future Trends Forum (FTF).

He works with Fortune 100 clients, governments, the UN and UNDP. Garrick is interested in how very large systems are able to transform themselves.

Garrick lives in London. Wearing his musical hat, Garrick composes for films, contemporary artists and performance. Ask him to play the piano for you if you get the opportunity!

Lightning Source UK Ltd.
Milton Keynes UK
UKHW011838100820
367994UK00006B/80/J

9 781648 713699